FOCUS:

UNDERSTANDING ECONOMICS IN CIVICS AND GOVERNMENT

COUNCIL FOR
Economic
Education

Teaching Opportunity®

*This publication was made possible through funding from
the U.S. Department of Education.*

AUTHORS

William Bosshardt
Associate Professor of Economics and
Director of the Center for Economic Education
Florida Atlantic University
Boca Raton, FL

Steven Miller
Associate Professor of Social Studies and Global Education
The Ohio State University
Columbus, OH

Mark C. Schug
Professor of Curriculum & Instruction, Emeritus
The University of Wisconsin-Milwaukee
Milwaukee, WI

Phillip J. VanFossen
James F. Ackerman Professor of Social Studies Education and
Associate Director of the Center for Economic Education
Purdue University
West Lafayette, IN

Funding

The Council for Economic Education gratefully acknowledges the funding of this publication by the United States Department of Education, Office of Innovation and Improvement, Excellence in Economic Education: Advancing K-12 Economic & Financial Education Nationwide grant award U215B050005-07. Opinions, findings, conclusions, or recommendations expressed in the publication are those of the authors and do not necessarily reflect the view of the U.S. Department of Education.

ISBN: 978-1-56183-662-8

CONTENTS

FOREWORD

Focus: Understanding Economics in Civics and Government is a core publication of the Council for Economic Education. This valuable instructional resource will help high school teachers actively engage their students in using the economic way of thinking to analyze many of the key topics addressed in high school economics and civics/government classrooms. Thoughtful consideration of the institutions and incentives that operate in modern market economic systems is central to citizens' ability to make informed decisions. While market systems generally provide well for organizing the production and distribution of scarce resources, there are many circumstances in which governments can help improve economic outcomes and advance societal goals. Lessons and activities that address the economic role of government, as well as the costs and benefits of alternative public policy options, can be found throughout this publication.

The Council for Economic Education believes that students can and should learn economics throughout the K-12 curriculum. The *Focus* series is designed to help teachers enhance student learning in a variety of subjects and at all grade levels. As with all Council instructional resources, activities in this publication are interactive, reflecting the belief that students learn best through active, highly personalized experiences with economics. The application of economic understanding to real-world situations and contexts dominates the lessons. In addition, the lessons explicitly teach the Council's widely adopted National Content Standards in Economics as well as the National Standards for Civics and Government, published by the Center for Civic Education.

The Council for Economic Education gratefully acknowledges funding provided for this publication by the United States Department of Education, Office of Innovation and Improvement, Excellence in Economic Education: Advancing K-12 Economic & Financial Education Nationwide grant award U215B050005-07.

The Council also gratefully acknowledges the efforts of the project director, Rich MacDonald, and the authors, drawn from the Council's talented network of affiliated Councils and Centers: William Bosshardt, Steven Miller, Mark Schug, and Phillip VanFossen.

> Joseph A. Peri
> Acting President and
> Chief Executive Officer
> Council for Economic Education

ACKNOWLEDGMENTS

PROJECT DIRECTOR:

Rich MacDonald
Council for Economic Education and
St. Cloud State University

EDITOR:

Richard Western

FIELD TEST TEACHERS:

Chad Coolman
Rogers City High School
Rogers City, MI

Jack Couch
Brooklyn Technical High School
Brooklyn, New York

Rene Gochenour
Benson High School Magnet
Omaha, NE

Rebecca Griffith
Avery County High School
Newland, NC

Strait Herron
South Pointe High School
Rock Hill, SC

Jill Koebernik
Wauwatosa East High School
Wauwatosa, WI

Ruth Lewis
Richwoods High School
Peoria, IL

Jim McCarthy
Ursuline Academy
Cincinnati, OH

Matt McWenie
Central High School
Phoenix, AZ

Natalie Scavone
Cayuga-Onondaga BOCES New Visions
Teacher Education
Auburn, NY

Henry Stobbs
Mohawk High School
Sycamore, OH

Lem Wheeles
A.J. Dimond High School
Anchorage, AK

CORRELATION OF LESSONS 1-10 TO THE NATIONAL CONTENT STANDARDS IN ECONOMICS, FROM THE COUNCIL FOR ECONOMIC EDUCATION

Standard	Standard Topic	Lesson 1	Lesson 2	Lesson 3	Lesson 4	Lesson 5	Lesson 6	Lesson 7	Lesson 8	Lesson 9	Lesson 10
Standard 1	Scarcity										
Standard 2	Decision-Making										
Standard 3	Allocation										
Standard 4	Incentives		X				X	X			
Standard 5	Trade		X				X				
Standard 6	Specialization										
Standard 7	Markets & Prices						X				
Standard 8	Role of Prices										
Standard 9	Competition and Market Structure									X	
Standard 10	Institutions	X									
Standard 11	Money										
Standard 12	Interest Rates										
Standard 13	Income										
Standard 14	Entrepreneurship										
Standard 15	Economic Growth										
Standard 16	Market Failure	X			X	X		X	X	X	X
Standard 17	Government Failure			X				X		X	X
Standard 18	Measuring Overall Economic Performance										
Standard 19	Unemployment & Inflation								X		
Standard 20	Fiscal & Monetary Policy				X						

CORRELATION OF LESSONS 11-20 TO THE NATIONAL CONTENT STANDARDS IN ECONOMICS, FROM THE COUNCIL FOR ECONOMIC EDUCATION

Standard	Standard Topic	Lesson 11	Lesson 12	Lesson 13	Lesson 14	Lesson 15	Lesson 16	Lesson 17	Lesson 18	Lesson 19	Lesson 20
Standard 1	Scarcity										
Standard 2	Decision-Making							X			
Standard 3	Allocation										X
Standard 4	Incentives	X	X							X	
Standard 5	Trade					X					
Standard 6	Specialization										
Standard 7	Markets & Prices										
Standard 8	Role of Prices									X	
Standard 9	Competition and Market Structure										
Standard 10	Institutions					X	X				
Standard 11	Money										
Standard 12	Interest Rates										
Standard 13	Income										
Standard 14	Entrepreneurship										
Standard 15	Economic Growth										
Standard 16	Market Failure	X		X	X	X	X				X
Standard 17	Government Failure	X		X	X	X	X	X			
Standard 18	Measuring Overall Economic Performance								X		
Standard 19	Unemployment & Inflation								X		
Standard 20	Fiscal & Monetary Policy								X		

CORRELATION OF LESSONS 1-10 TO THE NATIONAL STANDARDS FOR CIVICS AND GOVERNMENT (GRADES 9-12), FROM THE CENTER FOR CIVIC EDUCATION

Standard	Standard Topic	Lesson 1	Lesson 2	Lesson 3	Lesson 4	Lesson 5	Lesson 6	Lesson 7	Lesson 8	Lesson 9	Lesson 10
Standard I.A	Civic Life, Politics, and Government										X
Standard I.B	Limited/Unlimited Government	X	X		X						
Standard I.C	Nature and Purpose of Constitutions	X									
Standard I.D	Alternative Constitutional Governments										
Standard II.A	American Constitutional Government										
Standard II.B	American Society										
Standard II.C	American Political Culture				X						
Standard II.D	Values/Principles American Democracy										X
Standard III.A	Power/Responsibility in the U.S. Constitution									X	
Standard III.B	National Government Organization				X	X		X		X	
Standard III.C	State/Local Government Organization					X					
Standard III.D	Law in the American Constitutional System									X	
Standard III.E	Choice/Participation in the American System			X				X	X		
Standard IV.A	World Political Organization										
Standard IV.B	U.S. World Relations										
Standard IV.C	U.S and World Influence on Each Other										
Standard V.A	Citizenship										
Standard V.B	Citizens' Rights										
Standard V.C	Citizens' Responsibilities						X				
Standard V.D	Public and Private Civic Traits										
Standard V.E	Citizens in Civic Life			X					X		

CORRELATION OF LESSONS 11-20 TO THE NATIONAL STANDARDS FOR CIVICS AND GOVERNMENT (GRADES 9-12), FROM THE CENTER FOR CIVIC EDUCATION

Standard	Standard Topic	Lesson 11	Lesson 12	Lesson 13	Lesson 14	Lesson 15	Lesson 16	Lesson 17	Lesson 18	Lesson 19	Lesson 20
Standard I.A	Civic Life, Politics, and Government									X	
Standard I.B	Limited/Unlimited Government					X	X				
Standard I.C	Nature and Purpose of Constitutions		X			X					
Standard I.D	Alternative Constitutional Governments		X								
Standard II.A	American Constitutional Government		X								
Standard II.B	American Society										
Standard II.C	American Political Culture										
Standard II.D	Values/Principles American Democracy							X			
Standard III.A	Power/Responsibility in the U.S. Constitution										
Standard III.B	National Government Organization	X		X					X		
Standard III.C	State/Local Government Organization										
Standard III.D	Law in the American Constitutional System			X							
Standard III.E	Choice/Participation in the American System										
Standard IV.A	World Political Organization										
Standard IV.B	U.S. World Relations				X						
Standard IV.C	U.S and World Influence on Each Other								X	X	
Standard V.A	Citizenship										
Standard V.B	Citizens' Rights										X
Standard V.C	Citizens' Responsibilities										
Standard V.D	Public and Private Civic Traits										
Standard V.E	Citizens in Civic Life										

DOWNLOADING VISUALS, ACTIVITIES, AND RELATED MATERIALS

On the Web

To download the visuals and activities for each lesson, find online lessons to extend the student activities and find related material to each lesson, visit:

http://civics.councilforeconed.org

LESSON 1

HOW DO CONSTITUTIONS SHAPE ECONOMIC SYSTEMS?

Lesson 1
How Do Constitutions Shape Economic Systems?

INTRODUCTION

Constitutions are economic documents as well as political documents. This is certainly true of the U.S. Constitution. Our nation's founders believed that economic freedom and political freedom are essential for national prosperity and growth. Accordingly, they included provisions in the Constitution that establish and reinforce the conditions needed for a market economy.

The constitutions of other nations are also economic documents as well as political documents. In this respect, North Korea and South Korea provide an informative contrast. The two countries have much in common, including their location, access to natural resources, culture, and language. But the constitutions of the two countries provide for markedly different economic systems. The difference has proved to be important. One country has experienced near economic collapse while the other has enjoyed widespread growth and prosperity.

LESSON DESCRIPTION

In the first part of the lesson, the students examine the characteristics of a market economy and the economic provisions of the U.S. Constitution. Then they complete a grid which shows how the U.S Constitution establishes and supports those characteristics. In the second part of the lesson, the students consider a question: Why would North Korea and South Korea—two nations with much in common—experience very different economic outcomes? To answer this question, the students read excerpts from the constitutions of North Korea and South Korea and examine the differences between them.

CONCEPTS

- Constitution
- Incentives
- Innovation
- Private property
- Taxation
- Trade

OBJECTIVES

Students will be able to:

1. Identify the characteristics of a market economy.

2. Explain the economic provisions of the U.S. Constitution.

3. Compare and contrast the economic provisions of the constitutions of North Korea and South Korea.

CONTENT STANDARDS
Economics (CEE Standards)

- There is an economic role for government to play in a market economy whenever the benefits of a government policy outweigh its costs. Governments often provide for national defense, address environmental concerns, define and protect property rights, and attempt to make markets more competitive. Most government policies also redistribute income. (Standard 16)

Civics and Government (NSCG Standards, Grades 9-12)

- The relationship of limited government to political and economic freedom. (Standard I.B.4)

- Concepts of "constitution." (Standard I.C.1)

- Purposes and uses of constitutions. (Standard I.C.2)

TIME REQUIRED
90 minutes

MATERIALS

- A transparency of Visuals 1.1, 1.2, 1.3, 1.4, 1.5, and 1.6

- A copy for each student of Activities 1.1 and 1.2

PROCEDURE

1. Tell the class that the purpose of this lesson is to explore ways in which national constitutions shape economic systems and outcomes. Toward this end, the students will study the economic provisions of the U.S. Constitution and the effect of those provisions on the U.S. economy. Then they will compare the economic provisions of the constitutions of North and South Korea and learn about the economic performance of these two nations.

2. Display Visual 1.1 and distribute Activity 1.1. Direct the students' attention to Part A of Activity 1.1. Discuss the overview provided in Part A of the characteristics of a market economy. Explain how market economies stress the role of choices made by individual consumers and producers, with a limited, but important, role played by government.

3. Display Visual 1.2. Direct the students' attention to Part B of Activity 1.1. Part B elaborates on the provisions listed in Visual 1.2. Discuss the provisions. Explain how these provisions, taken together, establish the basic conditions needed for a market economy.

4. Ask the students to read Part C of Activity 1.1 and complete the grid. When the students have completed their work on the grid, display Visual 1.3 and discuss the students' responses.

5. Display Visual 1.4. Discuss the Visual, emphasizing the main point of contrast: the two countries are alike in many ways, yet they differ greatly in the performance of their economic systems. Ask the students to speculate: Why might the people of North Korea continue to suffer from severe economic problems while the people of South Korea prosper?

6. Distribute Activity 1.2. Ask the students to read Part A and B. Discuss the reading as necessary. Ask the students to answer the Questions for Discussion listed in Part C.

7. Display Visual 1.5. Using it as a point of reference, discuss the students' responses to the Questions for Discussion.

8. Display Visual 1.6. Ask:
How well has the economy of North Korea performed? How well has the economy of South Korea performed? How might the different levels of performance be explained?

(The economy of South Korea is 13 times larger than the economy of North Korea. The socialist model specified in the constitution of North Korea has apparently contributed little to the economic welfare of its people. In contrast, the more open, market-oriented economy of South Korea, established by its constitution, has led to substantial economic improvement.)

CLOSURE

Review the lesson by posing the following questions:

- What are the main characteristics of a market economy?

  (Private property; freedom of enterprise and choice, motivated by self-interest; competition; a system of markets and prices; and limited government.)

- What are some key economic provisions of the U.S. Constitution?

  (The commerce clause, coinage clauses, copyright clause, contract clauses, export clauses, searches and seizures clause, due process of law clauses, and reserved rights and powers.)

- In what ways are the constitutions of North Korea and South Korea different?

  (North Korea's constitution calls for the government to play a dominant role in the economy. It severely restricts private ownership of property and discourages individual enterprise. South Korea's constitution specifies that government plays an important regulatory role, but it allows a much larger role for individual enterprise, and it bans the outright nationalization of private property.)

ASSESSMENT

Multiple-Choice Questions

1. The export clause which states that "No tax or duty shall be laid on articles exported from any state" is a key economic feature of the

   A. **U.S Constitution.**

   B. South Korean Constitution.

   C. Fifth Republic of France.

   D. North Korean Constitution.

2. Which of the following characteristics is found in the North Korean constitution?

   A. "The economic order … is based on a respect for the freedom and creative initiative of enterprises and individuals in economic affairs."

   B. "Licenses to exploit, develop, or utilize minerals and all other important underground resources, marine resources, water power, and natural powers available for economic use may be granted for a period of time under the conditions as prescribed by law."

   C. **"There is no limit to the property which the State can own."**

   D. "The land and natural resources are protected by the State, and the State establishes a plan necessary for their balanced development and utilization."

Constructed-Response Questions

1. Michael Jablonski is interested in science. He will graduate from high school soon, and he plans to study biomedical science and business in college. He hopes to start his own business and to make it successful and profitable. His dream is to make his business a leader in finding new cures for serious diseases. Identify and explain two characteristics of a market economy that might help Michael to achieve his goals.

   (Michael hopes to exercise his freedom to choose and engage in enterprise. He is free to decide which occupation to pursue, and to obtain and organize the resources he will need to open his business. Michael is motivated in part by self-interest. He hopes to run a profitable business by doing good things for consumers. Michael will face competition in the biomedical field. Competition will give Michael an incentive to work hard at his business. There is no guarantee that he can do better than his competitors.)

2. North Korea and South Korea have experienced very different economic outcomes. Explain how the constitution of South Korea fostered economic success, compared to the dismal performance of the North Korean economy.

   (North Korea's constitution calls for the government to play a dominant role in the economy. It severely restricts private ownership of property and discourages individual enterprise. South Korea's constitution specifies that government plays an important regulatory role, but it allows a much larger role for individual enterprise, and it bans the outright nationalization of private property.)

Visual 1.1

Characteristics of a Market Economy

1. Private Property

2. Freedom of Enterprise and Choice

3. Motive of Self-Interest

4. Competition

5. A System of Markets and Prices

6. Limited Government

VISUAL 1.2

ECONOMIC PROVISIONS OF THE U.S. CONSTITUTION

- Commerce Clause

- Coinage Clauses

- Copyright Clause

- Contract Clauses

- Export Clauses

- Searches and Seizures Clause

- Due Process of Law Clauses

- Reserved Rights and Powers

Visual 1.3

Matching the Provisions of the U.S Constitution with the Basic Characteristics of a Market Economy

	Art. 1, Sec. 8	Art. 1, Sec. 9	Art. 1, Sec. 10	Amend. 4	Amend. 5	Amend. 9	Amend. 10	Amend. 14
Private Property	X	X	X	X	X			
Freedom of Enterprise and Choice	X	X	X					
Motive of Self-Interest	X							
Competition	X							
A System of Markets and Prices	X							
Limited Government		X	X	X	X	X	X	X

VISUAL 1.4
SOUTH KOREA AND NORTH KOREA

The countries of North and South Korea are similar in many ways:

- They share the same peninsula.

- They have easy access to the sea for trade.

- They have many of the same natural resources.

- They have a similar culture.

- They have a similar language.

But the two countries differ greatly in economic performance. North Korea is a very poor country. Its economy is stagnant and its people suffer from chronic malnutrition and poor living conditions. South Korea, by comparison, is a prosperous country. Its economy has flourished and its people live well, compared with their neighbors to the north.

What might explain this contrast?

Visual 1.5

Comparing Economic Provisions in the Constitutions of North Korea and South Korea

	North Korean Constitution	South Korean Constitution
1. Is private property protected?	No. Articles 21, 22, and 24 state that nearly all property is owned by the state or by state-endorsed cooperatives. Private property is restricted mainly to personal possessions and wages.	Yes. Article 126 states clearly that private enterprises may not be nationalized. In other words, they are to be privately owned.
2. Is freedom of enterprise encouraged?	No. Articles 21 and 25 call for a large role for the state in the production of goods and services, and almost no role for individuals.	Yes. Article 119 specifically calls for respect for the freedom and creative initiative of enterprises and individuals in economic affairs.
3. Is the role of government limited?	No. The government controls nearly all aspects of economic life. Articles 19, 21, and 24 help to make this clear.	Yes. There is a strong role for economic activity not controlled by the state, as suggested in Article 119 and 126. However, Articles 119, 120, and 122 call for a large regulatory role for government.
4. Is free trade encouraged?	No. Article 36 suggests that protectionism is the dominant goal of trade policy.	Yes. Article 125 suggests that international trade is encouraged.

VISUAL 1.6

COMPARING THE ECONOMIC PERFORMANCE OF NORTH KOREA AND SOUTH KOREA

1. North Korea

How has the economy of North Korea fared under its system?
Here is an excerpted report from the CIA World Fact Book
(https://www.cia.gov/library/publications/the-world-factbook/index.html).

- One of the world's most centrally planned and isolated economies, North Korea faces desperate economic conditions.

- Industrial capital stock (e.g., factories, equipment) is nearly beyond repair as a result of years of underinvestment and shortages of spare parts.

- Industrial output and power output have declined in parallel.

- Per Capita GDP in North Korea: $1,900 (2007 estimate).

2. South Korea

How has the economy of South Korea fared under its system?
Here is an excerpted report from the CIA World Fact Book
(https://www.cia.gov/library/publications/the-world-factbook/index.html).

- Since the 1960s, South Korea has achieved an incredible record of growth and integration into the high-tech, modern world economy.

- Four decades ago, South Korean GDP per capita was comparable with levels in the poorer countries of Africa and Asia. In 2004, South Korea joined the trillion dollar club of world economies. Today its GDP per capita is equal to the lesser economies of the European Union.

- Per Capita GDP in South Korea: $24,800 (2007 estimate).

Activity 1.1

The Market Economy of the U.S. Constitution

Directions: Read Part A and Part B.   Use information from Part A and B to complete the grid in Part C.

Part A. Characteristics of a Market Economy

1. Private Property

Labor resources, natural resources, capital resources (e.g., equipment and buildings), and the goods and services produced in the economy are largely owned by private individuals and private institutions, not by government.   Private ownership combined with the freedom to negotiate legally binding contracts permits people, within very broad limits, to obtain and use the resources they choose.

2. Freedom of Enterprise and Choice

Private entrepreneurs are free to obtain and organize resources for the production of goods and services, and to sell goods and services in markets of their choice. Consumers are at liberty to buy the goods and services that best satisfy their economic wants. Workers are free to seek any jobs for which they are qualified.

3. Motive of Self-Interest

The "Invisible Hand" that is the driving force in a market economy is each individual pursuing his or her self-interest. Consumers aim to get the greatest satisfaction from their purchases; entrepreneurs try to achieve the highest profits for their firms; workers want the highest possible wages and salaries; and owners of property attempt to get the highest possible prices from the use, rent, or sale of their resources.

4. Competition

Economic competition means that buyers and sellers act independently in the marketplace. Buyers and sellers are free to enter or leave any market as they choose. It is competition, not government regulation, that diffuses economic power and limits the potential abuse of that power as each economic unit attempts to further its own self-interest.

5. A System of Markets and Prices

Markets are the basic coordinating mechanisms in a modern market economy, not central planning by government. A market brings buyers and sellers of a particular good or service into contact with one another. The choices of sellers and buyers are registered on the supply and demand sides of various markets, and the outcome of these choices is the creation of a system of prices to allocate goods, services, and resources. These prices provide signals to participants in markets, helping them to make choices aimed at furthering their self-interest.

ACTIVITY 1.1, CONTINUED
THE MARKET ECONOMY OF THE U.S. CONSTITUTION

6. Limited Government

A competitive market economy promotes the efficient use of its resources. In most cases, the role of government in the economy is very limited, since market competition, through a system of economic incentives, has a self-regulating component that is subject to adjustments that promote efficiency. However, certain limitations and undesirable outcomes associated with the market system create the need for an active, but limited economic role to be played by government.

Part B. Economic Provisions in the U.S. Constitution

1. The Commerce Clause

- Article 1, Section 8 states that Congress shall have the power "To regulate commerce with foreign nations, and among the several states, and with the Indian tribes; ..."

- In authorizing the federal government to regulate interstate and international commerce, this clause prevents states from doing their own regulating of such commerce. If individual states were allowed to establish their own regulations, trade between states would be reduced, and specialization, which is fostered by trade, would be discouraged.

2. The Coinage Clauses

- Article 1, Section 8 states that Congress shall have the power "To coin money, regulate the value thereof " and "To provide for the punishment of counterfeiting the securities and current coin of the United States." Article 1, Section 10 gives Congress this power exclusively, stating that "No state shall...coin money."

- Imagine the confusion that would befall business or interstate travel if each state had its own currency. By eliminating such confusion, the coinage clauses reduce the costs of specialization and trade within the borders of the 50 states. They help to create a "free trade zone" within the United States, a goal only recently accomplished by the European Union, with its common currency, the euro.

3. The Copyright Clause

- Article 1, Section 8 states that Congress shall have the power "To promote the progress of science and useful arts, by securing for limited times to authors and inventors the exclusive right to their respective writing and discoveries."

- This clause encourages innovation by allowing authors and inventors to maintain control over their products and to benefit from the earnings their products generate, for a period of time. The prospect of obtaining a patent for an idea offers an incentive for people to invest the time, imagination, and resources needed to produce new goods or services. Patents and copyrights apply not only to material goods but also to creative and intellectual works including poetry, film, music, and computer programs.

ACTIVITY 1.1, CONTINUED
THE MARKET ECONOMY OF THE U.S. CONSTITUTION

4. The Contract Clauses

- Article 1, Section 10 states that "No bill of attainder or ex post facto law shall be passed" by Congress. Article 1, Section 10 states that "No state shall...pass any bill of attainder, ex post facto law, or law impairing the obligations of contracts."

- These provisions protect freedom of contract and authorize the enforcement of contracts. We are accustomed to the idea that parties engaged in voluntary exchanges will hold to their commitments, even if they do not know each other. If a business buys a shipment of new lawnmowers, it expects the lawnmower provider to supply the mowers, at the agreed-upon time and at the agreed-upon price, even if the lawnmower provider lives in another state and is a complete stranger to the buyer. In an environment of trust, many businesses operate with no formal contracts at all—just a handshake between the parties to the exchange. However, such an environment of trust is no accident. In fact, it remains rare in many parts of the world today. The U.S. Constitution encourages such trust by stating that contracts will be enforced by the courts. Without freedom of contract and enforcement of contracts as ensured by the Constitution, there would be little stability in financial arrangements. Uncertainty and lack of trust would discourage people from participating in economic life.

5. The Export Clauses

- Article 1, Section 9 states that "No tax or duty shall be laid on articles exported from any state." Article 1, Section 10 states that "No state shall without the consent of the Congress, lay any imposts or duties on imports or exports."

- These clauses make it unconstitutional for states to impose taxes on imports or exports. The Founders recognized that allowing states to exercise such power would reduce specialization and trade within the nation, thus reducing the standard of living for the nation. Like the coinage clauses, the export clauses have helped to create a "free trade zone" within the United States, a goal only recently accomplished by the European Union.

6. The Searches and Seizures Clause

- The Fourth Amendment to the Constitution states that "The right of the people to be secure in their persons, houses, papers, and effects, against unreasonable searches and seizures, shall not be violated."

- Would you be willing to run a grocery store in a country where the police could legally confiscate your business? Not likely. The Fourth Amendment protects people against unreasonable seizures of property. Only under special circumstances may the state conduct searches and remove private property.

7. Due Process of Law Clauses

- The Fifth Amendment to the Constitution states that "No person shall...be deprived of life, liberty, or property, without due process of the law." It also states that the government may not take private property for public use without paying "just compensation." The Fourteenth

ACTIVITY 1.1, CONTINUED
THE MARKET ECONOMY OF THE U.S. CONSTITUTION

Amendment, Section 1, applies the due process requirement to state governments: "nor shall any State deprive any person of life, liberty, or property, without due process of law."

- For most people, due process of law is associated with the rights of citizens when they are placed under arrest by the authorities. You have probably seen television shows in which individuals who have been arrested are notified that they have the right to an attorney, to remain silent, and so forth. These rights taken together are known as "due process of law." But, due process of law is not reserved only for criminal cases. It is also a fundamental economic freedom protected by the U.S. Constitution. It means that the government may not arbitrarily take property owned by individuals. For example, the government may not nationalize businesses or farms or take possession of homes without following specified legal procedures and paying compensation for any loss. Knowing this, property owners may use their property confidently, as they see fit, without fear that a disapproving government might confiscate it. This form of protection encourages people to invest in their property and allows them to retain any benefits they derive from the use of their property.

8. Reserved Rights and Powers

- The Ninth Amendment to the Constitution states that "The enumeration in the Constitution, of certain rights, shall not be construed to deny or disparage others retained by the people." The Tenth Amendment states that "The powers not delegated to the United States by the Constitution, nor prohibited by it to the States, are reserved to the states respectively, or to the people."

- The Founders assumed that fundamental rights and freedoms are inalienable rights held by individuals, not governments. Thus, any powers not specified as belonging to the state or national government are to remain with the people. Amendments Nine and Ten are meant to underscore the limited role of government in the U.S. economy.

Part C: Matching the Provisions of the U.S Constitution with the Basic Characteristics of a Market Economy

Directions: Use information from Parts A and B to assist you in matching the characteristics of a market economy to the economic provisions of the U.S. Constitution. Place an "X" in the space where you think the article or amendment of the U.S. Constitution serves to establish or support the economic characteristic.

ACTIVITY 1.1, CONTINUED

THE MARKET ECONOMY OF THE U.S. CONSTITUTION

Place an "X" in the space where you think the article or amendment of the U.S. Constitution serves to establish or support the economic characteristic.

	Art. 1, Sec. 8	Art. 1, Sec. 9	Art. 1, Sec. 10	Amend. 4	Amend. 5	Amend. 9	Amend. 10	Amend. 14
Private Property								
Freedom of Enterprise and Choice								
Motive of Self-Interest								
Competition								
A System of Markets and Prices								
Limited Government								

ACTIVITY 1.2

COMPARING THE CONSTITUTIONS OF NORTH KOREA AND SOUTH KOREA

Directions: Activity 1.2 compares the economic provisions of the constitutions of North Korea (officially known as the Democratic People's Republic of Korea, or DPRK) to South Korea (officially known as the Republic of Korea). Read Parts A and B. Use the information from Parts A and B to answer the Questions for Discussion in the grid in Part C.

Part A. The Constitution of North Korea

1. Overview

The current constitution of North Korea was patterned after those of other communist states. It calls for highly centralized decision making—within the government and the economy. Chapter 2 of the Constitution specifies how economic affairs are to be handled.

2. Excerpts from the Constitution of North Korea: Chapter 2, Economy

- **Article 19**

North Korea relies on socialist production relations and on the foundation of an independent national economy.

- **Article 20**

In North Korea, the means of production are owned only by the State and social cooperative organizations.

- **Article 21**

The property of the State belongs to the entire people.

There is no limit to the property which the State can own.

Only the State possesses all the natural resources, railways, airports, transportation, communication organs and major factories, enterprises, ports, and banks.

- **Article 22**

The property of social cooperatives belongs collectively to the working people within the organizations concerned.

Social cooperative organizations can possess land, agricultural machinery, ships, . . . factories, and enterprises.

The State shall protect the property of social cooperative organizations.

Activity 1.2, Continued

Comparing the Constitutions of North Korea and South Korea

- **Article 24**

Private property is confined to property meeting the simple and individual aims of the citizens.

Private property consists of socialist distributions of the result of labor and additional benefits of the State and society.

The products of individual sideline activities including those from the kitchen gardens of cooperative farmers and income from other legal economic activities shall also belong to private property.

The State shall protect private property and guarantee its legal inheritance.

- **Article 25**

The State shall provide all working people with every condition for obtaining food, clothing, and housing.

- **Article 36**

The State shall pursue a tariff policy with the aim of protecting the independent national economy.

Part B: Excerpts from the Constitution of South Korea

1. Overview

The current constitution of South Korea was patterned in part after those of western democracies; it also was strongly influenced by traditional Korean ideas. The constitution calls for a large regulatory role for the government, but it also protects basic economic and political freedoms.

2. Excerpts from the Constitution of South Korea: Chapter IX, The Economy

- **Article 119: Regulation and Coordination**

(1) The economic order of South Korea is based on a respect for the freedom and creative initiative of enterprises and individuals in economic affairs.

(2) The State may regulate and coordinate economic affairs in order to maintain the balanced growth and stability of the national economy, to ensure proper distribution of income, to prevent the domination of the market and the abuse of economic power, and to democratize the economy through harmony among the economic agents.

- **Article 120: Natural Resources**

Licenses to exploit, develop, or utilize minerals and all other important underground resources, marine resources, water power, and natural powers available for economic use may be granted for a period of time under the conditions as prescribed by law.

ACTIVITY 1.2, CONTINUED

COMPARING THE CONSTITUTIONS OF NORTH KOREA AND SOUTH KOREA

The land and natural resources are protected by the State, and the State establishes a plan necessary for their balanced development and utilization.

- **Article 122: Land Laws**

The State may impose, . . . under the conditions prescribed by law, restrictions or obligations necessary for the efficient and balanced utilization, development, and preservation of the land of the nation that is the basis for the productive activities and daily lives of all citizens.

- **Article 125: Foreign Trade**

The State fosters foreign trade, and may regulate and coordinate it.

- **Article 126: No Socialization**

Private enterprises may not be nationalized nor transferred to ownership by a local government, nor shall their management be controlled or administered by the State, except in cases as prescribed by law to meet urgent necessities of national defense or the national economy.

Activity 1.2, Continued

Comparing Economic Provisions in the Constitutions of North Korea and South Korea

	North Korean Constitution	South Korean Constitution
1. Is private property protected?		
2. Is freedom of enterprise encouraged?		
3. Is the role of government limited?		
4. Is free trade encouraged?		

LESSON 2

THE RELATIONSHIP BETWEEN ECONOMIC FREEDOM AND POLITICAL FREEDOM

LESSON 2

THE RELATIONSHIP BETWEEN ECONOMIC FREEDOM AND POLITICAL FREEDOM

INTRODUCTION

Citizens of the United States enjoy a great deal of political freedom (under our constitutional, representative democracy) and economic freedom (within our market-oriented economy). Is there a relationship between these two sorts of freedom? Many scholars say that there is. Self-government in a free society, they claim, is related to the presence of a free and open economic system. In other words, *political* freedom and *economic* freedom are inextricably linked. Noted sociologist Seymour Lipset, for example, claims that democracies are almost always found in countries with economic systems based on essentially free markets and private ownership of resources. Lipset concludes, in part, that "the more well-to-do a nation, the greater the chances that it will sustain democracy."[1] More recently, empirical studies in economics have demonstrated a causal link between political freedom and economic freedom.[2]

LESSON DESCRIPTION

To begin the lesson, students brainstorm examples of political and economic freedom. Then they examine several quotations describing the theoretical relationship between the two kinds of freedom, and they are asked if they believe such a relationship exists. In order to answer this question, the students examine the relationship by reference to evidence from two indices: the Freedom House *Freedom in the World* survey and the *Wall Street Journal*/Heritage Foundation *Index of Economic Freedom*. After a brief discussion of information from the indices, the students plot and analyze data for 30 randomly selected countries to determine

whether a relationship between the two types of freedom exists.

CONCEPTS

- Civil liberties
- Economic freedom
- Markets
- Political freedom
- Political rights

OBJECTIVES

Students will be able to:

1. Provide examples of political freedom and economic freedom.

2. Summarize the relationship between political and economic freedom as described by several authors.

3. Compare data on economic freedom and political freedom from a random sample of countries to determine what the relationship is between the two types of freedom.

CONTENT STANDARDS
Economics (CEE Standards)

- People respond predictably to positive and negative incentives. (Standard 4)

- Voluntary exchange occurs only when all participating parties expect to gain. This is true for trade among individuals or organizations within a nation, and among individuals or organizations in different nations. (Standard 5)

- Institutions evolve in market economies to help individuals and groups accomplish

---

[1] Seymour Lipset, *Political Man: The Social Basis of Politics* (Baltimore, MD: The Johns Hopkins University Press, 1981), p. 469.
[2] See, for example, W. Farr, R. Lord, and J. Wolfenbarger, "Economic Freedom, Political Freedom, and Economic Well-Being: A Causality Analysis," *Cato Journal, 18* (2), Fall 1998.

their goals. Banks, labor unions, corporations, legal systems, and not-for-profit organizations are examples of important institutions. A different kind of institution, clearly defined and enforced property rights, is essential to a market economy. (Standard 10)

Civics and Government (NSCG Standards, Grades 9-12)

- Students should be able to explain and evaluate competing ideas regarding the relationship between political and economic freedoms. (Standard I.B.4)

TIME REQUIRED
45-60 minutes

MATERIALS
- A transparency of Visuals 2.1, 2.2, 2.3, 2.4, and 2.5

- A copy for each student of Activity 2.1

PROCEDURE

1. Begin by asking the students to identify some examples of freedoms they enjoy in the United States. List several of their responses on the board. (*Answers will vary. Students might mention freedom of the press, freedom of movement, freedom of speech, etc. Most answers probably will be examples of* political *freedoms, as that concept is used in this lesson.*)

2. Tell the students that many of these examples are known more specifically as *political* freedoms. Label the list of political freedoms on the board under the heading, **Political Freedoms**. Ask the students to think of other political freedoms citizens of the United States have. Again, list these on the board under the same heading. (*Answers will vary but might include the right to vote, freedom of religion, freedom from religion, etc.*)

3. Now ask the students if they can think of any *economic* freedoms that citizens of the United States enjoy. (The students may already have identified some economic

freedoms in the first part of this exercise. If they have, move those examples over to the new list. Still, the students may need prompting here, so be prepared to suggest one or two new examples such as the right to own property.) List appropriate student responses on a separate section of the board under the heading **Economic Freedoms**. (*Answers will vary but might include individuals' freedom to seek employment of their choosing, freedom to buy goods in the store, freedom to start their own business, freedom from fraudulent business practices, etc.*)

4. Ask the students if they see any similarities between the freedoms on the two lists. Give them a few minutes to discuss this question among themselves.

5. Tell the students that many scholars—economists, political scientists, and others—believe that political freedom and economic freedom are related.

6. Place Visual 2.1 on the overhead. Reveal the first quotation. Ask the students to read it and to restate Friedman's thesis in their own words. (*Friedman states that at no time in history has a nation had political freedom without having economic freedom as well.*) Reveal the second quotation. Ask the students to read it and to restate Dahl's thesis in their own words. (*Dahl states that democracies exist only in nations that have market economies.*) Reveal the third quotation. Ask the students how the third quotation differs from the first two. (*Lipset provides a reason for believing that the thesis put forth in the first two quotations is true: that nations that are economically successful are more likely to sustain governments based on democratic ideals—that is, to enjoy political freedom.*)

7. Ask the students whether they agree with these authors or not. Also ask them to suggest some ways to test this hypothesis: that political freedom and economic freedom are causally related—that *one* is necessary for the *other* to be present.

8. State that one approach to testing the hypothesis would be to compare the amount of political freedom in various nations with the amount of economic freedom in those nations. Ask the students what evidence, from such a comparison, would suggest that the hypothesis holds. (*Nations with high levels of political freedom should have high levels of economic freedom, and vice versa.*) Note that this approach cannot prove a *causal* relationship between the two types of freedom. However, the comparisons might establish a predictable *correlation* between economic and political freedom.

9. Tell the students that each year an organization called the Freedom House publishes its *Freedom in the World Survey*, in which 192 nations are rated as Free, Partly Free, or Not Free. Similarly, the *Wall Street Journal*/Heritage Foundation's *Index of Economic Freedom* provides a measure of economic freedom in 161 nations. Tell the students that they will complete an activity comparing results from these two measures for 30 nations, randomly selected.

10. Distribute Activity 2.1 and ask the students to read up to the section titled "Political and Economic Freedom in Selected Countries." When they reach this section, they should stop.

11. Place Visual 2.2 on the overhead. Briefly review the data in each column. Make certain that students understand the *Index of Economic Freedom* (IEF) rating (e.g., Cuba, with a rating of 29.7, has very little economic freedom) and the *Freedom House* status (e.g., "Not Free" means citizens have very few civil and political freedoms).

12. Ask the students to complete the remainder of Activity 2.1.

A. Briefly review Table 2.1. Ask: What is the range (lowest to highest) of IEF ratings for Free countries? For Partly Free? For Not Free?

(*Free: 60.1 – 81.6; Partly Free: 48.4 – 68.7; Not Free: 29.7 – 55.1*)

B. Ask the students whether they see a correlation (based on the information presented here) between the IEF ratings and the political freedom ratings of these countries. What might that correlation be?

(*While some of the ranges overlap, Free countries generally have a higher midpoint in their range—more economic freedom—than Partly Free countries, and so on.*)

C. Ask the students to plot a bar graph for each country's IEF rating, using data from Table 2.1. When they have plotted the data, they should draw a vertical line to separate the Not Free countries from the Partly Free countries, and another line to separate the Partly Free countries from the Free countries.

(*See Visual 2.3*)

Ask: Do you see a correlation in the IEF ratings among these countries? What might that correlation be?

(*The bar graph plot shows that freer countries tend to have higher IEF ratings.*)

D. Ask the students to calculate (using data from Table 2.1) the average IEF rating for each of the Freedom House ratings: Not Free, Partly Free, Free:

Not Free average rating:___(45.31)_____

Partly Free average rating:__(58.27)_____

Free average rating:_____(69.66)_____

E. Ask the students to plot these averages, using bar graphs.

(*See Visual 2.4*)

F. Ask: Do you see a correlation between the average IEF ratings of these countries and their political freedom ratings? What might that correlation be?

(The average IEF rating for Free nations is higher than that of Partly Free or Not Free nations. This positive relationship means that countries in the Free category have, on average, greater economic freedom.)

G. Ask the students to write a two-paragraph response to this question: "Is there a relationship between political and economic freedom in the world today?" They should use their analyses of data and the quotations presented at the beginning of the lesson to develop their paragraphs.

(The paragraphs should include a summary of the data analyses conducted above and focus on the positive—but not perfect—correlation between the IEF rating and the Freedom House category.)

CLOSURE

Ask the students to recall what they have learned about the relationship between the *Index of Economic Freedom* (IEF) for a country and its Freedom House category (Free, Partly Free, Not Free). Place Visual 2.5 on the overhead with the last column covered. Ask the students to write out a prediction for the missing data in each table. Take an informal poll to determine how many students make accurate predictions.

ASSESSMENT

Multiple-Choice Questions

1. Generally speaking, the more political freedom citizens in a country have, the

    A. less economic freedom they will possess.

    B. **more economic freedom they will possess.**

    C. more difficult it is to predict the level of economic freedom.

    D. less likely they are to participate in their government.

2. Which of the following are political freedoms:

    A. **freedom of expression and belief, organizational rights, right to vote, and the rule of law.**

    B. freedom of individuals to seek employment of their choosing, freedom to buy goods in the store, and freedom to start their own business.

    C. private property rights, freedom from fraudulent business practices, and freedom to trade with others.

    D. none of these are political freedoms.

Constructed-Response Question

In class you discovered a relationship between economic and political freedom by using data for certain countries. Briefly explain why this relationship (while not perfect) was so strong. In other words, *why* are economic freedom and political freedom so closely linked? *(Answers will vary, but students may choose to elaborate on the quotations from Friedman, Dahl, and Lipset, found on Visual 2.1.)*

VISUAL 2.1

QUOTATIONS ON POLITICAL AND ECONOMIC FREEDOM

Quotation 1:

I know of no example in time or place of a society that has been marked by a large measure of political freedom and that has not also used something comparable to a free market to organize the bulk of economic activity.

> Milton Friedman, Nobel Prize-winning economist, *Capitalism and Freedom* (University of Chicago Press, 1962).

Quotation 2:

It is a historical fact that modern democratic institutions...have existed only in countries with predominantly privately-owned, market oriented economies, or capitalism, if you prefer the name.

> Robert Dahl, *After the Revolution: Authority in a Good Society* (Yale University Press, 1990).

Quotation 3:

The more well-to-do a nation, the greater the chances that it will sustain democracy.

> Seymour Lipset, *Political Man: The Social Basis of Politics* (The Johns Hopkins University Press, 1981).

VISUAL 2.2
POLITICAL AND ECONOMIC FREEDOM IN 30 RANDOMLY SELECTED COUNTRIES

Country	Index of Economic Freedom (IEF) Rating	Freedom House Status
Cuba	29.7	Not Free
Zimbabwe	35.8	Not Free
Myanmar (Burma)	40.1	Not Free
Turkmenistan	42.5	Not Free
Syria	48.2	Not Free
Chad	46.4	Not Free
Laos	49.1	Not Free
Algeria	52.2	Not Free
Russia	54.0	Not Free
Guinea	55.1	Not Free
Sierra Leone	48.4	Partly Free
Djibouti	52.6	Partly Free
Yemen	53.8	Partly Free
Burkina Faso	55.0	Partly Free
Turkey	59.3	Partly Free
Kenya	59.4	Partly Free
Albania	61.4	Partly Free
Madagascar	61.4	Partly Free
Nicaragua	62.7	Partly Free
Georgia	68.7	Partly Free
Mongolia	60.1	Free
Brazil	60.9	Free
Peru	62.1	Free
South Africa	64.1	Free
Czech Republic	69.7	Free
Australia	71.3	Free
Lithuania	72.0	Free
Germany	73.5	Free
Ireland	81.3	Free
United Kingdom	81.6	Free

VISUAL 2.3
IEF RATING BY FREEDOM HOUSE CATEGORY

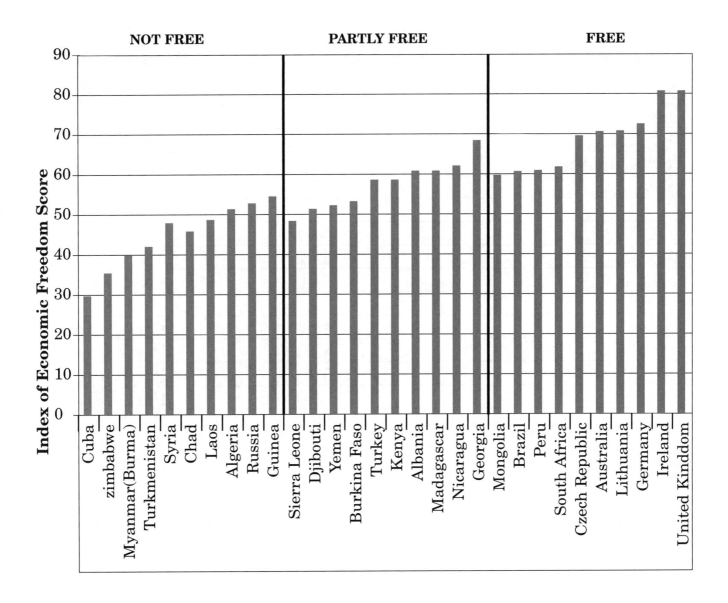

VISUAL 2.4

COMPLETED AVERAGE IEF RATING BY FREEDOM HOUSE CATEGORY FOR 30 RANDOMLY SELECTED COUNTRIES

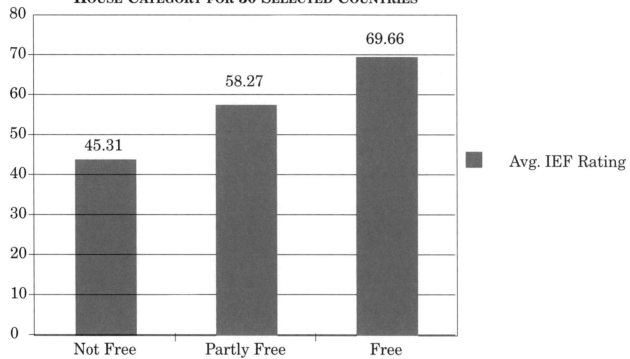

AVERAGE INDEX OF ECONOMIC FREEDOM (IEF) RATING BY FREEDOM HOUSE CATEGORY FOR 30 SELECTED COUNTRIES

VISUAL 2.5

TESTING THE RELATIONSHIP BETWEEN ECONOMIC AND POLITICAL FREEDOM

Country	Freedom House Category	Predicted IEF Rating	Actual IEF Rating
Iran	NOT FREE		43.1
South Korea	FREE		68.6
United States	FREE		82.0

Country	IEF Rating	Predicted Freedom House Category	Actual Freedom House Category
Norway	70.1		FREE
Estonia	78.1		FREE
Haiti	52.2		NOT FREE

FOCUS: UNDERSTANDING ECONOMICS IN CIVICS AND GOVERNMENT © COUNCIL FOR ECONOMIC EDUCATION, NEW YORK, NY

ACTIVITY 2.1

POLITICAL AND ECONOMIC FREEDOM: ANALYZING THE RELATIONSHIP

Directions: Read the brief descriptions of the *Freedom in the World* survey and the *Wall Street Journal*/Heritage Foundation *Index of Economic Freedom*. Next, review the data in Table 2.1. Complete the graphing tasks and answer the Questions for Discussion that follow.

Measuring Political Freedom

Each year since 1972, Freedom House (http://www.freedomhouse.org) has conducted the *Freedom in the World* survey. This survey analyzes the state of civil and political freedoms globally by gathering information on freedom in every country around the world. Freedom House defines freedom as "the opportunity to act spontaneously in a variety of fields outside the control of the government and other centers of potential domination."[3] It divides freedom into two broad categories: political rights and civil liberties. Political rights include the right to vote freely for distinct alternatives in legitimate elections, the right to compete for public office, the right to join political parties and organizations, and the right to elect representatives who have a decisive impact on public policies and are accountable to the electorate. Civil liberties, according to Freedom House, "allow for the freedoms of expression and belief, associational and organizational rights, rule of law, and personal autonomy without interference from the state."

The 2006 survey provides freedom ratings for 192 countries. In these ratings, countries are assigned two numerical ratings (on a scale of 1 to7): one for political rights and one for civil liberties. A rating of 1 indicates the *highest* degree of freedom; a rating of 7 indicates the *least*. Countries with combined average ratings between 1.0 and 2.5 are labeled Free; those with average ratings between 3.0 and 5.0 are labeled Partly Free; and those with average ratings between 5.5 and 7.0 are labeled Not Free.

Measuring Economic Freedom

Each year since 1995, *The Wall Street Journal* and The Heritage Foundation have produced the *Index of Economic Freedom* (IEF). The IEF measures the presence of 10 freedoms (from property rights to entrepreneurship) for 161 countries.

Here are the 10 economic freedoms that make up the IEF:

- Business freedom
- Trade freedom
- Monetary freedom
- Freedom from government
- Fiscal freedom

[3] Source: http://www.freedomhouse.org/template.cfm?page=351&ana_page=298&year=2006.

ACTIVITY 2.1, CONTINUED

POLITICAL AND ECONOMIC FREEDOM: ANALYZING THE RELATIONSHIP

- Property rights
- Investment freedom
- Financial freedom
- Freedom from corruption
- Labor freedom[4]

The IEF is a simple composite index based on an average of the 10 freedoms. The higher the IEF rating, the more economic freedom a country has. A country's IEF score can range from 0 (no economic freedom) to 100 (complete economic freedom). In 2008, IEF ratings ranged from 3 (North Korea) to 90.25 (Hong Kong).

Political and Economic Freedom in Selected Countries

The following table (Table 2.1) reports the Freedom House civil and political freedom rating and the *Wall Street Journal*/Heritage Foundation IEF rating for 30 nations selected randomly from the 161 for which both indices were available.[5]

---

[4] Source: http://www.heritage.org/research/features/index/chapters/htm/index2007_chap3.cfm.
[5] Note: Countries were chosen using simple stratified random sampling. Within each Freedom House category (Free, Partly Free, Not Free), 10 countries were selected at random.

ACTIVITY 2.1, CONTINUED

TABLE 2.1: POLITICAL AND ECONOMIC FREEDOM IN 30 RANDOMLY SELECTED COUNTRIES

Country	Index of Economic Freedom (IEF) Rating	Freedom House Status
Cuba	29.7	Not Free
Zimbabwe	35.8	Not Free
Myanmar (Burma)	40.1	Not Free
Turkmenistan	42.5	Not Free
Syria	48.2	Not Free
Chad	46.4	Not Free
Laos	49.1	Not Free
Algeria	52.2	Not Free
Russia	54.0	Not Free
Guinea	55.1	Not Free
Sierra Leone	48.4	Partly Free
Djibouti	52.6	Partly Free
Yemen	53.8	Partly Free
Burkina Faso	55.0	Partly Free
Turkey	59.3	Partly Free
Kenya	59.4	Partly Free
Albania	61.4	Partly Free
Madagascar	61.4	Partly Free
Nicaragua	62.7	Partly Free
Georgia	68.7	Partly Free
Mongolia	60.1	Free
Brazil	60.9	Free
Peru	62.1	Free
South Africa	64.1	Free
Czech Republic	69.7	Free
Australia	71.3	Free
Lithuania	72.0	Free
Germany	73.5	Free
Ireland	81.3	Free
United Kingdom	81.6	Free

ACTIVITY 2.1, CONTINUED

POLITICAL AND ECONOMIC FREEDOM: ANALYZING THE RELATIONSHIP

QUESTIONS FOR DISCUSSION

1. Briefly review Table 2.1. What is the range (lowest to highest) of IEF ratings for Free countries? For Partly Free? For Not Free?

2. Based on the information presented here, do you see a correlation between the IEF ratings and the political freedom ratings of these countries? What might that correlation be?

3. Use data from Table 2.1 to plot a bar graph for each country's IEF rating (see the Cuba example). When you have plotted the data, draw a vertical line to separate the Not Free countries from the Partly Free countries, and another line to separate the Partly Free countries from the Free countries.

   Do you see a correlation in the IEF ratings among these countries? What might that correlation be?

4. Use the data from Table 2.1 to calculate the average IEF rating for each of the Freedom House ratings: Not Free, Partly Free, Free:

   a.   Not Free average rating:_____

   b.   Partly Free average rating:_____

   c.   Free average rating:_____

   Using bar graphs, plot these averages for each of the three Freedom House categories.

5. Do you see a correlation between the average IEF ratings of these countries and their political freedom ratings? What might that correlation be?

6. Using your analysis of data and the quotations presented at the beginning of this lesson, write a two-paragraph response to this question: "Is there a relationship between political and economic freedom in the world today?" Explain your answer.

LESSON 3

VOTERS AND ELECTIONS

LESSON 3
VOTERS AND ELECTIONS

INTRODUCTION

Voter turnout in the United States influences the outcomes of elections. Politicians spend a great deal of time and energy trying to get their supporters to the polls. But why should this be a problem? Why don't all eligible voters vote? Economists who have studied this question believe that the answer has to do with the benefits and costs of voting. One sort of cost—opportunity cost—is especially helpful in explaining why some people choose not to vote.

LESSON DESCRIPTION

Students identify costs associated with voting. Then they make predictions about who might be more likely to vote based on their understanding of opportunity costs.

CONCEPTS

- Benefit
- Elections
- Opportunity cost

OBJECTIVES

Students will be able to:

1. List the costs and benefits of voting in an election.

2. Weigh costs and benefits to predict whether a person is likely to vote.

CONTENT STANDARDS

Economics (CEE Standards)

- Costs of government policies sometimes exceed benefits. This may occur because of incentives facing voters, government officials, and government employees, because of actions by special interest groups that can impose costs on the general public, or because social goals other than economic efficiency are being pursued. (Standard 17)

Civics and Government (NSCG Standards, 9-12)

- Students should be able evaluate, take, and defend positions about the roles of political parties, campaigns, and elections in American politics. (Standard III. E. 4)

- Students should be able to evaluate, take, and defend positions about the means that citizens should use to monitor and influence the formation and implementation of public policy. (Standard V. E. 3)

TIME REQUIRED

45 minutes

MATERIALS

- A transparency of Visuals 3.1, 3.2, 3.3, 3.4, and 3.5

PROCEDURE

1. Begin by noting that in a democracy, voting is an important civic right. Ask: Did everyone who was eligible to vote in the last presidential election actually vote? *(The answer is no, not everyone voted.)* If the right to vote is so important, why do some people choose not to vote? *(Answers will vary. Some answers may involve costs associated with voting, even if the students do not use that term.)* After some discussion of the students' answers, explain that the purpose of this lesson is to explore reasons why eligible voters do not always vote.

2. Tell the students that there are costs associated with voting. Ask:

   - What might these costs be?

     (The students might mention transportation costs, the cost of child care, the cost of time taken away from work etc. Explain that these costs might be called dollar costs. *Dollar costs might deter some people from voting. But*

other costs also may be important.)

- Apart from dollars spent, what other costs might people have to pay in order to vote? Hint: Think about how people might spend their time on election day if they decided not to vote.

  (People who do not take time to vote would have more time for working, shopping, recreation, etc.)

3. By reference to the students' answers, explain the concept of *opportunity cost*. The opportunity cost of doing something (voting, for example) is the highest-valued alternative a person gives up in choosing to do that particular something. A person whose most highly valued alternative is working (or at least the pay from work) would say that his or her opportunity cost of voting is lost time at work. Somebody else might identify sleeping as the most highly valued alternative; for that person, the opportunity cost of voting would be lost sleep. Emphasize the subjective nature of opportunity costs. The opportunity cost of voting will vary from person to person, and decisions about whether to vote or not will differ accordingly.

4. To summarize issues of costs related to voting, display Visual 3.1 and discuss it with the students. The Visual refers initially to Amendment 24 to the U.S. Constitution, which states that no dollar costs (in the form of poll taxes, for example) may be attached to voting in a federal election. The Visual then identifies other costs that voters may incur. Note that most of these costs—the opportunity costs of voting—involve the time it takes to register, learn about the candidates, and get to and from the polls. A hair stylist or cab driver, for example, might lose money for every hour spent away from work; for that person, the opportunity cost of voting might be lost income.

5. These examples may strike the students as somewhat hypothetical. Are prospective

voters in fact influenced by considerations of opportunity cost? How could we find out? To pursue the question, display Visual 3.2 and discuss its contents. The Visual shows results of a Census Bureau survey of actual reasons people gave for not voting in the 2004 national election. The list is presented in reverse order, based on the responses of all registered voters. The final column lists the separate percentage responses of individuals aged 18-24. Ask the students if there are any differences between the overall registration percentages and those for the younger population. *(Younger people were less likely to be ill, but less likely to know why they didn't vote and more likely to be busy. Younger people also tended to be out of town, perhaps at college, where they were not registered to vote.)* In reviewing the list, note that many of the items reflect judgments about increased costs of voting or decreased benefits from voting.

6. Still, despite the difficulties, many people do vote. Explore this point. Ask: why would any citizen vote when there are opportunity costs attached to voting and when it seems unlikely that any individual's vote will change the outcome of an election? *(Answers will vary. Some students may mention a civic duty to vote; others may think it important to express support for certain candidates.)*

7. Comment on these answers: They illustrate what some people have called "the paradox of voting." The paradox is that many people vote even when their votes are not likely to change the outcome of an election. (For more information, see the *expressive voting* entry in *The Encyclopedia of Public Choice* [electronic resource] / Dordrecht ; Boston : Kluwer Academic Publishers, c2004.) To prompt further discussion of this paradox, display and discuss Visual 3.3.

8. Given the subjective nature of opportunity costs, we would expect to find variation in

voting, with some people more likely to vote than others. Ask the students to speculate about this. Who tends to vote more? Who tends to vote less?

9. After some discussion of the students' responses, display Visual 3.4, which identifies various characteristics of voters. Note that the comparisons may not include all groups. Go over each comparison group in Visual 3.4 by asking the students which category of voters in each row was most likely to vote in the 2004 general election. Students don't need to guess the exact percentage for each category of voter, but they should attempt to identify which category of each comparison group was most likely to vote. The percentage-wise answers are found below in italics. In the discussion, challenge the students to think of reasons for the differences indicated, reminding them of the concept of opportunity cost. Many examples can be explained by the opportunity cost of voting. For example, lower-income voters may be workers who are paid at an hourly rate, and they may not be able to get away from work to vote without losing a significant amount of pay. Unemployed people may be worried more about finding work than voting, so they may view the costs of taking time to vote as too high. Homeowners are more settled than others and so are more likely to know how and where to register and vote; this familiarity with the setting reduces their opportunity cost of time needed to vote. Retirees also may have a lower opportunity cost regarding time, and so may be more likely to vote. Other examples may be explained by the benefits received. One example of a benefit is the sense of satisfaction some people find in meeting their civic duty to vote, which might explain why veterans tend to vote more than non-veterans. Other examples may be more difficult to understand, but even in these cases students often can propose interesting explanations.

Answers, in percentage of voting-age citizens:
Women (65.4); Men (62.1)
White (65.4); Black (60.0); Asian (44.1)
Native Born (64.5);
Naturalized Citizen (53.7)
Married (70.7); Never Married (52.0)
Divorced (58.4); Separated (47.5)
High Income (Over $100,000, 81.3);
Low Income (Less than $20,000, 48.3)
Employed (65.9); Unemployed (51.4)
Bachelor's Degree (77.5);
High School Degree (56.4)
Minnesotan (79.2); Floridian (64.3);
Hawaiian (50.8)
Veteran (73.5); Nonveteran (62.6)
Homeowner (68.7); Renter (48.3)
Old (age 65 to 74, 73.3);
Young (18 to 24 years old, 46.7)

Source: Census Bureau, "Voting and Registration in the Election of November 2004," publication P20-556. A version of this publication is produced for each federal election. The results of the 2008 election will be available in 2010.

10. Ask the students which groups of voters they would specifically try to attract if they were running for office. *(They should note that prospective voters who are more likely to turn out at the polls may have greater sway in forming the politicians' policies.)*

11. Ask the students what they think candidates for office might do to lower the opportunity cost of voting for their supporters? *(Offering transportation to the polls is one common proposal, especially for areas with large populations of elderly, retired voters. Offering help with absentee balloting also lowers the opportunity cost for voters who can't make it to the polls.)*

12. Display Visual 3.5. Note that many citizens fail to vote. Ask the students if they plan to register and vote when they turn 18. Remind them of the potential opportunity costs and ask what they think the benefits of voting will be for them.

CLOSURE

Review the following points with the students.

- Despite the fact that any one vote is unlikely to change the result of an election, many people voluntarily absorb the opportunity cost of voting.

- While opportunity cost is important in understanding why some people do not vote, many people vote despite the opportunity cost in order to gain the benefits—the sense of satisfaction that comes with meeting a civic obligation, for example, or with participating in an effort to affect change—that they associate with voting.

ASSESSMENT

Multiple-Choice Questions

1. Sue is paid an hourly wage of $10. She punches a time clock every day. Sam is paid an annual salary of $140,000 a year. He is allowed to take off two hours a day for lunch. For Sam and Sue, it will take two hours to vote. Sam votes on his lunch break, while Sue takes off work two hours early to get to the polls. What can be said about the costs and benefits of voting for these two citizens?

   A. Sue values voting more than Sam.

   B. Sam values voting more than Sue.

   C. **Sue's opportunity cost in terms of lost wages is higher than Sam's.**

   D. Sam's opportunity cost in terms of lost wages is higher than Sue's.

2. Which is not an opportunity cost of voting in a U.S. federal election?

   A. **A fee charged for voting**

   B. Wages lost while voting

   C. Time taken to learn about the candidates and their positions on issues

   D. Gasoline used to drive to the polls

Constructed-Response Questions

1. Have the students write a short essay supporting or opposing one of the following propositions:

   A. The United States government should pay people to vote in order to increase voter participation.

   B. The United States government should institute mandatory voting as is currently the policy in Australia, where failure to show up to vote can result in penalties (typically a fine of $20).

   C. The United States government should conduct an advertising campaign to encourage young people to vote.

   (The students should indicate, in responding to any of the propositions above, how the costs and benefits of voting are changed by the proposal in question.)

VISUAL 3.1

THE COSTS OF VOTING

1. *Dollar costs.* No dollar costs may be imposed by fees or taxation. Amendment 24 to the U.S. Constitution rules out dollar costs:

> Section 1. The right of citizens of the United States to vote in any primary or other election for President or Vice President, for electors for President or Vice President, or for Senator or Representative in Congress, shall not be denied or abridged by the United States or any state by reason of failure to pay any poll tax or other tax.

2. *Other costs.* While the Constitution prohibits monetary charges, this does not mean that voting is entirely without costs. Voters will incur *opportunity costs.* The opportunity cost of voting is what a voter gives up in choosing to vote. Here are some of the possible opportunity costs:

- Time taken to register.

- Time to find a voting location, or to vote via absentee ballet.

- Time taken to vote, which may also mean lost wages for voters who miss work; or babysitting or transportation costs.

- Time needed to investigate candidates and issues.

FOCUS: UNDERSTANDING ECONOMICS IN CIVICS AND GOVERNMENT © COUNCIL FOR ECONOMIC EDUCATION, NEW YORK, NY

Visual 3.2

Top Ten Reasons Registered Voters Gave for Not Voting in 2004

		All	18-24
10.	Transportation Problems	2.1%	1.9%
9.	Inconvenient Polling Place	3.0%	2.5%
8.	Forgot	3.4%	6.1%
7.	Registration Problems	6.8%	8.2%
6.	Don't Know or Refused to Answer	8.5%	15.2%
5.	Out of Town	9.0%	12.8%
4.	Didn't Like the Candidates	9.9%	6.4%
3.	Not Interested	10.7%	10.0%
2.	Illness or Disability	15.4%	2.8%
1.	Too Busy	19.9%	23.2%

In 2004, citizens aged 18 to 24 made up 12.6% of the voting-age population, but only 9.3% of voters.

Source: Census Bureau, *Voting and Registration in the Election of November 2004,* publication P20-556.

VISUAL 3.3

WHY DO PEOPLE VOTE?

• When the election is likely to be close and a person's vote may change the election result:

    ○ People may vote to support a particular politician.

    ○ People may vote to remove incumbents ("Throw the rascals out").

• When the election is not likely to be close and a person's vote is not likely to change the election result:

    ○ People may believe it is their civic duty to vote.

    ○ People may vote to voice their opinions regardless of the likely outcome.

    ○ People may vote in order to feel that they are a part of winning team.

VISUAL 3.4

WHO VOTES MORE?

Of all citizens, who voted most, percentage-wise, in the 2004 presidential election?

Men	or	Women		
White	or	Black	or	Asian
Naturalized Citizen	or	Native Born		
Married	or	Never Married		
Separated	or	Divorced		
Low Income	or	High Income		
Employed	or	Unemployed		
High School Degree	or	Bachelor's Degree		
Minnesotan	or	Floridian	or	Hawaiian
Veteran	or	Nonveteran		
Renter	or	Homeowner		
Young	or	Old		

Source: Census Bureau, *Voting and Registration in the Election of November 2004,* publication P20-556.

VISUAL 3.5

REPORTING VOTING, 1980-2004

Year	Voters as a Percent of the U.S. Citizen Voting-Age Population
1980	64.0
1984	64.9
1988	62.2
1992	67.7
1996	58.4
2000	59.5
2004	63.8

Source: Census Bureau, www.census.gov/population/www/socdemo/voting.html, Historical Time Series Table A-1.

LESSON 4

WHAT ARE THE ECONOMIC FUNCTIONS OF GOVERNMENT?

LESSON 4
WHAT ARE THE ECONOMIC FUNCTIONS OF GOVERNMENT?

INTRODUCTION

In order to ensure and support economic freedom as well as political freedom, the founders of the United States envisioned a limited role for the government in economic affairs. In a market economy such as the one established by the U. S. Constitution, most economic decisions are made by individual buyers and sellers, not by the government.

Still, the U.S. government's role in the economy is not trivial. It includes, most economists believe, responsibility for six major functions. The government (1) provides the legal and social framework within which the economy operates, (2) maintains competition in the marketplace, (3) provides public goods and services, (4) redistributes income, (5) corrects for externalities, and (6) takes certain actions to stabilize the economy.

Citizens, interest groups, and political leaders disagree about the proper scope of government activities within each of these functions. Over time, as society and the economy have changed, government activities in each area have generally expanded. Moreover, around the world, other societies with market economies have generally favored a larger economic role for government, sometimes endorsing actions beyond the six functions addressed in this lesson.

LESSON DESCRIPTION

The teacher introduces six economic functions of government in a brief lecture. In a guided practice activity, the students classify newspaper headlines according to the six functions. A brief reading introduces "liberal" and "conservative" views of the proper scope of government economic activity. The lesson concludes with students working in groups to develop liberal and conservative arguments about one of the newspaper headlines.

CONCEPTS

- Competition
- Economic stabilization
- Externality
- Income redistribution
- Public goods and services
- Social and legal framework

OBJECTIVES

Students will be able to:

1. Classify government economic activities according to the six economic functions of government.

2. Analyze governmental economic actions within the liberal/conservative framework.

CONTENT STANDARDS
Economics (CEE Standards)

- There is an economic role for government in a market economy whenever the benefits of a government policy outweigh its costs. Governments often provide for national defense, address environmental concerns, define and protect property rights, and attempt to make markets more competitive. Most government policies also redistribute income. (Standard 16)

- Federal government budgetary policy and the Federal Reserve System's monetary policy influence the overall levels of employment, output, and prices. (Standard 20)

Civics and Government (NSCG Standards, Grades 9-12)

- The relationship of limited government to political and economic freedom. (Standard I.B.4)

- Character of American political conflict. (Standard II.C.2)

• Major responsibilities of the national government in domestic and foreign policy. (Standard III.B.2)

TIME REQUIRED

90 minutes

MATERIALS

• A transparency of Visual 4.1

• A copy for each student of Activities 4.1, 4.2, and 4.3

PROCEDURE

1. Tell the students that the purpose of this lesson is to examine the economic functions of government. Ask the class to suggest some economic activities of local, state, and national governments. List several responses on the board. *(Possible responses include providing for national defense, providing low-cost meals at school, paying Social Security benefits, building and repairing roads, etc.)*

2. Point out that government *could* do all sorts of things. For example, it could provide everyone with an MP3 player, or provide everyone with an annual vacation at a theme park. Ask: What problems might arise if the government expanded its role along these lines? *(These new programs would cost a lot of money. To pay for them, people would have to pay higher taxes. Higher taxes would create economic inefficiencies. And people not interested in MP3 players or theme parks would object that their tax money was being wasted.)*

3. Pose another hypothetical example, this time concerning government regulation: Government imposes lots of rules in the economy—workplace safety regulations, for example. But some things still go unregulated. Why not regulate in every problem area? What would happen if the government decided that all new cars produced in the United States must be yellow, since yellow cars are easier for other drivers to see? What might be problematic about that? *(Many Americans would object*

to such a restriction of their freedom of choice. Finding one's own yellow car in a parking lot full of yellow cars might be difficult. The yellow-only rule might encourage people who don't like yellow to purchase cars manufactured outside the United States, or to repaint their yellow cars illegally.)

4. Review the examples discussed thus far, real and hypothetical: from governmental provisions for national defense to government-sponsored vacations for everybody. Explain that most Americans (not all) agree that government should do some of these things and should not do others, for various reasons. But what reasons? What general ideas might Americans look to for guidance in thinking about the government's proper, limited role in the nation's economy? Economists who study this question have a six-part answer. They generally contend (again, not all of them) that government has six legitimate functions to perform within the U.S. economy. The class now will turn to a consideration of these six functions.

5. Display Visual 4.1 and distribute copies of it (Visual 4.1 also serves as Activity 4.1). Explain each of the six economic functions of government. Solicit examples from the students for each function, and ask what would happen if government did not perform this function. Have the students write examples and notes on their copies of the activity.

   • Maintain the Legal and Social Framework:

     Define and enforce property rights. *(Government passes laws and establishes a court system. No one could sell property, invest, or have confidence in contracts if this legal system did not exist.)*
     Establish a monetary system. *(The federal government controls the amount of money circulating in the economy; it also regulates banks and other financial institutions. People*

would have to barter for the goods and services they wanted if this monetary system did not exist, and they might stay away from banks if banks were not regulated.)

- Maintain Competition:

  Create and enforce antitrust laws, and regulate natural monopolies.
  (The government sued Microsoft for monopoly practices; the government regulates the prices charged by companies that distribute natural gas to homes. Companies might charge higher prices and provide poor products if government policies did not promote competition.)

- Provide Public Goods and Services:

  Public goods and services are those that markets will not provide in sufficient quantities.
  (Examples include national defense, roadways, post offices and mail carriers, lighthouses, public defenders, public health clinics, public schools, and other important goods and services. Some important goods and services would be unavailable if the government did not provide them.)

- Correct for Externalities:

  Reduce negative externalities.
  (Negative externalities exist when some of the costs associated with production or consumption "spill over" to third parties— people other than the producer or consumer of the product. One example is pollution of lakes and rivers caused, for example, by industrial waste. The pollution affects everybody who uses the lakes and rivers, including those who had no part in producing or purchasing the products causing the pollution. Government regulates pollution. The environment would be far more polluted without government action.)

  Encourage increased production of goods and services that have positive externalities.

(Positive externalities exist when some of the benefits associated with production or consumption "spill over" to third parties— people other than the producer or consumer of the product. One example is public education. Government subsidizes education because its benefits flow to the students and to society in general. We would have fewer benefits linked to education without subsidization.)

- Stabilize the Economy:

  Reduce unemployment and inflation, and promote economic growth.
  (The federal government attempts to stabilize the economy through applications of fiscal policy [by raising or lowering taxes, or by government spending] and monetary policy [by controlling the money supply or by changing interest rates]. Without these actions, the economy might take much longer than it ordinarily does to recover from recessions.)

- Redistribute Income:

  Redistribute income from people who have higher incomes to those with lower incomes.
  (Redistribution usually involves higher tax rates for people with higher incomes. The tax revenue raised in this way helps to pay for various welfare programs, the Medicaid program, legal defense clinics, etc. Some people could not afford basic necessities without government redistribution programs.)

6. Distribute Activity 4.2. Explain that the 12 newspaper headlines are fictitious but realistic, each one referring to a government activity. The students are to classify each headline by writing in the letter of the economic function that fits it best. Check the students' answers and discuss the exercise in class.

Headlines

1. Federal Reserve Raises Key Interest Rate (E)

2. Congress Raises Tax Rates for Top Income Brackets (F)

3. EPA Plan to Reduce CO2 Emissions (D)

4. Homeland Security Funding Increased (C)

5. President Says More Spending Will Fight Recession (E)

6. Agency Blocks Merger of Two Airlines (B)

7. City Police Increase Neighborhood Patrols (A or C)

8. Lawsuit Establishes Patent Rights (A)

9. Legislature Passes Funding for Subsidized Housing (F)

10. New Info from Government Agency Helps Consumers Choose Wisely (A, B, or C)

11. Songwriter Sues Singer; Says Song Stolen (A)

12. County Funds Free Flu Vaccinations (D)

7. Distribute Activity 4.3. If appropriate, have a few students read the information aloud. Call on students to state specific liberal and conservative arguments, informed by Activity 4.3, and list these on the chalkboard. Check for understanding with the following two questions.

- Suppose a U.S. senator proposes legislation that increases taxes for higher-income taxpayers, in order to provide more funds for public education. Is this senator more likely to have a conservative view or a liberal view of the economic role of government? *(Liberal view.)*

- A Congressional leader argues that there should be a constitutional amendment that limits the size of the federal government. Is this policymaker more likely to be liberal or conservative? *(Conservative.)*

8. Explain that the class will examine headline 9 (*Legislature Passes Funding for Subsidized Housing*) in Activity 4.2, from the liberal and conservative perspectives. Divide the class into small groups. Designate each group as holding either a liberal or a conservative viewpoint. Each group should then discuss how a liberal or conservative would view headline 9. Ask the members of each group to select a spokesperson to report their findings. After the groups have completed their work, have the spokespersons present their arguments to the class as a whole.

9. Conclude this activity by pointing out that liberals and conservatives are at the opposing end of a spectrum. Many people find themselves to be located in different places along the spectrum.

CLOSURE

Call on the students to name the six economic functions of government. After each function is named, ask other students to give an example. Ask the class why, since there is broad agreement that government should perform these functions, there is disagreement sometimes about whether government should engage in particular activities.

ASSESSMENT
Multiple-Choice Questions

1. Public goods and services are

A. all goods and services paid for by government.

B. goods and services provided by publicly held companies.

C. **goods and services that would not be adequately provided by the market.**

D. goods and services that are available to the public.

2. Establishing and enforcing clearly defined property rights is an example of government

   A. **providing a social and legal framework.**

   B. maintaining competition.

   C. providing public goods and services.

   D. redistributing income.

3. Smoke from a factory drops ash all over your car. Government's economic function in this case is to

   A. stabilize the economy.

   B. maintain competition.

   C. provide public goods and services.

   D. **correct a negative externality.**

Constructed-Response Questions

1. Federal regulations now require Internet radio stations to pay substantial royalty fees (fees to the artists and songwriters) for the music that they play. Some stations were not able to pay the fees and have gone "off the air." What economic function of government is this an example of? Who benefits and loses from the regulation? What argument would you make for and against the regulation?

   (These regulations are an example of government policy aimed at establishing and enforcing property rights. The protection of property rights is an element of the legal and social framework government establishes. In this case, songwriters and artists benefit from the legal protection in question; the regulation maintains their property rights and enhances their incentive to produce music. Radio station operators and listeners lose. There are fewer Internet radio stations and less choice for listeners.)

2. Many city governments subsidize the construction of sports stadiums as a way to attract or hold on to sports teams. Write an argument for this practice, using the economic functions of government in support of your claim. Then present an alternative view, arguing against your initial claim.

   (Public support for sports stadiums might be regarded as an example of correcting for externalities. The economic argument for taxpayer-financed subsidization is that the sports teams provide substantial external benefits. The city gains visibility that might attract new businesses and visitors who will spend money in the city. Thus, many people benefit, including those who never attend any stadium events. Opponents argue that there is little "spill-over" benefit since people who attend stadium events do so instead of paying for other recreational activities, like going out to restaurants, museums, or shopping in local stores. Moreover, attending a stadium event seems to be a private activity, like going bowling or golfing or seeing a movie; those who want to participate in such activities should pay their own way.)

VISUAL 4.1/ACTIVITY 4.1

SIX ECONOMIC FUNCTIONS OF GOVERNMENT

1. Maintain the Legal and Social Framework

2. Maintain Competition

3. Provide Public Goods and Services

4. Correct for Externalities

5. Stabilize the Economy

6. Redistribute Income

ACTIVITY 4.2
CLASSIFYING GOVERNMENT ACTIONS

Directions: Below is a list of the six economic functions of government, followed by a set of 12 (fictitious) newspaper headlines. Decide which of the six economic functions is referred to, directly or by implication, in each headline. Classify each headline according to the six functions by writing in the letter of the economic function that best fits that headline.

The Six Economic Functions:
   A. Maintain the Legal and Social Framework
   B. Maintain Competition
   C. Provide Public Goods and Services
   D. Correct for Externalities
   E. Stabilize the Economy
   F. Redistribute Income

The Headlines:

____ 1. Federal Reserve Raises Key Interest Rate

____ 2. Congress Raises Tax Rates for Top Income Brackets

____ 3. EPA Plan to Reduce CO_2 Emissions

____ 4. Homeland Security Funding Increased

____ 5. President Says More Spending Will Fight Recession

____ 6. Agency Blocks Merger of Two Airlines

____ 7. City Police Increase Neighborhood Patrols

____ 8. Lawsuit Establishes Patent Rights

____ 9. Legislature Passes Funding for Subsidized Housing

____ 10. New Info from Government Agency Helps Consumers Choose Wisely

____ 11. Songwriter Sues Singer; Says Song Stolen

____ 12. County Funds Free Flu Vaccinations

Activity 4.3

What Role Should the Government Play in the Economy?

Although it is generally agreed that there is a role for the government to play in redistributing income in favor of the poor, providing public goods and services, and dealing with externalities, there is considerable disagreement over how far the government should go in these areas—and about additional areas for which some people believe the government should be responsible. Some people believe that "big government" is already a problem—that government is doing too much. Others believe that the government sector of the economy is being starved and that government should be allowed to do more. In the United States, the former view is associated with what is commonly called "conservative" political thinking; the latter view is associated with "liberal" political thinking.

The Conservative View

Conservatives believe that the government's role in the economy should be severely limited. They believe that economic and political freedom will be undermined by excessive reliance on government. Moreover, they question the government's ability to solve social and economic problems. They believe that faith in the government's power to solve these problems is unreasonable. They point to the slowness of government bureaucracy, the difficulty in controlling huge government organizations, the problems political considerations can breed, and the difficulties that arise when people try to learn whether government programs are successful or not. On the basis of these considerations, they argue that the government's role should be carefully limited. They call for more and better information about what government can reasonably be expected to do (and do well).

The Liberal View

While conservatives often question the government's ability to solve important social and economic problems, liberals often question the market's ability to solve such problems. They point to important limitations within the market system, and they claim that the government can do a great deal to overcome these limitations. Government can regulate private economic activity—for example, through minimum-wage laws. It can also provide goods and services that private businesses produce in insufficient quantities—for example, health care for the poor. In their advocacy for government programs of this sort, liberals tend to be less concerned than conservatives about the effects on personal freedom that may be a consequence of governmental intervention in the economy. They are more concerned with certain consequences of market activity—contending, for example, that the price system is unfair because it awards goods and services to those who can pay the price. In their view, people who acquire little in the way of goods and services through market activity are forced into lives of hardship. Liberals are, therefore, more concerned than conservatives about the unequal distribution of income produced by market activity and are more likely to propose government policies aimed at redistributing income in a manner that will reduce income inequality.

ACTIVITY 4.3, CONTINUED

WHAT ROLE SHOULD THE GOVERNMENT PLAY IN THE ECONOMY?

Questions for Discussion

1. Suppose a U.S. Senator proposes legislation that increases taxes for higher- income taxpayers in order to make more funds available for public education. Is this Senator more likely to have a conservative view or a liberal view of the economic role of government?

2. A Congressional leader argues that there should be a constitutional amendment that limits the size of the federal government. Is this policymaker more likely to be liberal or conservative?

Lesson 5

Government Spending

Lesson 5
Government Spending

INTRODUCTION

In the United States, spending by government at all levels has increased markedly over time. Spending by the federal government has increased from 3.4 percent of gross domestic product (GDP) in 1930 to 20.4 percent in 2006, having reached a peak of 43.6 percent during the wartime year of 1944. In addition, state and local government spending has increased to about 19.5 percent of GDP (19.3 percent in 2005). Thus, as a percentage of GDP, spending by government (measured as all government outlays) is a large and growing number. Some students may recognize that the government purchases category of GDP is a substantially smaller percentage of GDP, since government purchases do not include such items as transfer payments, which are included in the percentages referenced in this lesson.

The composition of spending by government has also changed as society has come to grips with new problems and priorities. At the height of spending on World War II, 86.7 percent of the federal budget was devoted to national defense. This has changed significantly over the past half-century, as the programs of the Great Society in the 1960s, among other things, have channeled a larger share of federal dollars toward non-defense items. Although the changes at the state and local levels have been less dramatic, during the last 30 years spending on welfare and corrections has increased, while education spending has declined as a fraction of outlays.

Another highly significant change in government spending, particularly at the federal level, is the relative increase in "mandatory" as opposed to "discretionary" spending. Mandatory spending is the portion of the federal budget that will be spent automatically unless Congress acts to change the relevant laws. Examples are "entitlement" spending, such as Social Security, and interest on the national debt. Discretionary spending

requires Congress to pass authorizations each year, including spending for most of the defense budget. Since the early 1960s, the ratio of mandatory to discretionary spending has changed from roughly 1:2 to 2:1.

This change is highly significant for several reasons. First, there is considerable controversy over how our society should deal with growth in mandatory spending. Second, growth in mandatory spending limits flexibility in spending for other priorities.

This lesson looks at past trends in government spending, which are used to make predictions about the path and composition of future spending. Note: The lesson focuses on trends and data pertaining to the time *before* the major changes in government spending that began as a response to the 2008 financial crisis and recession. The recent government anti-recessionary spending should be considered exceptional, as the data in this lesson show.

LESSON DESCRIPTION

Through cooperative learning, the students identify patterns and trends in spending by government at the federal, state, and local levels. They analyze potential problems posed by the growth in federal mandatory spending.

CONCEPTS

- Government spending
- Mandatory and discretionary spending

OBJECTIVES

Students will be able to:

1. Identify trends in government spending.
2. Recognize potential problems of, and solutions to, current trends in federal spending.

CONTENT STANDARDS
Economics (CEE Standards)

- There is an economic role for government in a market economy whenever the benefits of a government policy outweigh its costs. Governments often provide for national defense, address environmental concerns, define and protect property rights, and attempt to make markets more competitive. Most government policies also redistribute income. (Standard 16)

Civics and Government (NSCG Standards, Grades 9-12)

- Major responsibilities of the national government in domestic and foreign policy and financing government through taxation. (Standard III.B.2 and 3)

- Major responsibilities of state and local governments. (Standard III.C.3)

TIME REQUIRED

90 minutes

MATERIALS

- A transparency of Visual 5.1

- A copy for each student of Activities 5.1 and 5.2

PROCEDURE

1. Explain to the students that in this lesson they will learn some basic information about government spending at the federal, state, and local levels. They will explore various trends in government spending that will help them think about the current and future composition of government spending.

2. Write $2,655,435,000,000 and $13,061,100,000,000 on the chalkboard. Ask the class to read these amounts. (*2 trillion, 655 billion, 435 million dollars and 13 trillion, 61 billion, 100 million dollars*). Ask the class to guess what these numbers represent. (2006 *federal government spending and GDP, each expressed in current, or nominal, dollars.*) Explain that because these numbers are so large, we abbreviate them, usually in billions of dollars: $2,665.4 billion and $13, 061.1 billion. Explain that in order to compare spending by government from one time period to

another, we often express spending as a percentage of GDP: in this case, 2665/13061 = 20.4 percent.

3. Ask the students to name some things (such as goods and services or transfer payments) that government at all levels spends money on. Ask them to consider whether the expenditures mentioned occur at the federal, state, or local level. (*Answers will vary, but possible responses include federal spending—for national defense, Social Security, Medicare; state spending—for roadways, education, correctional facilities, parks; local spending—for education, community development, fire and police protection.*) Ask the students where governments get the money to pay for these items. (*Income taxes, payroll taxes, property taxes, sales taxes, borrowing.*)

4. Display Visual 5.1 and read the following excerpt from the Congressional Budget Office report (http://www.cbo.gov/doc.cfm?index=3521&type=0), while indicating the relevant points on the chart. Under the projections shown here, outlays (for Social Security, Medicare, and Medicaid) would rise from 8 percent of gross domestic product (GDP) today to 21 percent in 2075, which would exceed the share of GDP now absorbed by all federal revenues. Even if other major categories of federal spending remained fixed as a share of GDP, the growth of those programs would push total federal spending well above the level it has held to throughout much of the post-World War II period. Left unchecked, such spending could cause major deficits to emerge, propelling the government's debt and interest expenditures to unprecedented levels. The total cost of government, including interest expense, could more than double as a share of the economy, rising from 19 percent of GDP in 2002 to 40 percent in 2075.

5. Extend the discussion by asking:

- Where are the major areas of growth in spending shown on the chart? (*Medicare,*

Medicaid, Social Security, interest.)

- What does the projection assume about spending on other things? (*Other spending remains about the same.*)

- What problem for *you* does the projection pose? (*Taxes might have to be increased by a lot; much more of GDP may be devoted to government; payments for interest on the government debt may rise steeply.*)

6. Distribute copies of Activity 5.1 (Briefing Report) and copies of Activity 5.2 (Data) to all students. Explain that the class will be divided into groups of "experts," who will later be members of "home teams." It will be the job of the experts to brief the members in their home teams on their respective areas of expertise. Expert Group 1 will concentrate on the section of Activity 5.1 regarding trends in overall government spending. Expert Group 2 will focus on the second section of the activity, the composition of federal spending. Expert Group 3 will examine the composition of state and local government spending. Tell the students that the data are for "fiscal years," not calendar years. For example, federal government spending for 2006 is actually for October 1, 2005, through September 30, 2006. States generally use a fiscal year of July 1 through June 30. This can make a difference in interpreting the data.

7. Divide the class into expert teams. Each team should have no more than five members. For a class of 30 students, each expert-team topic will be researched by two teams. Have the teams examine the data and complete their section of the briefing report. Check the reports for accuracy.

8. After the experts have completed their work, group the class into several home teams, with each home team having two experts from each of the three expert teams. Have the experts brief their classmates on their findings. Home team members should complete the rest of the

sections of the briefing report, based on the information provided by the expert teams.

9. Have the teams report their findings from Activity 5.1. Use this discussion as the occasion to return to the problem posed by the relative increase in mandatory vs. discretionary spending. You may also want to note the projected effects of retiring baby boomers on future Social Security and Medicare spending.

Answers to Activity 5.1

Expert Group 1

In what year was each category of government spending as a percent of GDP highest?

    Federal spending?   Year _1983___
    Percent of GDP __23.5%___

    State and local spending?   Year _2003___
    Percent of GDP __20%___

    Total government spending? Year _1992___
    Percent of GDP __40.7%___

Trends
    (*Federal spending as a share of GDP declined through much of the 1980s and 1990s, but began increasing in the early 2000s. State and local spending as a percentage of GDP has increased three percentage points over the past 30 years. Total government spending as a share of GDP is now nearly 40 percent, having once been 35.4 percent [in 1979].*)

Has the percentage of spending gone up, down, or remained constant for the federal government?
    (*In 2006 and 1977, the percentage was about the same; but it varied substantially during that 30-year period.*)

What is your evidence for this conclusion?
    (*1977: 20.7%; 2006: 20.3%.*)

Has the percentage of spending gone up, down, or remained constant for state and local government?
    (*It has gone up.*)

What is your evidence for this conclusion? (Spending in the late 1970s was about 15.5% of GDP. By the mid-2000s, it was greater than 19% of GDP.)

Within the long-term trends, identify some short-term changes in spending. (Example: What happens around the time of recessions?) For each, speculate about the reason for the change.

(Answers may include the point that the percentage of government spending—both federal and state and local—tends to increase during recessions; during periods of sustained economic expansion, the percentage of government spending tends to decline as GDP grows more rapidly than spending.)

Expert Group 2

Answers will vary; here is a sample set of answers:

Category/Function	Trend	Evidence	Possible reason
Defense	*Down*	*About 6% in the mid-80s, falling to 3% prior to post-9/11 spending.*	*The nuclear arms race ended with the dissolution of the Soviet Union in the early 1990s; smaller number of military personnel in 1990s; increase in relative defense spending with the Iraq War and War on Terror in the 2000s.*
Domestic	*Down*	*Decreasing from around 4.7% of GDP to 3.5% of GDP.*	*The percentage of non-defense domestic discretionary spending had been reduced consistently until the early 2000s, when it started to grow; Homeland Security now appears in this category, which has led to an increase over the past several years.*
Social Security	*Constant*	*With little variation, SS spending has been about 4.3% of GDP.*	*The Baby Boom generation begins retiring around 2010, at which point this percentage will begin to rise.*
Medicare	*Up*	*Spending as a % of GDP has nearly tripled... from 1.1% to 2.9%.*	*Health care costs have increased relative to other costs; people are living longer; a growing share of the population qualifies for Medicare hospital insurance; creation of prescription drug program in 2000s.*
Medicaid	*Up*	*Spending as a % of GDP has nearly tripled... from .5% to 1.5%*	*Health care costs have increased relative to other costs.*

Expert Group 3

Answers will vary; here is a sample set of answers:

In what year was each category (as a percent of total spending) the highest?

Education?	Year 1977	Percent of Total Spending	31.7%
Welfare?	Year 2006	Percent of Total Spending	14.8%

Corrections (prisons)? Year 1997 and 2002

Percent of Total Spending   2.7%

Category / Function	Trend	Evidence	Possible reason
Education	Down, with recent small recovery.	Down from peak in 1977, although it has gone up almost 1 percentage point since 1992.	Education spending has been crowded out by spending in other categories; students in public higher education now pay for a larger share of the cost of their education.
Public Welfare	Up	Increase of about 4 percentage points.	States now play a larger role in public welfare programs, with block grants from the federal government becoming more popular.
Health	Up	About 1 percentage point higher than in 1977.	Health care spending has increased as health care costs have increased relative to the cost of other items.
Highways	Down	Lower by about 1.5 percentage points than in 1977.	Completion of many road systems in earlier periods has led to less costly maintenance and expansion projects for highways; there has been a slight shift toward public transportation budget priorities.
Corrections	Up	Spending as a percent of the total has doubled.	Growing prisoner populations from mandatory sentencing laws and more drug prosecutions.

CLOSURE

Display Visual 5.1 again and review the lesson in the context of this portrait of projected federal government spending. Ask the students to reflect on these future trends and to suggest solutions to some of the problems the trends imply. Answers might range from doing nothing to raising taxes to getting control of Medicare and Medicaid expenses, or some combination of policy proposals.

ASSESSMENT

Multiple-Choice Questions

1. In the last 30 years, as a percentage of total spending, the largest increase in state and local spending has been for

   A. education.

   B. fire protection.

   C. public welfare.

   D. highways.

2. Currently, the largest fraction of federal spending is devoted to

   A. Social Security.

   B. national defense.

   C. Medicare.

   D. foreign aid.

3. Projections of future federal spending in 2075 indicate that the largest category of federal spending as a percent of GDP (excluding interest on the debt) will likely be for

   A. disability programs.

   B. income security.

   C. national defense.

   D. Medicare.

Constructed-Response Questions

1. Imagine that your parent or guardian comments about a letter to the editor in the newspaper, complaining about how much government is spending. What are the three most important things you would tell her or him, and why is each one of these things important? *(Answers will vary, but should include reference to trends in spending, including the components of spending, at all levels of government).*

2. As an exercise in English class, you choose the option of writing a letter to your U.S. senators. You decide to write about the problem of mandatory and discretionary spending. What major points will you make in your letter? *(Answers will vary, but should include discussion of a larger share of federal government spending being accounted for by mandatory spending categories [such as Medicare, Social Security, and interest on the national debt] that cannot be limited without a change in current law).*

VISUAL 5.1
POSSIBLE FUTURE GROWTH IN FEDERAL GOVERNMENT SPENDING

(PERCENT OF GDP)

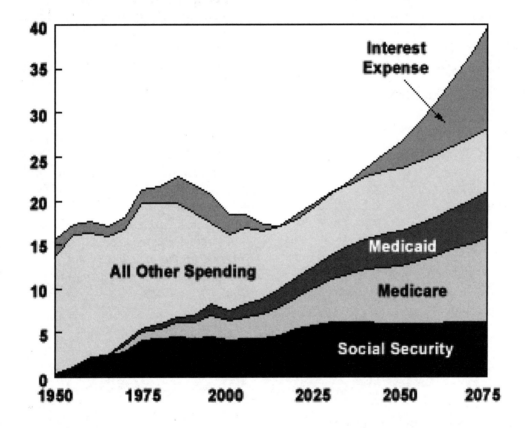

Source: Congressional Budget Office, *A 125-Year Picture of the Federal Government's Share of the Economy, 1950 to 2075.*

ACTIVITY 5.1

BRIEFING REPORT

Your teacher will assign you to an "Expert Group." Your group's task will be to complete the assigned section of this report, using the data your teacher has given to you. Next, your teacher will assign you to a "Home Team." You will have two tasks: (1) brief the members of your home team about your section of this briefing report; (2) complete the rest of this report with the information provided by the other members of your Home Team.

All Groups: Remember that even small changes in spending as measured as a percentage of GDP can be very significant. In 2006, one percent of GDP represented $130 billion!

Expert Group 1 (Trends in overall government spending)

Look at Table 1, "Government Spending, 1977-2006." Note that this table includes spending as a percent of GDP.

In what year was each category of government spending as a percent of GDP highest?

Federal spending?   Year _____   Percent of GDP _____
State and local spending?   Year _____   Percent of GDP _____
Total government spending?   Year _____   Percent of GDP _____

Look for any long-term trends in the data.

Has the percentage of spending gone up, down, or remained constant for the federal government?
_____

What is your evidence for this conclusion? _____

Has the percentage of spending gone up, down, or remained constant for state and local governments? _____

What is your evidence for this conclusion? _____

Within the long-term trends, identify some short-term changes in spending. (Example: What happens around the time of recessions?) For each, speculate about the reason for the change.

_____

_____

_____

_____

Expert Group 2 (Composition of federal spending)

Look at Table 2, "Federal Government Spending by Major Function, 1977-2006." Most of the categories shown in Table 2 are self-explanatory, but here are a few notes. *Mandatory spending* is the portion of the federal budget that will be spent automatically unless Congress acts to change the relevant laws. Examples are entitlement spending, such as Social Security, and interest on the national debt. *Discretionary spending* requires Congress to pass authorizations each

ACTIVITY 5.1, CONTINUED
BRIEFING REPORT

year, including spending for most of the defense budget. The column "Domestic" includes most of the domestic spending programs that Congress votes on for each budget, like highway construction and the space program. Mandatory spending includes the function called "Income Security," which includes many well-known programs like "Food Stamps" and other spending to support people with low incomes.

Be sure to brief your Home Team on mandatory and discretionary spending.

Look for any long-term trends in the data. Has spending as a percent of GDP gone up, down, or remained constant for mandatory and discretionary spending? For particular spending functions? What evidence demonstrates this? What reasons can you think of for the trends?

Category/Function	Trend	Evidence	Possible Reason

Expert Group 3 (Composition of state and local spending)

Look at Table 3, "Categories of State and Local Spending." The responsibilities of state and local governments are very different from those of the federal government. Note that education is mostly a state and local responsibility, as is police and fire protection, welfare, and many other functions.

Be sure to brief your Home Team on the categories of spending that are the responsibilities of state and local governments.

In what year was each category as a percent of total spending the highest?

Education?   Year _____   Percent of Total Spending _____

Welfare?   Year _____   Percent of Total Spending _____

Corrections (prisons)? Year _____   Percent of Total Spending _____

ACTIVITY 5.1, CONTINUED

BRIEFING REPORT

Look for any long-term trends in the data. Has spending gone up, down, or remained constant for particular spending functions? What evidence demonstrates this? What reasons can you think of for the trends?

Category/Function	Trend	Evidence	Possible Reason

ACTIVITY 5.2

DATA

TABLE 1: GOVERNMENT SPENDING, 1977-2006

(In current dollars and percent of GDP)

Year	GDP in $ billions	Federal Spending in $ billions	% of GDP	State and Local Spending in $ billions	% of GDP	Total Government Spending % of GDP
1977	1,974.3	409.2	20.7%	324.6	16.4%	37.2%
1978	2,217.0	458.7	20.7%	346.8	15.6%	36.3%
1979	2,500.7	504.0	20.2%	381.9	15.3%	35.4%
1980	2,726.7	590.9	21.7%	434.1	15.9%	37.6%
1981	3,054.7	678.2	22.2%	487.0	15.9%	38.1%
1982	3,227.6	745.7	23.1%	524.6	16.3%	39.4%
1983	3,440.7	808.4	23.5%	566.7	16.5%	40.0%
1984	3,840.2	851.9	22.2%	600.2	15.6%	37.8%
1985	4,141.5	946.4	22.9%	657.9	15.9%	38.7%
1986	4,412.4	990.4	22.4%	717.5	16.3%	38.7%
1987	4,647.1	1,004.1	21.6%	777.0	16.7%	38.3%
1988	5,008.6	1,064.5	21.3%	826.8	16.5%	37.8%
1989	5,400.5	1,143.8	21.2%	890.9	16.5%	37.7%
1990	5,735.4	1,253.1	21.8%	975.9	17.0%	38.9%
1991	5,935.1	1,324.3	22.3%	1063.3	17.9%	40.2%
1992	6,239.9	1,381.6	22.1%	1156.8	18.5%	40.7%
1993	6,575.5	1,409.5	21.4%	1213.7	18.5%	39.9%
1994	6,961.3	1,461.9	21.0%	1264.3	18.2%	39.2%
1995	7,325.8	1,515.9	20.7%	1351.4	18.4%	39.1%
1996	7,694.1	1,560.6	20.3%	1397.6	18.2%	38.4%
1997	8,182.4	1,601.3	19.6%	1460.6	17.9%	37.4%
1998	8,627.9	1,652.7	19.2%	1529.3	17.7%	36.9%
1999	9,125.3	1,702.0	18.7%	1625.9	17.8%	36.5%
2000	9,709.8	1,789.2	18.4%	1746.9	18.0%	36.4%
2001	10,057.9	1,863.2	18.5%	1899.2	18.9%	37.4%
2002	10,377.4	2,011.2	19.4%	2051.5	19.8%	39.1%
2003	10,808.6	2,160.1	20.0%	2164.2	20.0%	40.0%
2004	11,517.5	2,293.0	19.9%	2265.1	19.7%	39.6%
2005	12,265.8	2,472.2	20.2%	2372.1	19.3%	39.5%
2006	13,061.1	2,655.4	20.3%	2507.4	19.2%	39.5%

Shaded areas represent recession during part or all of the period.

Data on State and local expenditures from the Tax Policy Center:
http://www.taxpolicycenter.org/TaxFacts/Tfdb/TFTemplate.cfm?DocID=501&Topic2id=90&Topic3id=92.
Budget of the United States Government: Historical Tables Fiscal Year 2006
http://www.gpoaccess.gov/usbudget/fy06/hist.html.

ACTIVITY 5.2, CONTINUED

DATA

TABLE 2: FEDERAL GOVERNMENT SPENDING BY MAJOR FUNCTION, 1977-2006 (PERCENT OF GDP)

	Discretionary			Mandatory					
	Defense	Inter-national	Domestic	Social Security	Medicare	Medicaid	Income Security	Other Retirement & Disability	Other Programs
1977	4.9	0.4	4.6	4.2	1.1	0.5	1.8	1.6	1.2
1978	4.7	0.4	4.8	4.2	1.1	0.5	1.4	1.5	1.5
1979	4.7	0.4	4.6	4.1	1.1	0.5	1.3	1.5	1.3
1980	4.9	0.5	4.7	4.3	1.2	0.5	1.6	1.6	1.4
1981	5.2	0.4	4.5	4.5	1.4	0.6	1.6	1.7	1.4
1982	5.8	0.4	3.9	4.8	1.5	0.5	1.6	1.7	1.3
1983	6.1	0.4	3.8	4.9	1.6	0.6	1.9	1.7	1.3
1984	5.9	0.4	3.5	4.6	1.6	0.5	1.3	1.6	1.0
1985	6.1	0.4	3.5	4.5	1.7	0.5	1.3	1.5	1.4
1986	6.2	0.4	3.3	4.5	1.7	0.6	1.2	1.4	1.1
1987	6.1	0.3	3.1	4.4	1.7	0.6	1.2	1.4	0.9
1988	5.8	0.3	3.1	4.3	1.7	0.6	1.1	1.4	0.9
1989	5.6	0.3	3.1	4.3	1.7	0.6	1.1	1.4	1.0
1990	5.2	0.3	3.2	4.3	1.9	0.7	1.2	1.3	1.5
1991	5.4	0.3	3.3	4.5	1.9	0.9	1.5	1.4	1.7
1992	4.8	0.3	3.4	4.6	2.1	1.1	1.8	1.4	0.6
1993	4.4	0.3	3.4	4.6	2.2	1.2	1.8	1.3	0.2
1994	4.1	0.3	3.4	4.6	2.3	1.2	1.7	1.3	0.3
1995	3.7	0.3	3.4	4.5	2.4	1.2	1.6	1.3	0.1
1996	3.5	0.2	3.2	4.5	2.5	1.2	1.6	1.3	0.1
1997	3.3	0.2	3.1	4.4	2.5	1.2	1.5	1.2	0.1
1998	3.1	0.2	3.1	4.4	2.4	1.2	1.4	1.2	0.3
1999	3.0	0.2	3.0	4.2	2.3	1.2	1.4	1.2	0.4
2000	3.0	0.2	3.1	4.2	2.2	1.2	1.4	1.2	0.4
2001	3.0	0.2	3.2	4.3	2.4	1.3	1.4	1.2	0.4
2002	3.4	0.3	3.5	4.4	2.4	1.4	1.7	1.2	0.4
2003	3.7	0.3	3.6	4.4	2.5	1.5	1.8	1.2	0.5
2004	3.9	0.3	3.5	4.3	2.6	1.5	1.7	1.2	0.5
2005	4.0	0.3	3.6	4.2	2.7	1.5	1.6	1.2	0.6
2006	4.0	0.3	3.5	4.2	2.9	1.4	1.5	1.1	0.8

Source: Congressional Budget Office http://www.cbo.gov/budget/historical.shtml, Tables 8 and 10.

ACTIVITY 5.2, CONTINUED

DATA

TABLE 3: CATEGORIES OF STATE AND LOCAL SPENDING

Percentage of Total Spending
(Some categories excluded, numbers do not add to 100)

	1977	1982	1987	1992	1997	2002	2006
Education	31.7%	29.4%	29.2%	28.1%	28.6%	29.0%	29.0%
Public Welfare	10.6%	10.7%	10.3%	13.4%	13.7%	13.7%	14.8%
Hospitals	5.4%	5.8%	5.2%	5.1%	4.7%	4.3%	4.4%
Health	1.7%	2.0%	2.2%	2.5%	2.9%	2.9%	2.8%
Highways	7.1%	6.6%	6.7%	5.8%	5.6%	5.6%	5.4%
Police Protection	3.2%	3.1%	3.2%	3.1%	3.2%	3.1%	3.2%
Fire Protection	1.4%	1.3%	1.3%	1.3%	1.3%	1.3%	1.4%
Corrections	1.3%	1.6%	2.1%	2.5%	2.7%	2.7%	2.5%
Natural Resources	1.2%	1.3%	1.3%	1.1%	1.1%	1.1%	1.0%
Parks and Recreation	1.5%	1.4%	1.4%	1.4%	1.4%	1.5%	1.4%
Housing and Community Development	1.0%	1.6%	1.5%	1.5%	1.6%	1.5%	1.7%
Sewerage and Solid Waste	2.9%	2.8%	2.8%	2.9%	2.8%	2.5%	2.5%
Interest on General Debt	3.5%	3.8%	5.4%	4.8%	4.3%	3.7%	3.4%

U.S. Census Bureau, Annual Survey of State and Local Government Finances (01-Jun-07); State & Local Government Finance Data Query System. http://www.taxpolicycenter.org/taxfacts/displayafact.cfm?DocID=504&Topic2id=90&Topic3id=92. The Urban Institute-Brookings Institution Tax Policy Center. Data from U.S. Census Bureau, Annual Survey of State and Local Government Finances, Government Finances, Volume 4, and Census of Governments (Years). Date of Access: (22-Jul-08 12:48 PM).

CAN ELECTION FUTURES MARKETS BE MORE ACCURATE THAN POLLS?

LESSON 6

CAN ELECTION FUTURES MARKETS BE MORE ACCURATE THAN POLLS?

INTRODUCTION

Public opinion polls are an important part of American political life. Polling informs and influences political debate, the state of the economy, social trends, and more. Political scientists and polling companies have developed sophisticated techniques to make polling more accurate. Now, however, there is another approach to predicting election outcomes, and it may prove to be even more accurate than polling. This approach uses futures markets—in which people risk some of their own money— to predict the outcome of such things as presidential elections.

LESSON DESCRIPTION

The students examine results from opinion polls conducted near the end of the 2004 presidential campaign. They compare results from several national polls to those of the Iowa Electronic Markets (hereafter, the IEM), an online futures market, to predict the outcome of the 2004 race. They read and discuss a handout which allows them to compare the performance of opinion polls and the IEM in predicting election outcomes. Finally, the students learn how well the IEM performed in the presidential campaign of 2008.

CONCEPTS

- Futures markets
- Incentives
- Public opinion polls

OBJECTIVES

Students will be able to:

1. Explain how public opinion polls and futures markets are used to predict election outcomes.

2. Compare and contrast the market-based approach to the polling approach for predicting outcomes of presidential elections.

CONTENT STANDARDS

Economics (CEE Standards)

- People respond predictably to positive and negative incentives. (Standard 4)

- Voluntary exchange occurs only when all participating parties expect to gain. This is true for trade among individuals or organizations within a nation, and among individuals or organizations in different nations. (Standard 5)

- Markets exist when buyers and sellers interact. This interaction determines market prices and thereby allocates scarce goods and services. (Standard 7)

Civics and Government (NSCG Standards, Grades 9-12)

- Personal responsibilities. (Standard V.C.1)

TIME REQUIRED

30 minutes

MATERIALS

- A transparency of Visuals 6.1, 6.2, and 6.3

- A copy for each student of Activity 6.1

Note: You may wish to visit www.biz.uiowa.edu/iem/ to learn more about the IEM, a key element of this lesson. This site might also be a helpful tool for classroom use.

PROCEDURE

1. Set the stage: Explain that U.S. presidential elections are tremendously important to Americans and to others throughout the world. Because the elections are so important, many people work hard to try to predict their outcomes.

2. Tell the class that the purpose of this lesson is to compare two approaches for predicting the outcomes of presidential

elections. The first is to use the traditional and highly sophisticated opinion polls conducted by such well-known organizations as Gallup and Harris. The second is to use the Iowa Electronic Markets (IEM), an online futures market where contract payoffs are linked to election outcomes. Can a relatively simple market-based system outperform sophisticated opinion polls?

3. Display Visual 6.1, which summarizes 10 predictions made about the 2004 presidential race. Ask the students to compare the predictions of the nine national polls to the prediction of the IEM. *(The IEM outperformed seven of the nine national polls. Two polls, Harris Online and Fox News, having named Senator Kerry as the winner, were very far off. The IEM either tied or had the same percentage of difference as the CBS News N.Y. Times and CNN/USA Today polls.)* The IEM performed very well without identifying a random sample of likely voters or making one telephone call. How did the IEM do it?

4. Distribute Activity 6.1. Introduce it as a source of information about the two approaches to predicting election outcomes. Ask the students to read it. After they have completed the reading, ask:

- What are two challenges that polling companies face in their efforts to get accurate results?

   (Pollsters face many challenges. They must carefully identify random samples of people who best represent the opinions of the relevant population. They must make telephone calls at times when the people they want to talk to are likely to be at home. They must develop unbiased questions. And sometimes they must deal with evasion and dishonesty; the people they reach might not be truthful in their replies.)

- How does the IEM work to predict the outcomes of presidential elections?

   (The IEM enables individuals to buy and sell contracts reflecting their predictions. For example, the IEM operates a "winner-takes-all" market where contracts for the presidential candidate with the largest share of the popular vote pay one dollar [$1], while contracts for the losing candidate pay nothing. Each contract therefore has a maximum value of $1, and trading accounts can be opened for $5 to $500.)

- What is a futures market (such as the futures markets overseen by the CME Group)? How is a futures market like the IEM?

   (The CME Group is an entity formed by the merger of the Chicago Board of Trade [CBOT] and the Chicago Mercantile Exchange [CME]. It is a futures exchange where people buy and sell contracts for the future delivery of commodities and various financial instruments: corn, wheat, and soy beans as well as stock indexes, interest rates, and foreign exchange. The IEM provides a political futures market where people speculate on future election results, using relatively small amounts of money.)

- Why might the IEM produce better results than traditional opinion polls?

   (The IEM has two big advantages over traditional polls. First, people who buy candidate contracts through the IEM put their own money at risk. Buyers who put their money at risk have an incentive to be careful—to search for relevant information and try to make the right choice. Second, people who buy contracts through the IEM participate voluntarily. They have no incentive for misrepresenting their views.)

5. Display Visual 6.2. Review the final results of the 2008 presidential race. The IEM market appears again to have predicted the final outcome better than traditional polls.

6. Display Visual 6.3. Note that the IEM had shown Barack Obama with a consistent

lead throughout the election cycle, from the primaries to the general election.

7. If you wish to extend the lesson, go to the IEM website at www.biz.uiowa.edu/iem/ and examine the races that are currently being followed at the site.

CLOSURE

In closing, review the lesson by posing the following questions:

- What are some of the challenges facing the firms that conduct national polls?

(Pollsters must carefully identify random samples likely to represent the opinions of the relevant population, make telephone calls at times when the people they want to talk to may be home, and develop unbiased questions. Sometimes they must deal with interviewees who are not truthful in their replies.)

- What is the IEM?

(The IEM is a set of real-money futures markets where contracts on the outcomes of political and economic events are traded. The IEM allows individuals to buy and sell contracts reflecting their predictions. For example, the IEM operates a "winner-takes-all" market where contracts for the presidential candidates are bought and sold.)

- What are the advantages of the IEM over traditional polling?

(Unlike traditional opinion polls, the IEM does not work with randomly selected groups of people. It depends on informed individuals who have an incentive to make an accurate prediction: They can make money if they purchase the contract of the winning candidate. In the IEM, there are no problems of sampling, posing unbiased questions, or calling people at the wrong time of day. The IEM does none of these things. The individuals who buy contracts using the IEM also have no incentive to misrepresent their views.)

- What happens to the value of a presidential candidate's futures contract when the candidate experiences favorable news about the likelihood of winning the election?

(Favorable news about the likelihood of success for a presidential candidate will increase demand for the contract and will therefore increase the contract price. In this way, the IEM market is similar to other markets in which prices are determined by forces of supply and demand.)

ASSESSMENT

Multiple-Choice Questions

1. Which of the following are challenges facing firms that conduct opinion polls?

    A. Identifying non-random samples, interviewing a sufficient number of people, asking unbiased questions, reaching the correct people in an unbiased way.

    B. **Identifying random samples, interviewing a sufficient number of people, asking unbiased questions, reaching the correct people in an unbiased way.**

    C. Identifying random samples, conducting a sufficiently large number of interviews in shopping malls, asking biased questions, reaching the correct people in an unbiased way.

    D. Identifying random samples, finding the right number of interviewees in the telephone book, asking biased questions, reaching the correct people in an unbiased way.

2. Which approach is used by the IEM to predict the outcomes of presidential elections?

    A. The IEM is well known for the Nelson, Neumann, and Forsythe (NNF) poll, which operates much like the Gallup and Harris polls.

    B. The IEM allows traders to use an open auction of presidential candidate contracts who meet face-to-face in trading pits.

C. The IEM allows individuals to buy and sell candidate contracts on-line, reflecting their predictions about presidential races.

D. The IEM is well known for its regression analysis that has successfully predicted the outcomes of several presidential races.

Constructed-Response Questions

1. Compare traditional opinion polling to the IEM, noting advantages and disadvantages of each. In your discussion of the two methods, make use of information from the 2004 presidential election.

(Traditional opinion polls have several advantages. They use carefully designed methodologies that often [not always] produce accurate predictions. For example, six out of nine national polls predicted the correct outcome in the 2004 presidential race. But polling also has many disadvantages. It is difficult to identify random samples, make telephone calls at the right times, and develop unbiased questions. Moreover, people reached by pollsters might not be completely truthful in their replies.

The IEM has several advantages. Because it is not a poll, it avoids all the problems associated with conducting polls. In addition, the IEM provides an incentive for anonymous individuals to search for information on their own and choose the best candidate. In 2004, the IEM outperformed seven of the nine national polls. Markets like the IEM, if allowed to charge fees, could easily pay for themselves and thus be far more efficient than traditional polling. A disadvantage of the IEM might be that some people are skeptical of unregulated markets.)

2. The IEM is gaining a reputation for forecasting election results with great accuracy. Can you imagine other uses for this approach?

(The IEM approach can be used to make predictions in a variety of cases for which there will ultimately be a clearly defined answer. For example, the IEM offers a futures contract on Federal Reserve monetary policy, in which the future value of a federal funds rate futures contract is traded. The IEM has also experimented with contracts predicting the value of economic announcements, the reported quarterly profits of publicly traded firms, and even box-office earnings from newly released motion pictures. There are many policy variables to which this approach could be applied.)

VISUAL 6.1

COMPARING POLLS AND MARKETS

Final Pre-Election Predictions for the 2004 Presidential Election: Nine National Polls and the IEM*

Firm	When Conducted	Bush	Kerry	Nader	Other	Bush Lead
Election Result		50.7	48.3	0.3	0.7	2.4
Harris (Online)	10/29-11/1	47	50	1	2	-3.0
Fox News	10/30-10/31	46	48	1	5	-2.0
Gallup	10/31-11/1	49	49	1	1	0.0
Zogby	11/2	49.4	49.1	1	0.5	0.3
Harris (Telephone)	10/29-11/1	49	48	2	1	1.0
NBC News/ *Wall Street Journal*	10/29-10/31	48	47	1	4	1.0
ABC News *Washington Post*	10/28-10/31	49	48	1	3	1.0
CBS News *N.Y. Times*	10/29-10/31	49	47	1	3	2.0
CNN/*USA Today*	10/29-10/31	49	47	NA	4	2.0
Iowa Electronic Market (IEM)	11/1	51.4	48.6	NA	NA	2.8

* The polling results in this table were selected from a table prepared by Michael W. Traugott, "The Accuracy of the National Pre-Election Polls in the 2004 Presidential Election," *Public Opinion Quarterly, 69* (5), 2005. "NA" is not available. The Election Result row represents actual percentage of popular vote. All polling rows represent projected percentage of popular vote (with rounding in most cases). The IEM row is the implied probability of victory for each candidate from the IEM winner-takes-all market. The IEM vote share contracts on 11/1/2004 closed at Bush = 50.4 and Kerrey = 49.5.

VISUAL 6.2

RESULTS OF THE 2008 PRESIDENTIAL ELECTION

- The Iowa Electronic Markets predicted the final vote count in the 2008 presidential election to within a half percentage point.

- Prices on the IEM's Vote Share Market predicted that Barack Obama would receive 53.55 percent of the two-party presidential popular vote, and John McCain would receive 46.45.

- After the ballots were counted, Obama received 53.2 percent of the vote, and McCain received 46.8 percent, leaving an average error per contract of .3 percent.

- The average absolute error by public opinion polls, meanwhile, was 1.2 percent.

VISUAL 6.3

RESULTS FOR THE PRESIDENTIAL ELECTION: JUNE 2006-NOVEMBER 2008

- Through all the twists and turns of the primary campaign and the final campaign, the Iowa Electronic Markets consistently picked Barack Obama as the leader.

- As illustrated in the figure below, from June 2006 until November 2008, Barack Obama led by margins similar to the final election outcome.

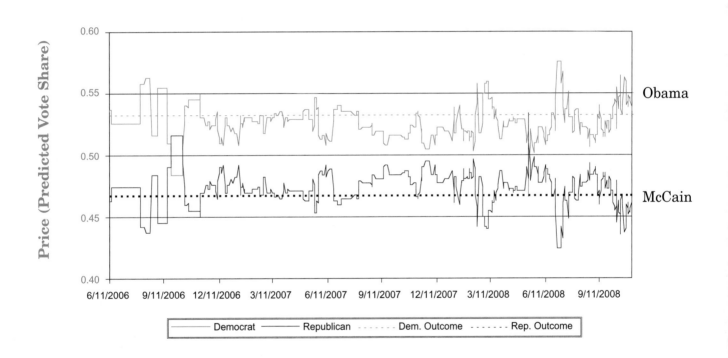

IEM 2008 Presidential Vote Share Market

Source: The Iowa Electronic Markets, Tippie College of Business, University of Iowa. Used with permission.

ACTIVITY 6.1

HOW ARE OPINION POLLS AND OPINION MARKETS DIFFERENT?

Directions: Read the following information. Then answer the Questions for Discussion.

Predicting Results by Conducting Public-Opinion Polls

Public opinion polls are a staple of American life. They are used to obtain information about a wide variety of questions, from what people want for breakfast to which candidate they support for president. Polls used to measure voter preferences have become very sophisticated, making use of several techniques developed by social scientists. National polling companies use these techniques to make their polls more accurate and unbiased. Here is an overview of some of the techniques.

Sampling

One major challenge for pollsters is to identify a random sample of voters. This cannot be done by talking to people in a shopping mall or asking people to call in to a television station. Probability sampling is the basis for all scientific survey research. The basic idea is that a small, randomly selected sample of a population can represent the opinions of all of the people in the population. The goal is to obtain the same results that would have been obtained had every member of the population been included in the survey.

Sample Size

Random selection of a sample is one issue polling companies face; sample size is another. For every poll, pollsters must determine how many interviews to conduct to insure that an adequate cross-section of randomly selected people will be included. It is not always necessary to work with a large number of people. A relatively small sample can represent a larger population adequately, provided that the sample meets other criteria for representativeness. In fact, a typical sample used in many national polls is 1,000.

Telephone Surveys

Pollsters use sophisticated computer programs to identify telephone numbers for the people to be included in a sample. Survey callers usually try to reach an adult living in the households identified by these numbers. Here, a certain sort of bias can be a problem. When there is no answer or the number is busy, the number typically is kept on file and called again later in the survey period. Pollsters use this re-dial procedure to correct for errors that could otherwise affect poll results, depending on who is at home at certain times. For example, older adults are more likely than others to be home at night. Younger single adults are less likely to be at home in the evening. Without the re-dial procedure, responses from younger voters might be underrepresented in the survey data.

Writing Good Questions

Writing good questions is hard. It requires a great deal of skill and experience. It also requires a determination to avoid introducing bias. The order in which questions are asked and the manner in which they are stated can affect the responses given. For example, in calls regarding a presidential race, it makes a difference whether the caller does or does not mention the party affiliation of the presidential candidates. Failure to mention party affiliation might bias the response. In some polls, like those commissioned by interest groups, people influenced by the wording of questions may guess at the expected answer and provide it.

ACTIVITY 6.1, CONTINUED

HOW ARE OPINION POLLS AND OPINION MARKETS DIFFERENT?

Lying, Voter Turnout, and Dollars

Pollsters face other problems as well. Some respondents lie to pollsters who call them, thus introducing error in the survey results. And while pollsters strive to obtain random samples of likely voters, it is extremely hard to predict who will in fact show up at the polls. For example, in the 2004 election, it was expected that more young people would vote than actually did. This expectation may have caused some polls to err by picking Senator Kerry over President Bush. Finally, it is expensive to conduct polls properly. It costs thousands of dollars to take all the steps needed to try to get things right. What if someone could get results of equal quality—or better results—without all the hassle and expense?

Predicting Results by Using Future Markets

There is an alternative to polling—a completely different approach to predicting elections. It involves using a political futures market. Trading in political futures involves none of the problems—statistical sampling, question design, and telephone contacts—that arise in opinion polling. Instead, futures markets allow interested individuals to make their own predictions regarding the outcomes of elections.

The Iowa Electronic Markets (IEM)

One example of a political futures market is the Iowa Electronic Markets (IEM). The IEM was developed in 1988 by three professors (Forrest Nelson, George Neumann, and Robert Forsythe) at the University of Iowa. It is a real-money, small-scale futures exchange. It allows individuals to buy and sell contracts reflecting their predictions about all sorts of events, including presidential races.

The IEM has various uses. It enables researchers to study market-based approaches to predicting outcomes. It also serves as an educational tool. It operates as part of a not-for-profit organization. No commissions or transaction fees are charged. Although the IEM is under the regulatory purview of the Commodity Futures Trading Commission (CFTC), it is not regulated by the CFTC or any other regulatory authority.

A futures contract is a legally binding agreement to buy or sell a commodity or financial instrument at a set future date. The price of the contract is determined by the bids of buyers and sellers in the market. The IEM operates something like the CME Group, a large futures contract exchange headquartered in Chicago. The CME Group enables people to buy and sell commodities like corn, wheat, and soy beans at a particular future date. It also permits the buying and selling of futures in certain financial instruments, including U.S. Treasury bonds and U.S. Treasury notes. Unlike the CME Group, however, the IEM is a *political* futures market where people can speculate on election results, using small amounts of money.

How does the IEM work? Let's imagine that it is the summer of 2012. The election of the U.S. president will take place on November 6, 2012. The IEM has just opened its "winner-takes-all" market where contracts for the presidential candidate with the largest share of the popular vote pay one dollar ($1), while contracts for the losing candidate pay nothing. You wish to buy a contract because you think you can predict who will win the contest between Candidate A and Candidate B.

ACTIVITY 6.1, CONTINUED

HOW ARE OPINION POLLS AND OPINION MARKETS DIFFERENT?

You contact the IEM website (www.biz.uiowa.edu/iem/) and open an account. (The most you can spend at IEM is $500.) The latest price for a futures contract on Candidate A is 62 cents. The price usually fluctuates, sometimes quite a lot, up until election day. With a Candidate A contract priced at 62 cents, Candidate A is considered to have a 62 percent probability of winning the election. If you buy a Candidate A contract and Candidate A does indeed win the election, the contract will pay you one dollar ($1) after the election. If Candidate B wins, you get nothing.

Let's say that you buy 500 Candidate A contracts at 62 cents each, for a total cost of $310. If Candidate A wins, your contracts will be worth $1 each, for a total of $500, giving you a gain of $190 on the $310 you spent. Of course, if Candidate B wins, you will lose the $310.

The presidential race in 2004 can help us understand how the IEM functioned when President George W. Bush ran against Massachusetts Senator John Kerry. In that year, the IEM's winner-takes-all market predicted a close race. On November 1, traders gave President Bush a 51.4 percent chance of winning, compared to a 48.6 percent chance for Senator Kerry. Throughout the summer, the IEM had shown a fairly close race. After the Republican Convention, the IEM showed Bush's probability of winning the election at 70 percent. That lead, however, dropped after the three presidential debates and continued to drop up until election eve. President Bush won with 50.7 percent of the popular vote; Senator Kerry lost with 48.3 percent. The winner-takes-all IEM market paid out $1 for each President Bush contract, and nothing for Senator Kerry contracts.

QUESTIONS FOR DISCUSSION

1. What are two challenges that public opinion companies face in their efforts to get accurate results? Explain your answer.

2. As a means for predicting the outcomes of presidential elections, how does the IEM work?

3. What is a futures market (such as the futures markets overseen by the CME group)? How is a futures market like the IEM?

4. Why might the IEM produce better results than traditional public opinion polls?

LESSON 7

TAXES CHANGE BEHAVIOR

Lesson 7
Taxes Change Behavior

INTRODUCTION

Many people view taxes merely as a means by which the government raises revenue in order to pay for the goods and services it provides. Taxes do raise revenue, but they do more than that. They also influence the behavior of individuals and firms. Some taxes are intended to change behavior. Other taxes cause unintended changes in behavior, often with unexpected consequences. In this lesson, the students examine selected taxes and predict ways in which these taxes might change people's behavior.

LESSON DESCRIPTION

The students review the economic functions of government, noting that taxes are necessary to pay for government activities. Then they consider how the government can influence behavior through taxation—by taxing sources of pollution to reduce emissions, for example, or by decreasing tax rates to encourage people to spend more. Looking at other examples, the students identify ways in which various taxes may change the behavior of those to whom they apply. They learn that taxes create incentives, and that people's responses to these incentives may have unexpected results.

CONCEPTS

- Excise tax
- Incentives
- Income tax
- Property tax

OBJECTIVES

Students will be able to:

1. Describe certain taxes levied in the United States.

2. Predict how taxes might change the behavior of consumers and producers.

3. Weigh the costs and benefits of various taxes.

CONTENT STANDARDS
Economics (CEE Standards)

- People respond predictably to positive and negative incentives. (Standard 4)

- There is an economic role for government in a market economy whenever the benefits of a government policy outweigh its costs. Governments often provide for national defense, address environmental concerns, define and protect property rights, and attempt to make markets more competitive. Most government policies also redistribute income. (Standard 16)

- Costs of government policies sometimes exceed benefits. This may occur because of incentives facing voters, government officials, and government employees, because of actions by special interest groups that can impose costs on the general public, or because social goals other than economic efficiency are being pursued. (Standard 17)

Civics and Government (NSCG Standards, 9-12)

- Students should be able to evaluate, take, and defend positions on issues regarding how government should raise money to pay for its operations and services. (III. B. 3)

- Students should be able to evaluate, take, and defend positions about the formation and implementation of public policy. (III. E. 6)

TIME REQUIRED

60 minutes

MATERIALS

- One set of cards from Activity 7.1

- A copy of Activity 7.2 for each group of three or four students

- A transparency of Visuals 7.1, 7.2, 7.3, and 7.4

PROCEDURE

1. Explain that the purpose of this lesson is to explore the functions of taxes and the manner in which taxes can change behavior—sometimes by design, sometimes unintentionally. To get started, ask the students why governments must tax their citizens. *(Answers will vary: the government doesn't need to tax at all; the government needs to pay for its activities; the government wishes to redistribute income, etc.)*

2. Display Visual 7.1, Part A, on the economic functions of government. Explain that the government has many roles to play in society. Visual 7.1 identifies only the economic functions. (Note: These economic functions are described in more detail in Lesson 4. Review these functions as necessary.)

3. Refer the students to Part B of Visual 7.1, which lists two roles of taxation. Take note of the most obvious purpose of taxation: taxes are needed to fund the government's activities. Give the students the following four examples, based on Part A of Visual 7.1:

   - Maintaining the Legal and Social Framework. The government uses tax revenue to pay for the country's law-enforcement and judicial system.

   - Providing Public Goods and Services. The government uses tax revenue to provide for national defense, one example of a public good.

   - Maintaining Competition. The government uses tax revenue in the enforcement of anti-trust laws.

   - Redistributing Income. The government uses tax revenue to provide services—health care through the Medicaid program, for example—to people who might not be able to obtain these

services on their own. Government programs like Medicaid have the effect of redistributing income from those who pay relatively more in taxes to those who receive benefits of the government programs.

4. Refer the students to the fifth and sixth functions of government listed on Visual 7.1 (Correcting for Externalities, Stabilizing the Economy). Ask the students the following questions regarding these functions:

   - Air pollution is caused in part by emissions from automobile engines. Suppose the government tripled the current tax on gasoline. What might this action accomplish, apart from the impact it would have on tax revenue? *(It would help to correct for an externality. It would increase the price of gas and thus cause many people to cut back on driving.)*

   - Suppose the government decreased income tax rates dramatically at a time when the economy was in a slump. What might this action accomplish, apart from the impact it would have on tax revenue? *(It would encourage many people to spend more, thus stimulating and perhaps helping to stabilize the economy.)*

   - Consider the latter two examples—the hike in the gasoline tax and the decrease in income tax rates—together. Apart from their effects on the collection of revenue, what else do taxes do? *(Taxes influence behavior, as stated in Part B of Visual 7.1.)*

5. Encourage discussion of the relationship between taxation and changing people's behavior by asking the students: Do you think the government can stop people from smoking? *(The government can require warnings to be printed on cigarette packages and advertisements; it can enact non-smoking laws covering restaurants and other public places; it can initiate lawsuits against tobacco companies, seeking pay-*

ment for health-care costs related to smoking; etc. If the students do not mention taxation here, remind them that cigarettes are taxed.)

6. Continue the discussion of taxation as a means by which government tries to discourage smoking. Ask: What effect do you think the taxation of cigarettes has on smokers? Does it cause them to reduce their smoking, or to quit smoking? *(The students probably will agree that taxes on cigarettes reduce smoking. They probably will disagree on the extent to which it reduces smoking.)*

7. Display Visual 7.2. Introduce the graph as an illustration of how economists analyze the effect of prices on consumers' decisions. Note that the demand curve shows how many cigarettes consumers are willing and able to purchase at each price. As the price of cigarettes increases, the quantity demanded decreases. For example, if the price of cigarettes increases from $4.30 to $4.80, then the quantity of cigarettes demanded goes down from 80 to 70. Note that the supply curve shows how many cigarettes firms are willing and able to produce at each price. As the price of cigarettes rises, the quantity of cigarettes supplied in the market increases. If there is no tax, the equilibrium price and the quantity exchanged are found where the supply curve and the demand curve intersect. In this case, the price is $4.30 and the quantity bought and sold is 80.

8. Display Visual 7.3. If the government imposes a tax on cigarette producers of $.80 per pack of cigarettes, this increases the cost of production. The supply curve with the tax shifts up by the amount of the tax: $.80 in this case. This shift of the supply curve is called a decrease in supply, since firms now are less willing to produce cigarettes at any given price. Use the graph to show how the equilibrium price has moved from point A to point B as the tax was imposed. The price increases from $4.30 to $4.80. Consumers therefore pay a price that is $.50 higher. The producers

receive $4.80 from consumers, but after paying the $.80 tax, the producer is left with $4.00, which is $.30 less than the producer received when no tax was paid. In effect, the $.80 tax is divided between the producers (who paid $.30) and consumers (who paid $.50). Point out to the students that while consumers pay more of the tax in this example, the actual division depends on which group is more sensitive to changes in price (in economic terms, the price elasticity of demand versus the elasticity of supply).

9. Note that the quantity exchanged has fallen after the tax was imposed. Ask the students: Do you believe that a tax on cigarettes will significantly reduce the quantity of cigarettes purchased? *(Students may say that cigarettes are addictive, so smokers will buy them no matter what. Acknowledge that the degree to which cigarette purchases are discouraged is open to debate – and some studies show that cigarette purchases are not very sensitive to changes in price. Still, the quantity exchanged will go down to some degree. Higher prices always result in less of a good being consumed—except in very unusual circumstances.)* Ask the students if a reduction in smoking is what law makers intended when they passed the tax. *(They will probably answer yes.)*

10. Tell the students that the tax on cigarettes is an example of an excise tax. Certain excise taxes (on cigarettes or liquor, for example) are often called *sin taxes*, since one purpose of these taxes is to discourage people from doing something that might be viewed as bad for them. Explain that, from an economist's standpoint, one important issue is whether the smoker bears all the costs of smoking. If the smoker bears all the costs associated with his or her smoking, then (economists believe) the market can determine the "best" quantity of cigarettes for society. In reality, the smoker does not bear all the costs; some costs spill over to others, in the form of second-hand smoke, clean-up activity, etc. Economists view second-hand

smoke as a negative externality that imposes costs (annoyance, health risks) on bystanders. For an economist, taxing an item that produces a negative externality is one way to reduce the harm that this item imposes on others.

11. Ask the students: Do you believe this intended change in behavior (less smoking) is good for society? *(Some students may say yes, since people—smokers and bystanders alike—will be healthier. Others may note that their economic freedom to buy what they want is reduced, or that producers of cigarettes will see lower sales.)*

12. Organize the class into groups of two to four people. Make sure that exactly 10 groups are formed. Remind the students that people pay many taxes, and that all taxes work to change people's behavior in some manner. Introduce Activity 7.1. Explain that each group of students will receive a card (the cards are provided in Activity 7.1). Each of the cards describes a tax that is similar to, or is a simplified form of, an actual tax paid in the United States in the last few years. Below the description of the tax on each card there is a proposal to change the tax. Distribute the cards to the student groups. Tell the students to have one person read his or her card to their group and then ask the group members to discuss the proposal.

13. Distribute Activity 7.2. Tell the students to work in their groups and answer the Questions for Discussion. Before the students begin, explain that tax evasion, while it certainly may be a consequence of increased taxes, is not the answer you are looking for in this case. Tax evasion is illegal. You are looking for thoughts about how people might *legally* change their behavior in response to a given tax. Tell the students to designate one person per group to report on the groups' answers when called upon.

14. After five or ten minutes, call for the groups' reports. *(Here are suggested answers; some of them are disputable, even among economists. The purpose here is to*

prompt thought and discussion about these issues. Sources are given for some of the information provided. Question 4 is left to the students' judgment. As the students go through the questions, summarize their answers on Visual 7.4.)

Answers for Activity 7.2

Card 1: Excise Tax on Gasoline

1. *An increase in the price of gasoline will result in less gas being consumed. People will drive less, buy cars that get better mileage, or car-pool.*

2. *The tax proposal may have been intended to reduce driving, but the revenues provide more funding for highways. This tax is an example of taxing according to benefits received.*

3. *Students might believe that using less gasoline is a good thing in that less driving might reduce pollution and congestion, which are negative externalities. Some will believe that reduced reliance on gasoline will provide increased economic security for the country. Some will note that transportation costs will be higher; thus some people will not be able to travel as much, or they will need to spend more to get to their jobs.*

Source for tax information: U.S. Department of Transportation, Federal Highway Administration, TABLE MF-121T, August 2008 Reporting Period, http://www.fhwa.dot.gov/ohim/mmfr/index.cfm.

Card 2: Estate Tax

1. *An increase in the estate tax from no tax (in 2010) to taxing estates over $1 million (beginning in 2011) could result in people dying to avoid paying the estate tax. While the change in behavior is not likely to be widespread—not every octogenarian millionaire will succumb—at the margin, everything else equal, the death rate is likely to be slightly higher in December of 2010 than in January of 2011. Some of the*

change in death rates might be accounted for by misreported dates of death—family members might fudge the actual dates somehow to avoid the tax—but some will also be caused by people dying to avoid taxes.

2. *The early death of citizens is obviously not the intended outcome here.*

3. *This change in behavior would not be a good thing for society.*

Source for whether this actually happens: W. Kopczuk and J. Slemrod, Dying to Save Taxes: Evidence from Estate-Tax Returns on the Death Elasticity, Review of Economics & Statistics, *85(2), May 2003, pp. 256-265.*

Card 3: Federal Income Tax on Wages

1. *An increase in the tax on wages will result in people working less. Some people will work fewer hours; some may decide not to work. Taxing work at such a high marginal rate will encourage some people to take more leisure time instead. (Some students may note that some individuals will work more to make up for lost income.)*

2. *The income tax on wages is not intended to dissuade people from working; it is intended to raise revenue or redistribute income.*

3. *If taxation significantly reduces the quantity of labor supplied, this change in tax policy may be viewed as bad for society in that production will be decreased.*

Card 4: Capital Gains Tax

1. *Eliminating the tax on capital gains would encourage people to invest in assets such as stocks or real estate. People would be more willing to make these investments because, with the change, they would be able to keep all of the gains arising from appreciation of the assets in question. With more funds flowing into stocks and other assets, firms would gain capacity to expand and modernize.*

2. *The hope behind such tax cuts is that they would spur the economy to grow at a faster rate: additional investment would lead to more capital formation and thus more rapid economic growth.*

3. *The issue of the fairness of such tax cuts is addressed in Lesson 11. The capital gains tax is a progressive tax. Eliminating the capital gains tax would make the tax system less progressive. The trade-off in this case is one between economic equity and economic growth.*

Card 5: Deductions for Children on Federal Income Taxes

1. *An increase in the deduction will lead to an increase in the number of children, since the cost of having a child will be subsidized in part by the government. In addition, the timing of births will be affected. Children will be more likely to be born in the last week of December as opposed to the first week of January, so that their parents can take advantage of the tax break. According to one estimate, "increasing the tax benefit of having a child by $500 raises the probability of having the child in the last week of December by 26.9 percent."**

2. *While the deduction is given to help families, it is not clear that larger families or ones with December birthdays are an expressed goal of the policy.*

3. *Should public policy encourage population growth? It is hard to say. Although each worker represents a resource for the country—and this pool of resources is enlarged when the population increases—traditional growth studies suggest that GDP per person declines when population growth rates rise.*

*Source: S. Dickert-Conlin and C. Amitabh, "Taxes and the Timing of Births," Journal of Political Economy, 107 (1), February 1999, p. 161.

Card 6: The Gas- Guzzler Tax

1. An increase in the gas-guzzler tax would reduce the number of lower fuel-efficiency cars purchased. A key question is what else might be purchased in their place. One way to avoid the tax would be to buy a more fuel-efficient car. However, a second way would be to buy an SUV or a light truck (which would get worse gas mileage). The intent of the tax was to discourage large, low-mileage cars in favor of high-mileage cars.

2. The intent was not to encourage the use of low-mileage SUVs or trucks.

3. Doubling the gas-guzzler tax might create an incentive for more people to move from cars to SUVs and trucks, which would not necessarily be good for society.

Gas-Guzzler Tax Information:
http://www.epa.gov/fueleconomy/guzzler/

Card 7: Tax on Fishing Rods

1. An increase in the tax on fishing rods will reduce the quantity of fishing rods purchased. People who fish will not buy a new rod as often, and some may turn to other outdoor sports.

2. The intent of the tax is probably not to reduce the number of people who fish, but rather to obtain money from people who fish and use the money to improve the quality of fishing resources in the states. This tax is an example of taxing according to benefits received.

3. Of course, doubling the tax may discourage too many people from fishing, leaving lakes filled with fish for fewer people who enjoy fishing. Fewer people interested in fishing might also mean that fewer people would care whether fish are nurtured or not, and that outcome would not be good for the fish.

Source: Federal Aid in Sport Fish Restoration Act,
http://www.fws.gov/laws/lawsdigest/fasport.html, U.S. Fish and Wildlife Service.

Card 8: Excise Tax on Wine

1. Like the tax on cigarettes, the tax on wine is a sin tax. Increasing the tax will reduce wine consumption. However, if the tax on other alcoholic beverages is not increased as well, then some drinkers will substitute beer or hard liquor for wine.

2. The goal of these taxes is to reduce the consumption of wine.

3. If the consumption of wine causes a negative externality (a cost to others—drunken driving, perhaps), then a tax is a reasonable policy to reduce wine consumption. Otherwise, a tax will reduce the benefits to society of having wine available at a lower price.

Source: http://www.ttb.gov/tax_audit/atftaxes.shtml

Card 9: Property Tax

1. An increase in the property tax will reduce the demand for homes in the city. This reduction in demand would be lower if other cities matched the tax increase. As the demand for homes decreases, the price of homes will drop.

2. Discouraging living in the city is not the intention of the tax. The intention is to provide revenue for the city, to be used to pay for city services.

3. Property taxes are an important source of revenue for many cities. The burden of the tax must be weighed against the benefits that the city provides. If city services such as schools, fire protection, and police protection are valued by the citizens of the city, then the additional benefits (in the form of enhanced services) may outweigh losses associated with declining property values.

Card 10: Tariff on Tennis Rackets

1. The price of imported tennis rackets would increase. U.S. tennis players would have to pay more to buy their favorite imported rackets. American racket producers would profit at the expense of the U.S. consumer.

2. *The intent of the tariff is to provide protection for U.S. producers, even though consumers are harmed.*

3. *The harm to consumers would outweigh the benefits to producers. In terms of efficiency, lower trade barriers are, in general, best for society.*

For information on tariffs of all types: Harmonized Tariff Schedule of the United States (2009), http://www.usitc.gov/tata/hts/bychapter/index.htm

15. After reviewing each group's card and the answers provided, ask the students which taxes they believe are good ones. *(This is an open-ended question. Answers may be based on whether the tax would cause favorable changes in behavior or whether the tax seems to be fair.)*

CLOSURE

Ask the students the following questions:

- Do taxes change behavior? *(They should answer yes.)*

- Can you name taxes that are intended to change behavior? *(The tax on wine and cigarettes, the gasoline tax, the gas-guzzler tax, the tariff on tennis rackets. These taxes all are intended to change behavior.)*

- Can you name taxes that cause unintended changes in behavior? *(Deductions for children, income taxes, estate taxes, taxes on fishing rods, the capital gains tax—although a capital gains tax cut may be intended to increase saving and investment. These taxes might change behavior in ways not intended by legislators.)*

Conclude the closure discussion by noting that good tax policy should anticipate reactions to the policy in question.

ASSESSMENT
Multiple-Choice Questions

1. A tax on imported goods is called

   A. an excise tax.

   B. a tariff.

   C. a millage rate.

   D. an incoming tax.

2. The federal tax on gasoline is an example of

   A. an excise tax.

   B. a tariff.

   C. a millage rate.

   D. a progressive tax.

3. If the government taxes a good, the price of the good will _____ and people will buy _____ of the good.

   A. increase, less

   B. increase, more

   C. decrease, less

   D. decrease, more

Constructed-Response Questions

1. You are in charge of tax policy in a small country. You are considering placing a 50 percent tax on either gasoline or apples to raise tax revenue. Which tax would you choose, and why?

   (Students should note that taxing either item will reduce its consumption. They should speculate that apple consumption might drop more than gasoline consumption. In terms of tax revenue, then, a gasoline tax might do better. Students might also decide that it would be a good thing to reduce consumption of gasoline, because using gasoline causes pollution. Consumption of apples does not have a negative externality.)

2. In early August, many states have sales-tax holidays on back-to-school supplies or clothing.   How do these tax holidays change consumers' behavior?   Are these tax holidays good policies? Why or why not?

    (During these tax holidays, people buy more of the goods in question than they ordinarily do. Students may decide that that is a good thing—that the tax holidays help to make important goods more affordable for needy families.   This benefit to families might outweigh the state's loss of tax revenue.)

VISUAL 7.1
GOVERNMENT AND TAXES

Part A. The Economic Functions of Government

1.   Maintaining the Legal and Social Framework

2.   Providing Public Goods and Services

3.   Maintaining Competition

4.   Redistributing Income

5.   Correcting for Externalities

6.   Stabilizing the Economy

Part B. Roles of Taxation

1.   Taxes provide funding for government activities

2.   Taxes influence behavior

VISUAL 7.2

How Do Taxes Change Behavior?

The Market for Cigarettes:

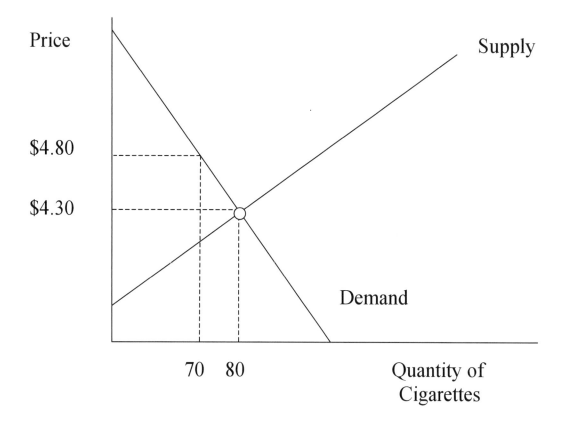

The graph shows the supply of and demand for cigarettes. The equilibrium price of cigarettes is $4.30. The equilibrium quantity exchanged is 80.

VISUAL 7.3

HOW DO TAXES CHANGE BEHAVIOR?

Tax on Cigarettes:

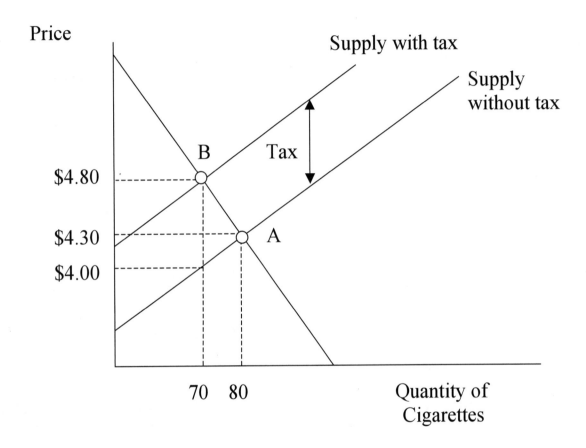

The graph shows the effects of an $.80 tax on each pack of cigarettes. The supply curve shifts by the amount of the tax (a decrease in supply). Equilibrium in the market moves from point A to point B.

VISUAL 7.4

SUMMARY SHEET

Tax Policy	Intended Behavior Change?	Behavior Change a Good Thing?	Should We Implement the Proposal?
Increase Excise Tax on Gasoline			
Estate Tax Increase			
Increase Federal Income Tax			
Decrease Capital Gains Tax			
Increase Deductions			
Increase Gas-Guzzler Tax			
Increase Excise Tax on Fishing Rods			
Increase Excise Tax on Wine			
Increase Property Taxes			
Increase Tariff on Tennis Rackets			

ACTIVITY 7.1
CARDS

Directions to the teacher: See Lesson Procedure 12. Distribute one card to each student group.

Card 1: Excise Tax on Gasoline

Description: The federal excise tax on gasoline is 18.4 cents per gallon. Most revenue from the tax goes to fund federal highways. State taxes on gasoline range from 7.5 cents per gallon to 36 cents per gallon.

Proposal: Both the federal and state governments will double the excise tax on gasoline.

Card 2: Estate Tax

Description: The U.S. federal estate tax is to be repealed in the year 2010. This means that the families of people who die in 2010 will not be subject to paying a tax on their estate.

Proposal: Beginning in 2011, estates above $1,000,000 will be subject to an estate tax.

Card 3: Federal Income Tax on Wages

Description: The federal government taxes wage income. The amount of this tax can be as high as a marginal tax rate of 35% for high-income households (wage income above $357,700 in 2008). This means that for each additional dollar earned, 35 cents is paid as federal tax.

Proposal: Increase the marginal tax rate in the top tax bracket to 70%.

Activity 7.1, continued

Cards

Card 4: Capital Gains Tax

Description: Capital gains taxes are taxes that are paid when an asset such as stock or a house has appreciated in value and is sold for a higher price. Currently, most long-term capital gains on stock are taxed at 15%.

Proposal: Congress will eliminate the tax on all capital gains.

Card 5: Deductions for Children on Federal Income Tax Forms

Description: For each child in a household, a deduction (reduction in taxable income) is given. In 2008, this deduction was $3,500 per qualifying child. If a family had a taxable income of $75,000, a child would reduce the family's tax bill by $875.

Proposal: Double the deduction for children.

Card 6: Gas-Guzzler Tax

Description: The federal government taxes passenger cars under 6,000 pounds that do not get at least 22.5 miles per gallon. This law does not apply to light trucks or SUVs. An automobile whose mileage is 22 miles per gallon or lower would be subject to a tax of $1,000.

Proposal: The federal government will double the tax on gas guzzlers.

Card 7: Excise Tax on Fishing Rods

Description: The federal government places a 10% excise tax on fishing rods and other fishing equipment. The proceeds from the tax, over $400 million in 2008, go to state programs to develop and enhance fishing resources.

Proposal: The federal government will increase the excise tax on fishing rods to 20%.

ACTIVITY 7.1, CONTINUED
CARDS

Card 8: Excise Tax on Wine

Description: The federal government imposes a tax of 21 cents per bottle of wine. Some states have additional taxes on wine; other states regulate the sale of wine.

Proposal: Increase the federal tax on wine to $1.00 a bottle.

Card 9: Property Taxes

Description: A city currently charges a tax on the value of property in the city. The millage rate charged by the city is 5 mills per dollar of value, which is equivalent to $5 of tax for every thousand dollars of value. A mill is one thousandth; thus a property valued at $100,000 would pay $500 in tax.

Proposal: The city will increase the millage rate to 10 mills.

Card 10: Tariff on Tennis Rackets

Description: The United States charges a tariff of 3.9% on tennis rackets imported from many countries.

Proposal: The United States will increase the tariff to 20%.

ACTIVITY 7.2

THE TAX PROPOSALS: QUESTIONS FOR DISCUSSION

1. How do you suppose peoples' behavior would change if the tax proposal on your card was implemented? Describe specifically how people would change their behavior in response to the change in the tax.

2. Do you suppose the tax proposal was intended to change peoples' behavior in this way? Explain your answer.

3. Is this change in behavior a good thing for society? Why or why not?

4. Would you implement this tax proposal? Why or why not?

FOCUS: UNDERSTANDING ECONOMICS IN CIVICS AND GOVERNMENT © COUNCIL FOR ECONOMIC EDUCATION, NEW YORK, NY

LESSON 8

ECONOMIC MISERY AND PRESIDENTIAL ELECTIONS

LESSON 8
ECONOMIC MISERY AND PRESIDENTIAL ELECTIONS

INTRODUCTION

Many factors influence voters as they decide how they will vote. The economic policies advocated by candidates and political parties are important factors in these decisions. No matter what policies a presidential candidate may propose, however, an incumbent candidate is often blamed for or credited with how well the economy is doing, whether or not the incumbent's policies were actually the cause of the condition in question. Many voters base their decisions narrowly on how the nation's economy is affecting them at the time. Therefore, in a presidential campaign in which an incumbent is vying for re-election, certain key measures of economic performance can help to predict the election outcome. This lesson shows how two economic measures, the Misery Index and the growth rate in real GDP per capita, can be used to make predictions about presidential elections.

LESSON DESCRIPTION

The students examine economic data in order to predict the results of presidential elections.

CONCEPTS

- Inflation
- Misery Index
- Real GDP
- Real GDP per capita
- Unemployment
- Voting and elections

OBJECTIVES

Students will be able to:

1. Identify economic conditions likely to influence voter opinion.

2. Examine economic data to make predictions about presidential elections.

CONTENT STANDARDS
Economics (CEE Standards)

- Costs of government policies sometime exceed benefits. This may occur because of incentives facing voters, government officials, and government employees, because of actions by special interest groups that can impose costs on the general public, or because social goals other than economic efficiency are being pursued. (Standard 17)

- Unemployment imposes costs on individuals and nations. Unexpected inflation imposes costs on many people and benefits some others because it arbitrarily redistributes purchasing power. Inflation can reduce the rate of growth of national living standards, because individuals and organizations use resources to protect themselves against the uncertainty of future prices. (Standard 19)

Civics and Government (NSCG Standards, 9-12)

- Students should be able evaluate, take, and defend positions about the roles of political parties, campaigns, and elections in American politics. (III. E. 4)

- Students should be able to evaluate, take and defend positions about the means that citizens should use to monitor and influence the formation and implementation of public policy. (V. E. 3)

TIME REQUIRED

60 minutes, plus time for the students to complete Activity 8.1 as homework

MATERIALS

- A copy of Activity 8.1, 8.2, and 8.3 for each student

- A transparency of Visuals 8.1, 8.2, and 8.3

PROCEDURE

1. Tell the students that in a future class period they will be considering economic factors that influence the outcomes of presidential elections. In order to do this as accurately as possible, they will need to collect information from someone who is of voting age (18 years or older).

2. Give each student a copy of Activity 8.1. Assign the students to collect the information called for from one person of voting age. Set a due-date for completion of the task, and clarify the directions as necessary. The person from whom the information is collected does not need to be a member of the student's household. Parents, guardians, relatives, neighbors, co-workers, friends—all can serve as subjects for this interview. And even if the next presidential election is far off, it is important that the interviewees identify the issues that are, will be, or have been most important to them when considering which candidate to support for president. This activity is not intended to determine whether or not a person has voted in an election (or for whom she or he voted). Instead, it is designed to help students identify issues that are important to adults of voting age.

3. Collect the students' completed forms from Activity 8.1 and organize the responses for use during a forthcoming class period. As you review the responses, highlight common answers and central tendencies that stand out. When you resume work on the activity with the class, write these common answers on the board, with notations to show the number of times each was mentioned in responses to Activity 8.1.

4. Call on the students to comment on the election issues you have listed on the board. How many of these are economic issues? *(Answers will vary, but several economic issues [e.g., unemployment, inflation, the federal budget deficit, income inequality, tax policy, Social Security, trade policy, etc.] will likely appear on the list. Other issues [e.g., the environment, immigration, energy, and educational policy] also have economic implications.)* By reference to the economic issues listed, emphasize the point that the state of the economy weighs heavily in voters' minds as they decide which candidate to support. Quote the old political adage, "People tend to vote their pocketbooks."

5. Ask the students: Do you think the economy is in good shape today? *(Accept any answer.)* Press further: What data do you use to support your answer? *(Many answers are possible, but be sure to steer the discussion toward measures of the unemployment rate, the inflation rate, and real GDP as important determinants of the current state of economic activity. As necessary, explain that GDP is a measure of overall production, inflation measures the percentage change in average prices, and the unemployment rate captures the percentage of those who are working or wish to work but cannot currently find a job.)*

6. Display Visual 8.1. Use it to explain that some economic indicators are especially important in predicting election results. In particular, growth in real GDP per capita—growth in the value of final goods and services produced per person—is an important indicator of whether an incumbent president (or the candidate from the incumbent party) will be reelected. The growth in real GDP per capita is found by dividing real GDP for each year by the country's population and then finding the percentage change from one year to the next. A second indicator, the Misery Index, also can be used to predict an election result. In any given year, the Misery Index is the sum of the inflation rate and unemployment rate. As the name of the Misery Index implies, high rates of unemployment and/or high inflation rates can cause economic misery. Economic misery usually means trouble for incumbent candidates.

7. Divide the class into groups of three or four students. Distribute a copy of Activity 8.2 to each student. Briefly

review the columns in the table. (Note: You may wish to update the table with current data. If you do so, note that this table uses *annual* data. Annual unemployment and inflation [using the Consumer Price Index] data can be found by searching the website www.bls.gov, while annual levels of real GDP per capita can be found at the website www.bea.gov. As noted above, the annual growth rate of real GDP per capita can be computed by calculating the percentage change in the levels of this series, using "chained dollars," from one year to the next).[1]

8. As you review the columns in Activity 8.2, ask:

   • What year since 1957 had the highest unemployment rate? *(1982)*

   • What year had the highest inflation rate? *(1980)*

   • What year had the highest Misery Index? *(1980)*

   • How does this compare to the Misery Index now? *(Use current data.)*

9. Distribute a copy of Activity 8.3 to each student. Ask the students, working in their groups, to complete Part I of Activity 8.3, using information provided in Table 8.2. *(Answers: 1960, Kennedy, Lose; 1964, Johnson, Win; 1968, Nixon, Lose; 1972, Nixon, Win; 1976, Carter, Lose; 1980, Reagan, Lose; 1984, Reagan, Win; 1988, Bush, Win; 1992, Clinton, Lose; 1996, Clinton, Win; 2000, Bush, Lose; 2004, Bush, Win; 2008, Obama, Lose.)* Since the rest of the sheet depends upon correct answers, check the students' answers. As necessary, explain which party was the incumbent and who won each election.

10. Tell the students that they will now try to predict who will win a presidential election. More than that: They will try to create a rule that can be used to make such predictions. They will begin by considering an example. Display Visual 8.2 and discuss the rule that it proposes: "The incumbent party usually wins if the growth rate of real GDP per capita is greater than 0% during the year of the election." Call on the students to check this rule against Table 8.2. How well does the rule stand up to the data? *(Not particularly well. While it predicts correctly all six of the incumbent wins, it is incorrect on six of the seven losses that were actually registered. It yields a correct prediction for a loss only in 1980; it incorrectly predicts a win for actual losses in 1960, 1968, 1976, 1992, 2000 and 2008. Overall, the rule correctly predicts only 7 of 13 elections.)*

11. Tell the students, working in groups, to complete Part II of Activity 8.3. Clarify the task as necessary. They must try to create two rules. One rule should be based on the real GDP per capita growth rate, the other on the Misery Index. You may want to provide hints—such as concentrating on current-year information for the real GDP per capita growth rule, and on changes from the year prior to the election year for the Misery Index. If the students have trouble coming up with these rules, show them the first two rules in Visual 8.3 and have them copy these rules to Part II of Activity 8.3.

12. Call on the students, group by group, to share their proposed rules with the class. Ask the class to decide which of the proposed rules work the best. Be sure that the students base their evaluations on how

[1] The term "chained dollars" is now frequently found in tables of macroeconomic data. This term comes from a procedure known as "chain-weighting," which is a means by which statistical agencies convert economic data to "real" measures. Therefore a reference to "chained dollars" implies that the data are expressed in real, inflation-adjusted form (using constant prices instead of current prices). In most cases, it is unnecessary for students to know this, other than its use to differentiate between nominal and real measures.

successfully each proposed rule does in fact predict winners. Also, the students should reject any rules that are not based on economic reasoning. While many such rules have been suggested from time to time—for example, picking winners by reference to the score of the Washington Redskins' last home game—any successful rule should be based on acceptable economic theory.

13. If you have not already shown the students the first two rules in Visual 8.3, display them now. Ask:

- How well does the real GDP per capita growth rule in Visual 8.3 predict election outcomes? *(The rule is correct in 10 of 13 elections. It is incorrect for the years 1968, 1976, and 2000.)*

- How well does the Misery Index rule in Visual 8.3 predict election outcomes? *(The rule is correct in 11 of 13 elections. It is incorrect for the years 1976 and 1992.)*

14. Continue the inquiry. Ask: Given the first two rules in Visual 8.3, which election was the most difficult to predict? *(The 1976 election. Real GDP per capita growth was 4.3 percent. Inflation and unemployment, while high, were down significantly from the previous year. From an economic standpoint, these two facts make this election the hardest to predict by application of the two proposed rules. Non-economic factors probably mattered a great deal in this election. The incumbent was Gerald Ford, who had been appointed by President Nixon. President Nixon, who had earlier resigned as a result of the Watergate scandal, was ultimately pardoned from criminal prosecution by President Ford. It was not a good time for a candidate to be associated with the Nixon administration or the Republican party.)*

15. Turn to the last rule in Visual 8.3: the Guaranteed Loss Rule. Note that not all losses would have been predicted by this rule. Nevertheless, whenever the rule's two conditions have been met, the incumbent

party has always lost (in 1960, 1980 and 2008). An incumbent party is in trouble when the Misery Index has increased and real output per person has grown by less than 2.5 percent in an election year.

16. Will these rules continue to perform well? If the timing is appropriate, ask the students to use the Misery Index rule and the Real GDP per Capita Growth Rule to predict the outcome of a forthcoming presidential election.

CLOSURE

Use the following questions to review the lesson:

- Based on the data you have examined in this lesson, do you believe that economic conditions have a strong impact on presidential elections? *(The answer should be yes; the economy usually does influence presidential elections.)*

- Is the incumbent party necessarily to blame for poor economic performance in the run-up to an election, or is it necessarily responsible for good economic performance? *(Answers will vary. Conventional wisdom holds that the President receives too much credit when the economy is doing well and shoulders too much blame when the economy is performing poorly.)*

ASSESSMENT
Multiple-Choice Questions

1. The misery index is the sum of the

   A. inflation rate and the growth rate of real GDP.

   B. unemployment rate and the growth rate of real GDP.

   C. **inflation rate and the unemployment rate.**

   D. inflation rate, the unemployment rate, and the growth rate of real GDP.

2. Inflation was the highest in

   A. the late 1960s and early 1970s.

B. **the late 1970s and early 1980s.**

C. the late 1980s and early 1990s.

D. the late 1990s and early 2000s.

3. Which one of the following growth rates is most likely to be lowest for the U.S. economy?

A. Growth rate of nominal GDP

B. Growth rate of nominal GDP per capita

C. Growth rate of real GDP

D. **Growth rate of real GDP per capita**

Constructed-Response Question

1. Assume that you are the president of United States. You are coming up for reelection next year. A bill that significantly increases government spending for projects across the country is awaiting your signature. While the increase in government spending will lower unemployment for the next year or two, you fear that it also will lead to significantly higher inflation in two years time. Given what you know about the correlation between the Misery Index and election outcomes, should you sign the bill?

(The students should note that by signing the bill, the president increases his or her probability of reelection. The policy, while reducing unemployment, will come at a cost of inflation in the future. To evaluate the policy overall, the students need to weigh the benefits of lower unemployment and reelection against the prospect of higher inflation in the future.)

VISUAL 8.1

SOME KEY ECONOMIC INDICATORS

SOME KEY ECONOMIC INDICATORS

- Unemployment Rate: The percentage of people in the labor force who are unemployed.

- Inflation Rate: The percentage increase in the overall price level.

- Real GDP: the value of all final goods and services produced in a country in a year, expressed in terms of constant dollars.

TWO STATISTICS BASED ON THESE INDICATORS

- Misery Index: The sum of the unemployment rate and the inflation rate.

- Growth rate in real GDP per capita: The percentage change in real GDP per person.

VISUAL 8.2

AN ECONOMIC RULE THAT DOES NOT WORK WELL

A Real GDP per capita growth rule:

The incumbent party usually wins if . . .

The growth rate of real GDP per capita is greater than 0% during the year of the election.

VISUAL 8.3

SOME ECONOMIC RULES THAT WORK WELL

A Real GDP per capita growth rule:

The incumbent party usually wins if . . .

The growth rate of real GDP per capita is greater than or equal to 2.5% during the year of the election.

A Misery Index rule:

The incumbent party usually wins if . . .

The Misery Index has not increased from the year prior to the election.

A Guaranteed Loss Rule:

The incumbent party has always lost if

(1) the real GDP per capita growth is less than 2.5%

AND

(2) the misery index has increased from the year prior to the election to the year of the election.

ACTIVITY 8.1

THE THREE MOST IMPORTANT ISSUES IN A PRESIDENTIAL ELECTION

Directions: Ask an adult of voting age (18 years of age or older) the following three-part question. (This adult can be a family member, a guardian, a friend, a relative, a co-worker, or anyone else who may be willing to share his or her views about important issues in a presidential election. Make sure to indicate that you are NOT asking whether the interviewee plans to vote, or has voted in a prior election. You are also NOT asking for whom the interviewee has voted in the past, or may support in the future.)

The question:

Please indicate the three issues that are most important to you as you decide who will get your vote in a U.S. presidential election.

Issue 1: _____

Issue 2: _____

Issue 3: _____

ACTIVITY 8.2

ELECTIONS AND THE ECONOMY

The following table includes information about three key measures (growth in real GDP per capita, unemployment rate, and inflation rate) of the annual performance of the U.S. economy since 1957.

TABLE 8.2

Year	Growth in Real GDP per Capita (in %)	Unempl. Rate (in %)	Inflation Rate (in %)	Misery Index	Real GDP per Capita Growth Rule	Misery Index Rule	Candidates	Incumbent Party Wins or Loses?
1957	0.2	4.3	3.3	7.6				
1958	-2.6	6.8	2.8	9.6				
1959	5.3	5.5	0.7	6.2				
1960	0.4	5.5	1.7	7.2	_____	_____	Kennedy / Nixon	_____
1961	0.7	6.7	1	7.7				
1962	4.4	5.5	1	6.5				
1963	2.9	5.7	1.3	7				
1964	4.5	5.2	1.3	6.5	_____	_____	Johnson / Goldwater	_____
1965	5.1	4.5	1.6	6.1				
1966	5.3	3.8	2.9	6.7				
1967	1.4	3.8	3.1	6.9				
1968	3.8	3.6	4.2	7.8	_____	_____	Humphrey / Nixon / Wallace	_____
1969	2.1	3.5	5.5	9				
1970	-1.0	4.9	5.7	10.6				
1971	2.1	5.9	4.4	10.3				
1972	4.2	5.6	3.2	8.8	_____	_____	McGovern / Nixon	_____
1973	4.8	4.9	6.2	11.1				
1974	-1.4	5.6	11	16.6				
1975	-1.2	8.5	9.1	17.6				
1976	4.3	7.7	5.8	13.5	_____	_____	Carter / Ford	_____
1977	3.6	7.1	6.5	13.6				
1978	4.5	6.1	7.6	13.7				
1979	2.0	5.8	11.3	17.1				
1980	-1.4	7.1	13.5	20.6	_____	_____	Carter / Reagan / Anderson	_____
1981	1.5	7.6	10.3	17.9				
1982	-2.9	9.7	6.2	15.9				
1983	3.6	9.6	3.2	12.8				
1984	6.3	7.5	4.3	11.8	_____	_____	Mondale / Reagan	_____

ACTIVITY 8.2, CONTINUED

ELECTIONS AND THE ECONOMY

TABLE 8.2, CONTINUED

Year	Growth in Real GDP per Capita (in %)	Unempl. Rate (in %)	Inflation Rate (in %)	Misery Index	Real GDP per Capita Growth Rule	Misery Index Rule	Candidates	Incumbent Party Wins or Loses?
1985	3.2	7.2	3.6	10.8				
1986	2.5	7	1.9	8.9				
1987	2.5	6.2	3.6	9.8				
1988	3.2	5.5	4.1	9.6	_____	_____	Dukakis / Bush	_____
1989	2.6	5.3	4.8	10.1				
1990	0.7	5.6	5.4	11				
1991	-1.5	6.8	4.2	11				
1992	2.0	7.5	3	10.5	_____	_____	Clinton / Bush / Perot	_____
1993	1.3	6.9	3	9.9				
1994	2.8	6.1	2.6	8.7				
1995	1.3	5.6	2.8	8.4				
1996	2.5	5.4	3	8.4	_____	_____	Clinton / Dole	_____
1997	3.3	4.9	2.3	7.2				
1998	3.0	4.5	1.6	6.1				
1999	3.3	4.2	2.2	6.4				
2000	2.5	4	3.4	7.4	_____	_____	Gore / Bush	_____
2001	-0.3	4.7	2.8	7.5				
2002	0.6	5.8	1.6	7.4				
2003	1.6	6	2.3	8.3				
2004	2.7	5.5	2.7	8.2	_____	_____	Kerry /Bush	_____
2005	2.0	5.1	3.4	8.5				
2006	1.8	4.6	3.2	7.8				
2007	1.0	4.6	2.8	7.4				
2008	0.2	5.8	3.8	9.6	_____	_____	Obama/McCain	_____

FOCUS: UNDERSTANDING ECONOMICS IN CIVICS AND GOVERNMENT © COUNCIL FOR ECONOMIC EDUCATION, NEW YORK, NY

ACTIVITY 8.3

A WORKSHEET ON ELECTIONS AND THE ECONOMY

Directions: Working with others in your group, use information from Table 8.2 to answer the following questions, as directed by your teacher.

Part I. Who Won?

1. Circle the winner of each presidential election.

2. Under the column "Incumbent Party Wins or Loses?" Write "Win" or "W" if the incumbent party won the election. Write "Lose" or "L" if the incumbent party lost the election. In each set of listed candidates, the first candidate mentioned is the Democratic candidate and the second candidate is the Republican candidate. In three contests, there was a third-party candidate who is listed as the last entry. To get started, note that the president prior to the Kennedy/Nixon election was Eisenhower, who was a Republican. Therefore, since Kennedy won the presidential election, your group should enter "Lose" in the appropriate spot in the last column of Table 8.2, since the incumbent party lost the election.

Part II. Predictions

1. Create a Real GDP per capita Growth Rule based on the instructions your teacher gives you.

   Real GDP per capita Growth Rule:

   The incumbent party usually wins if the real GDP per capita growth

   _____ .

2. For each election, write "Win" or "W" in the column under Real GDP per capita Growth Rule if the rule predicts the incumbent party will win. Write "Lose" or "L" in the column if the rule predicts the incumbent party will lose.

   This real GDP per capita Growth Rule is correct _____ out of 13 times.

3. Create a Misery Index Rule based on the instructions your teacher gives you.

   Misery Index Rule: The incumbent party usually wins if the misery index

   _____ .

4. For each election, write "Win" or "W" in the column under Misery Index Rule if the rule predicts the incumbent party will win. Write "Lose" or "L" in the column if the rule predicts the incumbent party will lose.

   The Misery Index Rule is correct _____ out of 13 times.

THE MARKET GOES TO COURT: KEY ECONOMIC CASES AND THE UNITED STATES SUPREME COURT

LESSON 9
THE MARKET GOES TO COURT: KEY ECONOMIC CASES AND THE UNITED STATES SUPREME COURT

INTRODUCTION

When we think of landmark cases decided by the U.S. Supreme Court, we tend to think of famous cases involving education (e.g., *Brown v. Board of Education*), civil liberties (e.g., *Miranda v. Arizona*), or religious freedom (e.g., *Lemon v. Kurtzman*). However, many key Supreme Court cases have had their origins in economic issues or in issues related to our market economy and the role of the government within it. Indeed, one of the first landmark cases (*McCulloch v. Maryland*) dealt with the federal government's power to establish and regulate interstate commerce.

In such cases, the Supreme Court wields the power of judicial review—that is, the power to declare laws unconstitutional. Judicial review has often been brought to bear on legislation intended to regulate business, encourage competition, or protect property rights.

Many of the economic cases heard by the Court have dealt, directly or indirectly, with either the Fourteenth Amendment or the Commerce Clause (Article 1, Section 8) of the U.S. Constitution. In cases involving the Fourteenth Amendment, the Court has often considered whether state laws unreasonably violated economic liberties. In some cases dealing with the Commerce Clause, the Court has considered whether, or to what extent, Congress has authority to regulate the national economy. (Since the New Deal in the 1930s, the Court has generally upheld Congressional exercises of authority under the Commerce Clause.) Perhaps the most notable economic cases brought before the court were the "trust-busting" cases (e.g., *Standard Oil of New Jersey v. United States*) in which the Court considered whether Congress could regulate (via the Sherman Anti-Trust Act, for example) anti-competitive business practices. Recent notable cases have involved copyrights and intellectual property rights, especially in

the context of peer-to-peer electronic and music-file sharing. This lesson looks at different types of economic cases and how they have been adjudicated by the U.S. Supreme Court.

LESSON DESCRIPTION

The students participate in a reader's theater activity. This activity conveys information about the role of the Supreme Court, and it introduces four types of economic cases heard by the Court. Then the students read four case studies (one of each type) and work in small groups to complete a data chart summarizing the four types of economic cases. This lesson can serve as a review/extension activity for a unit on the U.S. Supreme Court.

CONCEPTS

- Maintaining competition
- Monopoly
- Property rights
- Regulation
- Role of government

OBJECTIVES

Students will be able to:

1. Define and give examples of the four types of economic cases heard by the Supreme Court.

2. Categorize sample cases according to the four types.

3. Review the role of the Supreme Court in the system of shared powers described in the U.S. Constitution.

CONTENT STANDARDS
Economics (CEE Standards)

- Competition among sellers lowers costs and prices, and encourages producers to produce more of what consumers are willing and able to buy. Competition among buyers increases prices and allocates goods and services to those people who are willing and able to pay the most for them. (Standard 9)

- There is an economic role for government in a market economy whenever the benefits of a government policy outweigh its costs. Governments often provide for national defense, address environmental concerns, define and protect property rights, and attempt to make markets more competitive. Most government policies also redistribute income. (Standard 16)

- Costs of government policies sometimes exceed benefits. This may occur because of incentives facing voters, government officials, and government employees, because of actions by special interest groups that can impose costs on the general public, or because social goals other than economic efficiency are being pursued. (Standard 17)

Civics and Government (NSCG Standards, Grades 9-12)

- Students should be able to explain how the United States Constitution grants and distributes power to national and state government and how it seeks to prevent the abuse of power. (Standard III.A.1)

- Students should be able to evaluate, take, and defend positions on issues regarding the purposes, organization, and functions of the institutions of the national government. (Standard III.B.1)

- Students should be able to evaluate, take, and defend positions on issues regarding the major responsibilities of the national government for domestic and foreign policy. (Standard III.B.2)

- Students should be able to evaluate, take, and defend positions on the role and importance of law in the American political system. (Standard III.D.1)

TIME REQUIRED

45-60 minutes

MATERIALS

- A transparency of Visuals 9.1 and 9.2

- A copy for each student of Activities 9.1 and 9.2

PROCEDURE

1. Tell the students that this lesson will focus on key economic cases that have been decided by the U.S. Supreme Court. Among other things, these cases demonstrate important economic concepts and principles related to such topics as competition, regulation, trade, imperfect competition, and property rights.

2. To get started, write *Napster* and *File-sharing* on the board. Ask:

   - Are you familiar with Napster? (*Napster was a file-sharing service that paved the way for decentralized file-sharing programs such as Kazaa.*)

   - Did you know that the U.S. Supreme Court, while not deciding a case involving Napster directly, has heard cases that deal with illegal music downloads, computer software, etc.? (*Answers will vary. Inform the students that a key case on file-sharing will be discussed in this lesson.*)

3. Turn to a more detailed look at the Supreme Court. Ask: Who can tell me something about the composition of the U.S. Supreme Court and its jurisdiction? (*Answers are found on Visual 9.1.*) After the students have responded, display Visual 9.1. Briefly review the origin, members, and jurisdiction of the Supreme Court.

4. Distribute a copy of Activity 9.1 to each student. Assign roles and have the students make a note of who will be reading each role. Note that at certain points all students are to read aloud. Once everyone's role is assigned, read the play aloud in class. Note: teachers may want to rearrange the classroom so that the readers appear to be entering a building (the Supreme Court) which has the frieze "Equal Justice Under Law" on its facade.

5. Display Visual 9.2. Review the four types of economic cases with the students (*Regulation, Competition, Interstate Commerce, Copyrights/Patents*) by revealing each in turn.

6. Distribute Activity 9.2. Ask the students to read the directions and the four case

studies silently. Once they have finished reading, assign them to groups (four students per group, if possible) to complete the accompanying data chart.

7. Briefly review the students' answers. Answers should include the following:

Data Chart: Economic Cases by Type

Case	Type of Case	Reason for the Case	Court Findings
West Coast Hotel v. Parrish (1937)	*Regulation*	*Washington state passed a minimum wage law. West Coast Hotel refused to pay the minimum wage. Ms. Parish sued for back wages due her. West Coast Hotel claimed the law violated the Fourteenth Amendment's Due Process Clause.*	*The Court's opinion held that the Fourteenth Amendment does not prohibit states from enacting "reasonable" regulations in pursuit of the public good. The minimum wage law was constitutional because it was a reasonable attempt to regulate in order to protect the health and welfare of workers.*
Gibbons v. Ogden (1824)	*Interstate Commerce*	*New York State Legislature passed a law giving Robert Fulton (and others, including Aaron Ogden) a monopoly on steamship travel between New York state and New Jersey. Gibbons operated a ferry licensed by a 1793 act of Congress regulating coastal trade. The state of New York—citing its law giving Fulton's ferry company monopoly control over New York waterways—denied access to Gibbons.*	*In his majority opinion, Chief Justice Marshall wrote that the Commerce Clause allowed the federal government to regulate <u>all</u> commerce, including that within the borders of a state.*
Metro-Goldwyn-Mayer Studios Inc. et al. v. Grokster, Ltd., et al. (2005)	*Copyrights/Patents*	*MGM and other companies sued Grokster (which distributes the file-sharing program Morpheus) for facilitating the theft of copyrighted music and movies. According to MGM, over 90% of the material exchanged using Grokster's file-sharing software was copyrighted material and, therefore, copyright infringement occurred every time users exchanged the information.*	*The Supreme Court, in a unanimous decision, ruled that the providers of software that enabled "file-sharing" of copyrighted works may be held liable for any copyright infringement that takes place using that software.*

Case	Type of Case	Reason for the Case	Court Findings
Standard Oil Co. of New Jersey v. United States (1911)	Competition	Standard Oil owned more than 90% of the oil refining companies in the United States. It used this broad scope of ownership to manipulate the transportation rates it was charged by railroads. Standard also used its size against competitors in a number of other ways that were considered "anti-competitive": underpricing, threatening suppliers who worked with Standard's competitors, etc. The government prosecuted Standard Oil as a trust under the relatively new Sherman Antitrust Act. Standard Oil then challenged the Sherman Act as unconstitutional.	The Court found that the Sherman Antitrust Act was within Congress' Constitutional authority under the Commerce Clause. The Court found that "restraint of trade" referred to a wide range of contracts that resulted in "monopoly or its consequences." The Court identified three consequences of resulting monopolies: (1) higher prices, (2) reduced output, and (3) reduced quality.

CLOSURE

Read the following case summary to the students. Ask them to place the case into one of the four economic categories developed in this lesson.

United States v. E. C. Knight (1895)

Just after the Sherman Antitrust Act was passed, the American Sugar Refining Company bought out four other sugar refineries, giving it 98 percent control over American sugar production. The U.S. government sought to invalidate American Sugar's purchase in a lower federal court on the grounds that it violated the Sherman Antitrust Act. The lower court dismissed the case, and the government appealed to the Supreme Court.

Once the students have determined which type of case this was (*Competition*), read the following, which highlights the Court's finding:

In this early case involving the Sherman Act, the court found that the Constitution's Commerce Clause allows Congress to "regulate commerce ... among the several States," and that these manufacturing operations—because they occurred entirely in one state—were not "interstate commerce." In short, Congress has the power to regulate trade to encourage competition, but not necessarily manufacturing. This decision was later overturned in a number of cases including the *Standard Oil* case (1911).

ASSESSMENT

Multiple-Choice Questions

1. Generally speaking, the four types of economic cases heard by the Supreme Court are

   A. **regulation, competition, copyrights/patents, interstate commerce.**

   B. regulation, economic liberties, copyrights/patents, interstate commerce.

   C. regulation, competition, market failures, interstate commerce.

   D. regulation, competition, copyrights/patents, government failures.

2. The Commerce Clause can be found in which part of the U.S. Constitution?

A. The Fourteenth Amendment

B. Article 1

C. Article 2

D. Article 3

Constructed-Response Questions

1. "The Commerce Clause is the most important economic aspect of the U.S. Constitution."

   Do you agree or disagree? Take and defend a position on this statement. Explain your position.

   (Answers will vary. Students who agree with this statement should point out that many economic cases that have reached the U.S. Supreme Court have had to do with interpretation of this clause of the Constitution. Among other things, this clause addresses the regulation of commerce across state lines, thus determining to a considerable extent how large a role the government may play in economic affairs. Students who disagree may point out that many recent cases have focused on intellectual property rights, copyright infringement, patent protection, etc. This area of litigation is likely to become increasingly important as the U.S. economy continues to shift to a service-providing economy that is, among other things, very dependent upon transfer of information services.)

2. Choose one of the cases discussed in the lesson and explain why you believe this case had more impact than the others on the American economic system.

   (Answers will vary. In support of their answers, students should use evidence from the case details outlined in the lesson.)

Visual 9.1

Overview of the Supreme Court

Origins

Article 3, Section 1 of the U.S. Constitution provides that "[t]he judicial Power of the United States, shall be vested in one supreme Court, and in such inferior Courts as the Congress may from time to time ordain and establish."

Members

- The Chief Justice

- Eight Associate Justices

- Lifetime appointments for the Justices

Jurisdiction

- Judicial Review (established in *Marbury v. Madison*): The power to decide on the constitutional validity of a legislative or executive act.

- According to the Constitution (Art. 3, Sect. 2), the Supreme Court can hear cases involving:

  i. laws of the United States (Federal laws)

  ii. Treaties

  iii. Ambassadors, other public Ministers and Consuls

  iv. Lawsuits to which the United States shall be a Party

  v. Controversies between two or more States or between a State and Citizens of another State or between Citizens of different States. . .

VISUAL 9.2

TYPES OF ECONOMIC CASES HEARD BY THE U.S. SUPREME COURT

Regulation

Cases that deal with the power of Congress, or the state legislatures, to regulate aspects of the economy. Such cases have involved minimum-wage issues, the right to contract, economic liberties, etc.

Competition

Cases that deal with whether Congress, or the state legislatures, can pass legislation promoting competition in the market. Such cases typically involve questions of monopoly power (arising, for example, under the Sherman Antitrust Act).

Interstate Commerce

Cases that deal with the power of Congress to regulate commerce that crosses state lines. The Court has held that Congress can regulate in such cases when not doing so would have a significant, negative effect on trade and commerce.

Copyrights/Patents

Cases that deal with the intellectual property deriving from creative efforts (e.g., inventions, artwork, books, movies, software, etc.). Such cases have considered both individual claims of copyright and the definition of *invention*.

ACTIVITY 9.1

SEE YOU IN COURT: AN INTRODUCTION TO THE ECONOMIC DECISIONS OF THE U.S. SUPREME COURT

Directions: In the following activity, several students play a role. The teacher will assign students to play particular roles; other students are to read along and play the role of "ALL" by reading the lines of "ALL" aloud when they appear in the play.

Characters
(portrayed by:)

_____ Narrator

_____ Mr. Jones, Economics Teacher

_____ Ms. Smith (Supreme Court Docent)

_____ Mr. Brown (Supreme Court Docent)

_____ Madison (Student)

_____ Lilly (Student)

_____ Zach (Student)

_____ Clay (Student)

_____ Alex (Student)

_____ Jeff (Student)

_____ Kristin (Student)

_____ Bethany (Student)

Narrator: The setting is outside of the U.S. Supreme Court building in Washington, D.C. A group of high school seniors is visiting Washington for their senior class trip. Their chaperone is Mr. Jones, their economics teacher. Before the class goes into the building, Mr. Jones has a few words to say.

Mr. Jones: All right class, before we go into this hallowed hall, who can remind us of the important role the Supreme Court plays in our system of government? Madison?

Madison: The Supreme Court is at the top of one of the three branches of government, the judicial branch. It acts as an important check against the powers of Congress and the President because it can review laws to see if they are constitutional or not.

Mr. Jones: Very good, Madison! Yes, the Court plays a very important part in our system; its actions represent one way in which power is shared among the three branches of government. But it is a court, after all, and so

ACTIVITY 9.1, CONTINUED

SEE YOU IN COURT: AN INTRODUCTION TO THE ECONOMIC DECISIONS OF THE U.S. SUPREME COURT

it is concerned not just with reviewing laws, but also with making sure justice is done. Look above this door here [points to the frieze above the Supreme Court building]. What is written in the stone?

ALL: "EQUAL JUSTICE UNDER LAW"!

Mr. Jones: Excellent! Remember that as we begin our tour…. Alright, settle down, here come our docents.

Ms. Smith: Welcome to the Supreme Court! Let's all quiet down as we go inside. We must keep in mind that very serious business goes on behind these doors.

Mr. Brown [once all students are inside]: Again, welcome to the Supreme Court. I wonder, did anyone notice what was written above the doorway as we came in?

ALL [slightly perturbed…]: "EQUAL JUSTICE UNDER LAW"!

Mr. Brown [a little surprised]: Well, that's right! [Turning to Mr. Jones] Your teacher has done an excellent job with you!

Ms. Smith: Who can tell me what kind of cases the Supreme Court hears in this building?

Lilly: We learned that the Supreme Court is the "court of last resort" for all cases that have to do with federal law….

Clay:… and that it can hear cases that involve arguments between states, or ambassadors from other countries….

Alex: …and that the Court has the power of judicial review…to judge whether laws are constitutional or not….

Ms. Smith: That's right…this is certainly a smart group of seniors!

Mr. Jones: OK, but I'm an economics teacher and these are students from my senior-level economics class. Have any of the Court's cases involved economic issues? I mean issues that affect the nation's economy or how companies do business?

Mr. Brown: Of course. In fact one of the early landmark cases in the Court's history— *McColloch v. Maryland*—dealt with whether Congress could create a national bank, something we take for granted today with our Federal Reserve System.

Ms. Smith: Does anyone know what happened in this case? It was from a long, long time ago, nearly 200 years ago.

Jeff: Something about Maryland not wanting any banks that weren't from their own state….

Kristin: …and they were taxing banks from other states. I think Maryland argued that nowhere in the Constitution was Congress given the authority to create a bank.

Ms. Smith: Excellent! Yes, but the Court found that Congress could create a bank and that no state had the right to impede valid constitutional exercises of power by the federal government—in this case, Congress.

Mr. Jones: OK, so even early on in its history, the U.S. Supreme Court decided cases that impacted our economy. Certainly not allowing a national bank would have had a tremendous negative impact on the early economy.

Bethany: Are there other Supreme Court cases that deal with the economy?

ACTIVITY 9.1, CONTINUED

SEE YOU IN COURT: AN INTRODUCTION TO THE ECONOMIC DECISIONS OF THE U.S. SUPREME COURT

Mr. Jones [adding to Bethany's good question]: And don't many of the economic cases have to do with the Commerce Clause, found in Article 1, Section 8 of the Constitution?

Bethany: Hey, I remember that from the Government final we took last semester. Isn't that the clause that says Congress can regulate "Commerce with foreign Nations, and among the several States, and with the Indian Tribes"?

Mr. Brown: You are both right. Many cases are related to the Commerce Clause, including one of the most famous cases, *Gibbons v. Ogden*.

Ms. Smith: In this case, the Court ruled that under the Commerce Clause, Congress had power to regulate any aspect of commerce that crossed state lines, including modes of transportation. Since *Gibbons* was decided way back in 1824, Congress has continued to increase its power over a number of national issues.

Madison: Are there any other types of economic cases?

Mr. Brown: In addition to the Commerce Clause cases, cases that deal with the economy generally fall into three other categories....

Lilly: I remember the Court just decided something about MP3 files and music downloads.

Mr. Brown: Yes, that's right, in *MGM v. Grokster*, the Court found that using peer-to-peer software for sharing music files was copyright infringement against the artists and record companies. This is a second type of case, those that deal with copyrights and patents.

Zach: What about monopolies? I remember my parents talking about the Microsoft case. Wasn't that about monopolies?

Ms. Smith: That particular case did not make it to the Supreme Court, but a number of famous cases have. These cases dealt with whether Congress could encourage competition in the economy—by outlawing monopolies—or not. The Court has found in a number of cases that Congress can pass laws to better promote competition by eliminating monopolies.

Mr. Jones: Are there any other types of cases?

Mr. Brown: The last type has to do with regulating the economy. In one famous case, *West Coast Hotel v. Parrish*, the Court found that states could regulate businesses by requiring companies to pay a minimum wage.

Mr. Jones: OK class, let's do a quick review. What are the four types of economic cases the Court has taken on?

ALL: REGULATION, COPYRIGHTS AND PATENTS, COMPETITION, AND INTERSTATE COMMERCE.

Mr. Jones: And one of the greatest economic powers Congress has is found in the...

ALL: COMMERCE CLAUSE, IN ARTICLE 1, SECTION 8!!

Ms. Smith: What a wonderful group! Would you all like to follow me and see the "highest court in the land"?

Jeff: I thought the Supreme Court *was* the highest court. Is there another?

Mr. Brown: She's making a joke—that's the name the Justices have given to the *basketball* court in the gym on the top floor of this building. Get it: "highest court in the land"?!? Come along....

ACTIVITY 9.2

TYPES OF ECONOMIC CASES BROUGHT BEFORE THE U.S. SUPREME COURT[1]

Directions: The four case studies that follow are examples of the four different types of economic cases on which the U.S. Supreme Court has ruled. Read all four silently. Your teacher will then assign you to a study group, and you and other members of your group will use these case studies to complete the accompanying data chart. As you read, pay close attention to what distinguishes each of the four types of cases.

West Coast Hotel v. Parrish (1937)

Background:

In 1932, a law entitled "Minimum Wages for Women" was passed by the Washington State Legislature. The law required companies to pay minimum wages for women and children in order to protect their well-being. The law created a special commission to determine what the minimum-wage levels should be. A housekeeper at the West Coast Hotel, Elsie Parrish, sued the hotel in a state court, claiming that it had not paid her the law's minimum wages. The hotel's defense was that the Washington State law was unconstitutional. A Washington State court found the law unconstitutional and ruled for the hotel. On appeal, the Washington State Supreme Court reversed the state-court ruling and directed the hotel to pay back wages to Ms. Parrish. The hotel appealed to the U.S. Supreme Court, which issued its opinion in 1937.

The Court's Opinion:

The Supreme Court, in a 5-4 decision written by Chief Justice Charles Evans Hughes, found that the law did not violate the U.S. Constitution. West Coast Hotel argued that the law violated the Fourteenth Amendment's Due Process Clause, which states that no state "shall deprive any person of life, liberty, or property, without due process of law." The hotel argued that the law deprived employers and employees of the "liberty" of contract negotiation without due process of the law. The Court's opinion held that the Fourteenth Amendment does not prohibit states from enacting "reasonable" regulation in pursuit of the public good. In part due to the impact of the Great Depression, the Court held that it was sometimes reasonable for governments to set a wage floor. Thus, the minimum wage law was constitutional because it was a reasonable attempt to regulate commerce in order to protect the health and welfare of workers.

[1] Sources for these case studies include K. Hall, *The Oxford Companion to the Supreme Court of the United States* (Oxford: Oxford University Press, 1992); FindLaw.com (http://www.findlaw.com/); and Oyez (http://www.oyez.org/).

ACTIVITY 9.2, CONTINUED

TYPES OF ECONOMIC CASES BROUGHT BEFORE THE U.S. SUPREME COURT

Gibbons v. Ogden (1824)

Background:

This was an early landmark case in which the Court said that the U.S. Constitution trumped state law. The case developed when the New York Legislature passed a law giving Robert Fulton (and others, including Aaron Ogden) a monopoly on steamship travel between New York State and the state of New Jersey.

Thomas Gibbons, the owner of another steamship company, was operating a ferry which had been licensed by a 1793 act of Congress regulating coastal trade. The state of New York—citing its law giving Fulton's ferry company monopoly control over New York waterways—denied access to Gibbons. Ogden obtained an injunction from a New York court against Gibbons to keep his ferry company out of New York. Gibbons then sued to overturn the injunction. The case was then appealed to the United States Supreme Court.

The Court's Opinion:

The majority opinion, written by Chief Justice John Marshall, greatly expanded the federal government's ability to regulate commerce. Earlier court decisions found that the federal government had power over only *interstate* commerce. In this case, however, Marshall found that the U.S. Constitution's Commerce Clause allowed the federal government to regulate *all* commerce, including commerce within the borders of a state:

> The mind can scarcely conceive a system for regulating commerce between nations which shall exclude all laws concerning navigation…. a Congressional power to regulate navigation is as expressly granted as if that term had been added to the word 'commerce.'

Marshall also concluded that the power of Congress to regulate commerce should extend to all aspects of it, overriding state law to the contrary:

> If, as has always been understood, the sovereignty of Congress, though limited to specified objects, is plenary as to those objects, the power over commerce with foreign nations and among the several states is vested in Congress as absolutely as it would be in a single government, having in its constitution the same restrictions on the exercise of the power as are found in the Constitution of the United States.

Metro-Goldwyn-Mayer Studios, Inc., et al. v. Grokster, Ltd., et al. (2005)

Background

In October 2001, MGM and other major music and movie companies sued Grokster and StreamCast (which distributes the file-sharing program Morpheus) for facilitating the theft of copyrighted music and movies. According to MGM, over 90 percent of the material exchanged using Grokster's file-sharing software was copyrighted material and, therefore, copyright infringement

ACTIVITY 9.2, CONTINUED

TYPES OF ECONOMIC CASES BROUGHT BEFORE THE U.S. SUPREME COURT

occurred every time users exchanged the information. MGM contended that Grokster contributed to this infringement by making the file-sharing software available to the public.

In 2003, a federal court concluded that the file-sharing software could be used for legitimate purposes and thus rejected the entertainment companies' arguments. The federal court determined that such legitimate use was protected under the 1984 Sony Betamax ruling. The case was appealed to the U.S. Supreme Court.

The Court's Opinion:

The Supreme Court, in a unanimous decision written by Justice David Souter, ruled that the providers of software that enabled "file-sharing" of copyrighted works may be held liable for any copyright infringement that takes place using that software:

> We hold that one who distributes a device with the object of promoting its use to infringe copyright, as shown by clear expression or other affirmative steps taken to foster infringement, is liable for the resulting acts of infringement by third parties.

As a result of the Court's decision, Grokster announced that it would no longer offer its peer-to-peer file sharing service. A posting on the Grokster web site stated:

> The United States Supreme Court unanimously confirmed that using this service to trade copyrighted material is illegal. Copying copyrighted motion picture and music files using unauthorized peer-to-peer services is illegal and is prosecuted by copyright owners.

Standard Oil Co. of New Jersey v. United States (1911)

Background:

During a 20-year period in the 1880s and 1890s, the Standard Oil Company of New Jersey bought more than 90 percent of the oil refining companies in the United States. The company used this overwhelming market control to manipulate the rates it was charged by railroads. By undercutting the production costs of refining in this way, Standard Oil was able to put pressure on smaller refiners in a number of ways that were considered "anti-competitive": under-pricing, threatening suppliers who worked with Standard's competitors, etc. The U.S. government prosecuted Standard Oil as an illegal trust under the relatively new Sherman Antitrust Act. Standard Oil then challenged the Sherman Act as unconstitutional. The key issue before the Court was whether Congress could prevent a company from acquiring other companies in the same industry by legal means if those acquisitions violated the anti-competition clauses of the Sherman Act.

ACTIVITY 9.2, CONTINUED

TYPES OF ECONOMIC CASES BROUGHT BEFORE THE U.S. SUPREME COURT

The Court's Opinion:

The Court found that the Sherman Antitrust Act was within Congress' Constitutional authority under the Commerce Clause, and that the term *restraint of trade* referred to a wide range of contracts including some that do not harm the public. The Court noted that the Sherman Act referred to contracts that resulted in "monopoly or its consequences." The Court identified three consequences of resulting monopolies: (1) higher prices, (2) reduced output, and (3) reduced quality. The Court held that business practices violated the Sherman Act only when such practices restrained trade "unduly" by resulting in one of these three consequences. Any other definition, the Court stated, would jeopardize normal contracts, thus infringing the liberty of contract. The Court also endorsed the rule of reason first described in *Addyston Pipe and Steel Company v. United States* (1898), and found that Standard Oil Company went beyond the limits of this rule.

Data Chart: Economic Cases by Type

Case	Type of Case	Reason for the Case	Court Findings

FOCUS: UNDERSTANDING ECONOMICS IN CIVICS AND GOVERNMENT © COUNCIL FOR ECONOMIC EDUCATION, NEW YORK, NY

LESSON 10

AN ECONOMIC ANALYSIS OF HEALTH CARE POLICY

LESSON 10
AN ECONOMIC ANALYSIS OF HEALTH CARE POLICY

INTRODUCTION

Medical care in the United States is often considered to be the best in the world. In 2007, average life expectancy for Americans had increased to 78 years (75.15 years for males and 80.97 years for females). U.S. physicians are highly educated and have access to the most advanced medical equipment and technologies. Still, health care problems loom large in the United States. The two largest problems involve lack of universal access and increasing costs. About 47 million Americans do not have health insurance. And costs are high: Health care spending overall, it is estimated, will double to $4.1 trillion by 2016, consuming 20 percent of GDP.

LESSON DESCRIPTION

The students discuss the strengths and weaknesses of health care in the United States. As "members" of the Surgeon General's Task Force on the Economics of Health Care Policies, they consider how the laws of supply and demand can be used to analyze and shape health care policy. They study four criteria for judging health care policies; then they apply these criteria in an examination of three general plans: Pay or Play, Tax Credits, and National Health Insurance. They draw conclusions, determining which plans accomplish which goals.

CONCEPTS

- Conflicts among values and principles
- Normal good
- Role of government in a market economy
- Scarcity

OBJECTIVES

Students will be able to:

1. Apply the laws of supply and demand in analyzing health care issues.

2. Identify and apply economic criteria for

use in evaluating three health care policies.

CONTENT STANDARDS
Economics (CEE Standards)

- There is an economic role for government to play in a market economy whenever the benefits of a government policy outweigh its costs. Governments often provide for national defense, address environmental concerns, define and protect property rights, and attempt to make markets more competitive. Most government policies also redistribute income. (Standard 16)

- Costs of government policies sometimes exceed benefits. This may occur because of incentives facing voters, government officials, and government employees, because of actions by special interest groups that can impose costs on the general public, or because social goals other than economic efficiency are being pursued. (Standard 17)

Civics and Government (NSCG Standards, Grades 9-12)

- The purposes of politics and government. (Standard I.A.3)

- Fundamental values and principles. (Standard II.D.3)

- Conflicts among values and principles in American political and social life. (Standard II.D.4)

TIME REQUIRED

60 minutes

MATERIALS

- A transparency of Visuals 10.1 and 10.2
- A copy for each student of Activities 10.1 and 10.2

PROCEDURE

1. Tell the class that the purpose of this lesson is to use economic analysis to examine

the strengths and weaknesses of three different approaches to providing health care in the United States.

2. Display Visual 10.1. Use the points it presents to introduce students to some of the health care issues facing the United States today. Stress the point that the increasing cost of health care is especially worrisome when one considers that the nation faces many other priorities as well: defending against terrorist attacks, improving education, providing for transportation, protecting the environment and so forth. How much are we willing to trade off in order to provide widespread, government-provided health care?

3. Distribute Activity 10.1. This reading asks the students to imagine that they have been appointed to the Surgeon General's Task Force on the Economics of Health Care Policies. Ask each student to read Parts I and II of the activity and respond to the questions at the end of the exercise. After the students have completed this task, ask:

    *   What is the fundamental economic problem in health care?

        (Scarcity is the fundamental problem we face in health care. The resources devoted to the production of health care have other valuable uses. As a result, we have to make choices about how, and to whom, health care is to be allocated.)

    *   What sort of health care system do other market economies provide?

        (Answers will vary, but in the nations of Western Europe, for example, hospitals and clinics are operated by the government and paid for by taxes.)

    *   Many market economies, such as those in Western Europe and Japan, offer universal health care paid for completely by government tax revenue. What is the fundamental advantage of universal health care systems? What is the fundamental disadvantage?

(Answers will vary, but it should be noted that universal health care programs provide health care to all citizens at no direct cost to them. Tax revenues typically do not keep pace with the quantity of health care that is demanded when it is provided at no direct cost. As a result, shortages frequently result.)

*   Explain two factors that influence the demand for health care.

    (Students might make the following points regarding demand: Health care is a normal good. This means that as incomes rise, people demand more health care. Because health care is considered to be a necessity, demand for health care is inelastic. American consumers of health care depend heavily on third-party payers. Third-party payment severs the link between consumers and producers of health care, therefore increasing demand for health services. Moreover, health insurance is a form of employee compensation that is not subject to federal taxation.)

*   Explain two factors that influence the supply of health care.

    (Students might make the following points regarding supply: The high cost of medical education limits the supply of physicians; new health-care technology tends to be expensive because it often takes years to develop and it is subject to many regulations.)

*   According to the analysts who prepared the Memorandum, is it the existence of a market or the lack of a market that is the problem in health care?

    (The fundamental problem according to these analysts is that health care is provided outside the context of a vibrant free-market system. In a well-functioning market, consumers weigh the price of a good or service against its quality. Producers innovate to provide consumers with the quality they want at a price they are willing to pay.

Producers hope to benefit by earning profits. However, this does not always occur in the health care market. There are two approaches to addressing this problem: We can take steps to encourage more competition in the health care market, so that it functions like other competitive markets, or we can consider the health care market as a special case that does not operate in the way other markets do and adopt policies that address this special status.)

5. Distribute Activity 10.2. Discuss the four criteria for judging health care plans and the descriptions of the three policy alternatives. Ask the students to complete the Decision Grid.

6. Display Visual 10.2. Compare the students' responses on the Decision Grid to those that are suggested in the Visual. Ask:

   • Does the analysis suggest a clear conclusion about which alternative is better? (*Not likely. These are highly complicated issues.*)

   • Should all the criteria be equally weighted? (*Answers will vary. Some students will think that limiting the role of government is less important than increasing accessibility. Others may disagree. Answers to these questions depend, at least in part, on the students' personal values. While economic analysis can help students make an informed decision, there are no right and wrong answers to complex policy issues that require students to make value judgments.*)

CLOSURE

Review the lesson by posing the following questions:

• What are some of the advantages and disadvantages of health care in the United States today?

(While medical care in the United States is often considered the best in the world, about 47 million Americans do not have health insurance. Health care spending is rapidly increasing.)

• Explain various factors that influence the demand for health care.

(As incomes rise, people demand more health care. Demand for health care is largely inelastic; consumers of health care show only limited sensitivity to increases in health care prices. American consumers of health care depend heavily on third-party payers. Health insurance is a form of employee compensation that is not subject to federal taxation.)

• Explain various factors that influence the supply of health care.

(The supply of health care is determined in part by the supply of physicians, which is influenced in turn by the high cost of medical education. In health care, new technologies tend to be expensive because they often take years to develop and are subject to many regulations.)

• What are some criteria that economists might use to judge health care policies?

(Improved accessibility, increased role of individual consumers, increased price competition, and a limited role of government.)

ASSESSMENT
Multiple-Choice Questions

1. Health care is considered to be a normal good because as

   A. incomes increase, people want less.

   B. incomes increase, people want more.

   C. costs increase, people buy less.

   D. costs increase, people buy more.

2. Which approach to health care is used by most Western European economies?

   A. Pay or Play

   B. Tax Credits

   C. Vouchers

   D. National Health Insurance

3. Which of the following is a factor that influences the demand for health care?

   A. Insufficient number of physicians

   B. **Third-party payer systems**

   C. Physician influenced supply

   D. Limited number of hospitals

Constructed-Response Questions

1. Poorer Americans are less likely than others to have health insurance. One remedy for this situation would be to issue government-provided vouchers to low-income Americans, which they could use to purchase health insurance. Use the Decision Grid with the four criteria used in Activity 10.2 to analyze this policy proposal.

2. Explain why single-payer systems such as those in Western Europe and Japan often lead to shortages of health care and long lines for patients.

(In these countries, tax revenues typically do not keep pace with the quantity of health care that people demand when it is provided for them at no direct cost. Since the price of health care is so low, people demand a great deal of it. Shortages frequently result. Tax payers resist paying the real costs of health care under these circumstances. To deal with the shortages, governments develop rules and policies to allocate health care services. The consequence is that patients sometimes must wait in line for important medical procedures.)

	Improve Accessibility	*Increase Role of Individual Consumers*	*Increase Price Competition*	*Limit the Role of Government*
Vouchers	*A voucher would improve accessibility but would not provide universal care. Some people would still opt out.*	*It would increase the opportunity for individual consumers to make decisions, but consumers would still be spending a government-provided voucher rather than their own income.*	*Probably would provide some increase in price competition as health insurance providers seek ways to serve the low-income market.*	*The role of government remains somewhat limited. While tax revenues would have to be increased, any new government agency created to manage the voucher program could be limited in size and scope.*

VISUAL 10.1
HEALTH CARE IN THE UNITED STATES

The Good News

- Medical care in the United States is often considered to be the best in the world.

    - In 2007, average life expectancy for Americans had increased to 78 years.

    - U.S. physicians are highly educated and use the most advanced medical equipment and technologies.

The Bad News

- Accessibility and costs are major problems.

    - About 47 million Americans do not have health insurance.

    - The lack of health insurance is concentrated among poorer Americans.

    - Many young people with good health choose not to buy health insurance.

    - Health care spending overall is expected to double to $4.1 trillion in 2016, consuming 20 percent of GDP.

VISUAL 10.2
A DECISION GRID ON HEALTH CARE POLICY CHOICES

Directions: Rate each of the three health care plans below according to the four criteria shown in the top row of the grid. For each criterion, rate each plan from 1 to 3, with 1 being the lowest rating and 3 being the highest. Give reasons for your ratings.

	Improve Accessibility	Increase Role of Individual Consumers	Increase Price Competition	Limit the Role of Government
Pay or Play	**Rating: 2 Reason:** Employees and most others would be covered.	**Rating: 2 Reason:** Most individual consumers would still depend on third- party payers.	**Rating: 2 Reason:** Limited or no increase in price competition.	**Rating: 2 Reason:** Expands the role of government to tax and administer the program.
Tax Credits	**Rating: 1 Reason:** Expands the number of people with health insurance but allows others to opt out.	**Rating: 3 Reason:** Increases the role of individual consumers to make decisions about purchasing the plan they wish to have.	**Rating: 3 Reason:** The expanded role of consumers will increase price competition among insurance providers.	**Rating: 3 Reason:** Since no new tax is imposed and no new agency is established, it would maintain a limited role of government.
National Health Insurance	**Rating: 3 Reason:** All citizens would be covered.	**Rating: 1 Reason:** Since consumers would not pay directly for health care services, the role of consumers would be reduced.	**Rating: 1 Reason:** Provides no increase in price competition since government is the only payer.	**Rating: 1 Reason:** Significantly expands the role of government. Taxes will have to be increased and new agencies will have to be established.

ACTIVITY 10.1

SURGEON GENERAL'S TASK FORCE ON THE ECONOMICS OF HEALTH CARE POLICIES

Directions: Imagine that you have been appointed to the Surgeon General's Task Force on the Economics of Health Care Policies. Read the information in Part I about the work of the Task Force. Then read the Memorandum in Part II and respond to the Questions for Discussion.

Part I

In Today's News

The following is a news item from *USA Today*, January 1, 2010, Washington D.C.

Surgeon General to Provide Economic Analysis of Health Care Policies

Dr. Antonio Bonds, Surgeon General of the United States, has nearly reached final recommendations for the President and the nation on health care policy in the United States. The United States, after conducting several state-level experiments, is now ready to adopt a national plan. Dr. Bonds, in turn, commissioned the Task Force on the Economics of Health Care Policies to assist him in reaching a decision.

Dr. Bonds, an economist as well as a medical doctor, has insisted that the members of the Task Force use economic analysis to study health care problems and policies.

Part II

Welcome to the Surgeon General's Task Force on the Economics of Health Care Policies

You have just been appointed by Dr. Antonio Bonds, Surgeon General of the United States, to the Surgeon General's Task Force on the Economics of Health Care Policies. The purpose of the Task Force is to give advice to Dr. Bonds and the nation on how best to improve health care in the United States.

Read the following memorandum from the Task Force Economics Division. This memorandum provides an economic analysis of health care policy in the United States. Discuss the questions that follow.

Economics Division Memorandum on Health Care

To: Members of the Surgeon General's Task Force on the Economics of Health Care Policies

From: Research Staff, Surgeon General's Task Force on the Economics of Health Care Policies, Economics Division

Date: January 1, 2010

Activity 10.1, continued

Surgeon General's Task Force on the Economics of Health Care Policies

The Fundamentals of Health Care

The fundamental problem we face in health care is that health care is scarce. The resources devoted to the production of health care—the people, hospitals, prescription drugs, clinics, and technology—have potential, valuable uses in other sectors. In other words, while peoples' desires for health care are basically unlimited, the resources needed to provide health care are limited. As a result, we have to make choices about how, and to whom, health care is to be allocated.

The need to allocate scarce resources raises difficult problems. Most goods and services produced in our economy come from the private sector, and most people like it that way. Few Americans would want their condos, cars, or cantaloupes to be produced by the government. But when it comes to health care, people often think differently. To many, the allocation of medical care on the basis of price seems unethical. As a result, many nations with market economies (Canada, Japan, the United Kingdom, and nearly all of the nations of Western Europe) have opted for socialized approaches to medical care.

In many of these countries, hospitals and clinics are operated by the government and paid for by taxes. Physicians, nurses and other health care providers are government employees. Since tax revenues typically do not keep pace with the quantity of health care that people demand when it is provided for them at no direct cost, shortages frequently result. To deal with the shortages, governments develop rules and policies to allocate health care services. The consequence is that patients sometimes must wait in line for important medical procedures.

Demand for Health Care

In the case of shortages and other problems in the health care sector, the laws of demand and supply help to explain what is going on. We should begin by acknowledging that health care is a normal good. This means that as incomes rise, people demand more health care. Per capita income in the United States was $43,500 in 2006. That level of per capita income, by itself, explains in good measure why Americans now demand more and better health care.

Demand for health care is also affected by the notion that it is a necessity. There are few good substitutes for medical care. Thus demand for health care is inelastic. When prices increase for the latest cancer treatment or the newest diagnostic device, many people still want the treatment. Their decisions about expensive treatments are influenced by the fact that they often do not bear all of the out-of-pocket costs.

Since health care is regarded as a necessity, it might seem that we should regard it as different from other economic goods and, therefore, provide for it in a different manner. But health care is not the only necessity about which consumers make choices. Food and housing are necessities, too, but most Americans don't turn to others to manage their purchase of food and housing. They don't ask their employers to pay their rent or buy their groceries. Instead, they decide what sort of housing they wish to have and what sort of food they wish to eat. The concept of necessity does not explain why health care should be thought of as unique.

ACTIVITY 10.1, CONTINUED

SURGEON GENERAL'S TASK FORCE ON THE ECONOMICS OF HEALTH CARE POLICIES

Demand for health care in the United States is bolstered by payment methods. American consumers of health care depend heavily on third-party payers. Most families have health insurance paid for, at least in part, by an employer. As a result, they do not feel the "bite," in direct costs, of the health care they consume. Vernon Smith, 2002 Nobel Laureate in Economics, describes it this way:[1]

> A is the customer. B is the service provider. B informs A what A should buy from B, and a third entity, C, pays for it from a common pool of funds. Stated this way, the problem has no known economic solution because there is no equilibrium. There is no automatic balance between willingness to pay by the consumer and willingness to accept by the producer that constrains and limits the choices of each.

Moreover, consumers of health care do not shop around for medical care as they do for other goods and services. They may be deterred from doing so by a sense of urgency about the need for prompt treatment. They may also believe that the information they would need to do comparison shopping is complex and not readily available. And in part, the disinclination to shop is explained by widespread reliance on third-party payers. Why spend time shopping for a low price when somebody else is paying the bill?

Health insurance itself has a special status in the United States. About two-thirds of working adults have health insurance through group insurance programs offered by their employers. The insurance is part of their compensation packages. And it is a form of compensation that is not subject to federal income taxation.

The Supply of Health Care

Like demand, the supply of health care is also influenced by several factors. Among other things, the supply of health care is dependent upon the total number of physicians that are willing and able to offer their services. In the United States, the preparation (education, training, and experience) needed to become a physician makes it very costly to pursue a career as a medical doctor. Medical education ordinarily requires four years of undergraduate college work, four years of medical school, an internship, and perhaps three more years of training in a medical specialization. It is a long, difficult road to take, and, according to an article in the *New England Journal of Medicine,*[2] it has become increasingly expensive over the past several years. Medical school tuition since 1984 has increased by 317 percent at public schools and by 151 percent at private schools. Accompanying this increase has been an enormous increase in the average amount of student debt. The average debt in 1984 was $22,000 for medical students in public schools and $26,000 for medical students in private schools. By 2004, the average debt had increased to $105,000 and $140,000, for public-

---

[1] Vernon L. Smith, "Trust the Customer!" *The Wall Street Journal*, March 8, 2006, p. A20.
[2] Gail Morrison, "Mortgaging Our Future: The Cost of Medical Education," *New England Journal of Medicine,* January 13, 2005, pp. 117-119.

ACTIVITY 10.1, CONTINUED

SURGEON GENERAL'S TASK FORCE ON THE ECONOMICS OF HEALTH CARE POLICIES

and private-school students, respectively. The high cost of medical education no doubt discourages some capable people from becoming physicians.

Another supply problem has to do with technology. Technology in health care is often very expensive, for a special set of reasons. In other sectors of the economy, when a technological break-through occurs and a new product comes to the market, the initial price is usually high. Hand-held calculators and desktop computers, for example, appeared in stores initially as relatively expensive products. In most sectors, however, market forces soon take over and work to reduce prices. High prices early on attract additional producers. Competition increases. Production techniques improve. Supply increases, and prices come down.

In health care, it is different. New technologies in health care often take years to develop, and they are subject to many regulations. Like other new products, they come into the market initially at a high price. But we don't typically see market pressures bringing prices down as quickly in health care as they do in other sectors. Why not? The explanation has to do with the nature of health care, where stakes are high. Consumers facing acute medical problems demand prompt access to the latest technology—the latest robot-assisted surgery, the least invasive treatment for a herniated disk, or the newest cancer treatment. They do not want to wait around for new producers to enter the market, increase competition, increase supply, and reduce prices. This preference by patients is made easier, of course, when someone else is paying for the treatment in question.

The Lack of a Vibrant Market

Supply and demand analysis reveals peculiarities in the market for health care services in the United States. But the fundamental problem is not that health care is provided within a market system. It is that we try to provide health care outside the context of a vibrant, free-market system. In a vibrant market, consumers weigh the price of a good or service against its quality. If the quality isn't provided at the right price, they walk away. Producers pay close attention to these decisions. They innovate to provide consumers with the quality they want at the price they are willing to pay. Providers who are successful remain in business and expand, while providers who are not successful are driven out.

Could such a dynamic operate in health care? Many examples suggest that it could. For example, consumers interested in using contact lenses let it be known early on that they wanted contact lenses that were easy to wear, easy to use, disposable, and inexpensive. Producers such as Johnson and Johnson responded by developing disposable contact lenses. These were a big hit with consumers, and Johnson and Johnson was highly rewarded in the marketplace. Other illustrations can be found in the eye glass industry and, more recently, in the market for Lasik eye surgery. In the Lasik eye surgery market—for a procedure not typically covered by insurance—market forces have driven prices down and generated significant competition among physicians for new customers.

ACTIVITY 10.1, CONTINUED

SURGEON GENERAL'S TASK FORCE ON THE ECONOMICS OF HEALTH CARE POLICIES

So, one of the challenges for this task force is to recommend the adoption of policies that encourage continued innovation in the health care market, but do so in a way that produces high-quality, affordable care for American families. Some of the questions we need to consider are listed below.

Questions for Discussion

1. What is the fundamental economic problem in health care?

2. What sort of health care system do many other market economies provide?

3. Many market economies, such as those in Western Europe and Japan, offer universal health care paid for completely by tax revenues. What is the fundamental advantage of universal health care systems? What is the fundamental disadvantage?

4. Explain two factors that influence demand for health care.

5. Explain two factors that influence the supply of health care.

6. According to the analysts who prepared the Memorandum, is it the existence of a market or the lack of a market that is the problem in health care?

Activity 10.2

The Surgeon General's Task Force on the Economics of Health Care Policies

Directions: After studying the Memorandum prepared by the Economics Division, the members of the Surgeon General's Task Force on the Economics of Health Care Policies decided that one promising way to improve health in the United States would be to expand coverage to nearly everyone. They also proposed to strengthen market forces in the health care industry. In an effort to meet these goals, the members of the Task Force established four criteria to help them judge health care plans. Read the criteria and the description of the three policy alternatives. Then use the grid to rate the policies according to how well they meet the criteria.

The Criteria

1. **Does the proposed health care policy improve accessibility and reduce the number of people without health insurance?** Any reform for health care must present realistic plans to reduce the number of people who are uninsured. Would the proposed reform, for example, reduce the cost of acquiring health insurance, thus providing an incentive for more people to obtain coverage?

2. **Does the proposed health care policy increase the role of individual consumers in making health care decisions?** Would the proposed reform, for example, reduce the role of third-party payers of health care expenses? Such a move would provide incentives for consumers to economize when it comes to using health care. Plans that shift responsibility for purchasing health insurance from employers to consumers would provide a step in this direction.

3. **Does the proposed health care policy increase price competition?** What incentives are provided to encourage new producers to enter the market? Allowing Americans to buy health insurance from vendors in any one of the 50 states would substantially increase price competition among insurance providers. Would the proposed policy open up opportunities of this sort?

4. **Does the health care policy limit the role of government?** Does the policy set the stage for a government-driven system, or will it lead to market-oriented solutions that will result in a stronger role for consumers and more innovation? Increased health care costs are often cited as a reason to increase the role of government in paying for those costs. Over time, however, governments responsible for health care costs will take steps to control those costs by increasing rules and regulations. The result may be less competition, poorer quality, and unhappy consumers.

The Three Policy Alternatives

1. **Pay or Play.** Some states have experimented with versions of Pay or Play. In this approach all employers are required to provide health insurance for their workers, or pay a special payroll tax or other fee. In Massachusetts, employers must provide health insurance to their employees or pay a fee of $295 per month per full-time employee. In other states, new payroll taxes of about 11 percent are being considered. A state agency would be set up to administer the program.

ACTIVITY 10.2, CONTINUED

THE SURGEON GENERAL'S TASK FORCE ON THE ECONOMICS OF HEALTH CARE POLICIES

2. **Tax Credits.** Other experiments involve providing individuals with incentives to obtain their own health insurance. Here, the federal government would provide a tax credit, for example, of $2,500 for a single person or $5,000 to families, to be used for purchasing health insurance. In another plan for the use of tax credits, the federal government would provide a standard tax deduction for all those who purchase health insurance. In one proposal, individuals would receive a $7,500 deduction and families would receive a $15,000 deduction.

3. **National Health Insurance.** Perhaps the most controversial plan is to establish a system of national heath insurance along the lines of the Canadian plan. In such a system, the federal government would provide a basic package of health care to every individual at no direct charge. The system would be paid for out of tax revenues rather than insurance premiums. While the government would not own heath care facilities such as hospitals and clinics, and it would not directly employ doctors and nurses, it would pay the expenses for all approved medical procedures.

Complete the Decision Grid

Directions: Rate each of the three health care plans (discussed above) according to the four criteria shown in the top row of the grid. For each criterion, rate each plan from 1 to 3, with 1 being the lowest rating and 3 being the highest. Give reasons for your ratings.

	Improve Accessibility	Increase Role of Individual Consumers	Increase Price Competition	Limit the Role of Government
Pay or Play	Rating: Reason:	Rating: Reason:	Rating: Reason:	Rating: Reason:
Tax Credits	Rating: Reason:	Rating: Reason:	Rating: Reason:	Rating: Reason:
National Health Insurance	Rating: Reason:	Rating: Reason:	Rating: Reason:	Rating: Reason:

HOW SHOULD GOVERNMENTS STRUCTURE THE TAX SYSTEM?

LESSON 11
HOW SHOULD GOVERNMENTS STRUCTURE THE TAX SYSTEM?

INTRODUCTION

Collecting revenue through taxation creates complicated and controversial issues for governments. Governments need tax revenue in order to operate. In addition to supplying revenue, however, a tax system should also be viewed as fair. But what is fairness in taxation? There are a number of ways to think about this question. Economists often approach it by applying the principle of *vertical equity*. According to this principle, a fair system of taxation is one in which households with higher incomes will pay a larger share of their incomes in taxes than households with lower incomes. Most people believe that vertical equity implies a progressive tax system. This sounds straightforward, but in practice governments often find it difficult to achieve vertical equity in their tax systems. This lesson looks at issues associated with equitable taxation, focusing on the ideal of vertical equity and on certain tradeoffs that may be involved in efforts to reach that ideal.

LESSON DESCRIPTION

In a group activity, the students decide on a method of taxation for a hypothetical country. After they have developed a tax system, they discuss their reasons for designing the system they have created. They learn whether their system is progressive, regressive, or proportional.

CONCEPTS

- Average tax rate
- Horizontal equity
- Marginal tax rate
- Progressive tax
- Proportional tax
- Regressive tax
- Taxation
- Vertical equity

OBJECTIVES

Students will be able to:

1. Develop a simple tax system.

2. Distinguish between progressive taxes, proportional taxes, and regressive taxes.

3. Use the concept of vertical equity in describing and evaluating tax systems.

CONTENT STANDARDS
Economics (CEE Standards)

- People respond predictably to positive and negative incentives. (Standard 4)

- There is an economic role for government to play in a market economy whenever the benefits of a government policy outweigh its costs. Governments often provide for national defense, address environmental concerns, define and protect property rights, and attempt to make markets more competitive. Most government policies also redistribute income. (Standard 16)

- Costs of government policies sometimes exceed benefits. This may occur because of incentives facing voters, government officials, and government employees, because of actions by special interest groups that can impose costs on the general public, or because social goals other than economic efficiency are being pursued. (Standard 17)

Civics and Government (NSCG Standards, Grades 9-12)

- Students should be able to evaluate, take, and defend positions on issues regarding how government should raise money to pay for its operations and services. (III. B. 3)

TIME REQUIRED

120 minutes

MATERIALS

- A transparency of Visuals 11.1, 11.2, 11.3, and 11.4

- One calculator for each group of five students

- One set of role-playing cards from Activity 11.1 for each group of five students

- One copy of Activity 11.2, 11.3, and 11.4 for each group of five students

PROCEDURE

1. As necessary, introduce or review the concept of taxation. Explain briefly that governments need money in order to pay for the services they provide: education, fire protection, national defense, and so on. Governments obtain money by taxation—by imposing various taxes on individuals and corporations.

2. Explain that the purpose of this lesson is to explore different ways in which governments structure their tax systems. Different tax structures affect taxpayers in different ways, thus raising issues of fairness and efficiency.

3. Display Visual 11.1 and ask the students to read the first quotation. Explain that the U.S. Constitution gives Congress the right to collect taxes for the public good. Reveal the next two quotations. They express different points of view regarding taxation, ranging from the view that taxes are merely the cost of providing for the things we have come to expect in today's society to the view that any taxation deprives citizens of the right to do what they please with their lives and money. Reveal the final quotation, from Napoleon Bonaparte, and discuss it briefly. Tell the students that they will participate in an activity in which their task is to write a tax law.

4. Divide the class into groups of five. (If the class is not divisible by five, make as many groups of five as possible; assign the remaining students to serve as observers of a group.) Group by group, distribute the role-playing cards from Activity 11.1, and the calculators. In each group, each student must get a different card. Instruct the students to keep the information on their cards to themselves for now. In addition, distribute one copy of the tax law simulation instructions (Activity 11.2) and a blank copy of the tax law form (Activity 11.3) to each group.

5. Explain that, within the groups, each group member should play the role of the head-of-household described on his or her card. The five people in each group represent five households (in one country) who must figure out how to raise $50,000 to pay for their country's government services. Allow the students to read the instructions among themselves.

6. After the groups have read the instructions, summarize the main points and clarify terms that the students may not understand:

   - Each group must come up with a tax scheme that the group members believe is reasonable and that raises the required $50,000.

   - Groups may tax wage income by setting tax rates.

   - Groups may charge a tax on capital gains. (A capital gains tax is a tax on the appreciation of an asset such as stock or real estate.)

   - Groups may give families a tax credit (which is a reduction in taxes) for each child in a given household.

   - Tell the students that they will be judged against people with a similar background who are in other groups. Students who pay less in taxes than those from the same background in a different group will be judged successful.

7. After the students have read the instructions to the Activity, display Visual 11.2 to reinforce their understanding of their task.

Visual 11.2 presents an example (according to the instructions on Activity 11.2) that may help the students as they work to fill in the forms and determine how certain tax rates affect them.

Notes to the teacher:

- As necessary, remind the students that in their calculations they may need to convert percentages to decimals, and vice versa. Also, you may wish to offer incentives to encourage the students to complete their task successfully. For example, you might award a small prize (or provide some other award) to each of the five individuals who wind up paying the least amount of taxes in their income class. (For example: A Chan head of household will be a winner if that Chan pays less than the Chans in other groups.)

- The following table summarizes how the total wage income for each bracket

is calculated. This information is for the teacher's reference only. In reading this table, you may wish to refer to the following example: The Chan family has earned $45,000 this year. The first $25,000 falls in the first tax bracket and is taxed at the rate for that bracket. The next $20,000 is taxed at the rate for the second tax bracket. The "Total Wage Income in Bracket" is the total of the five families' incomes in each bracket. For example, only three families have incomes high enough to reach the second tax bracket: the Chans, the Dasguptas, and the Engles. The sum of the income in this second bracket is $70,000. In the simulation, the students know the total amount of wage income in each bracket, so they can calculate how much tax revenue their taxes will yield. The students do not know how each family makes (unless they share this information within their group).

Income Bracket	Abbots	Bosmans	Chans	Dasguptas	Engles	Total Wage Income in Bracket
$0-25,000	$10,000	$25,000	$25,000	$25,000	$25,000	$110,000
$25,000-$50,000	$0	$0	$20,000	$25,000	$25,000	$70,000
$50,000+	$0	$0	$0	$20,000	$50,000	$70,000
Total Wage Income	$10,000	$25,000	$45,000	$70,000	$100,000	$250,000

8. Tell the students that they will have 15 minutes to discuss and agree on their tax law. For the law to be enacted, it must be written out on Activity 11.3 and be signed by each of the five members of the group. In signing their names, the students should use their own first name and the last name of the person they are playing. Tell the students to begin their deliberations. For simplicity, you may wish to tell the students that they should not have a

negative tax payment for any family. This is probably most relevant in the case of the Abbots, who could possibly have child tax credits in excess of income tax owed.

9. During the deliberations, circulate to make sure the students understand the idea of different tax brackets. They may need help with the calculations needed to arrive at a tax law that raises exactly $50,000. Tell the students it will be no problem if their tax rates raise a bit more than

$50,000, due to rounding. If you see that students in a group are struggling, remind them that they need to raise $50,000 from wages of $250,000 and capital gains of $25,000, so they have $275,000 of income that is taxable. This means their tax rates have to be, on average, about 18 percent ($50,000 / $275,000). Remind them that if they want to tax some brackets or capital gains at a rate lower than 18 percent, the rate then will have to be higher than 18 percent on other tax brackets or on capital gains. Obviously, an infinite number of combinations work. The students will have to use a bit of trial and error. The table below lists some examples that raise $50,000.

Example Name	Tax Rate for Lowest Bracket	Tax Rate for Middle Bracket	Tax Rate for Highest Bracket	Capital Gains Tax Rate	Child Tax Credit
Flat Tax on Wage Income	20%	20%	20%	0%	$ 0
Extremely Regressive, But With Child Tax Credit	50 %	0%	0%	0%	$1,250
Extremely Progressive	0%	0%	50%	60%	$ 0
Flat Tax on All Income	18.2%	18.2%	18.2%	18.2%	$ 0
Compromise?	10%	20%	30%	20%	$ 250

10. After 15 minutes, tell the groups that they should have their tax laws written. If a group has not written and passed a law, tell the members of the group that their country's government has gone bankrupt and they are not eligible to receive any prizes. Also, they must fill in 20 percent for all brackets, 0 for the capital gains tax rate, and 0 for the child tax credit.

11. Tell the students it is time to pay their taxes. Hand out a set of tax forms (from Activity 11.4) to each group. Have each person figure his or her taxes on the appropriate family form, using the group's tax law (or the rate of 20 percent on wage income if the group has not come to an agreement). Have the students calculate their average tax rate and their marginal tax rate, and enter the results at the bottom of their tax forms.

12. Collect the tax laws from each group and record them on Visual 11.3. Point out that the tax rates you are recording are the **_marginal_** tax rates for each income bracket. A marginal tax rate is the percentage of an additional dollar of income that is paid in tax. The marginal tax rate is important since people may make decisions based on this rate. The decision to earn an extra dollar of income, or not to, may depend on the marginal rate.

13. Ask a member of the Engle family: If you earned one more dollar in wage income, how much would you have to pay in taxes? _(The answer will be the tax rate for the_

highest bracket.) Note that this is the marginal rate for the member of the Engle family. Remind the students that the marginal rate is different from the ***average*** tax rate. The average tax rate is the household's total tax divided by its total income. Ask the Engle family member: Is the marginal rate or the average rate larger for you? *(If the tax system is **progressive**, the marginal rate will be higher; if it is **proportional**, the marginal and average rates will be equal; if it is **regressive**, the marginal rate will be lower than the average rate.)*

14. Display Visual 11.4. Explain the differences among regressive, proportional, and progressive tax systems. Explain that the principle of **vertical equity** provides one way to consider fairness. It suggests that people with higher incomes should face a heavier tax burden. That is, it implies a progressive tax system. Another way to judge fairness is according to the principle of **horizontal equity**, which implies that people with equal incomes all should face the same tax burden. For example, a tax proposal to exempt all teachers' wage income from income taxes would violate the horizontal tax equity standard, since teachers would not pay the same tax as other taxpayers with the same income.

15. Ask the following questions on the economics of taxation.

   • What kind of tax system (progressive, regressive or proportional) did your group try to achieve? *(Student answers will vary.)* Why? *(Some students may suggest a progressive tax system since they believe that wealthier people can afford a higher rate. Others may suggest that a proportional tax is easy to administer. Wealthier students may suggest that a regressive system worked well for them and so they lobbied for such a system. If the students' tax systems are very similar, share with the students some of the extreme examples listed in the table above to illustrate the range of possible variations in tax systems.)*

• Did your group decide to give a tax credit for children? *(Answers will vary. The tax credit will most likely be supported by the Abbot and Dasgupta families.)* Why? *(Some students will suggest that these families have additional expenses and so deserve a tax break. Their ability to pay taxes is reduced because they have more dependents. Students may also suggest that they want to support the concept of a family. Other students may suggest that having children is a personal decision which should not influence tax policy.)*

• Did your group decide to tax capital gains? *(Answers will vary. The Dasgupta and Engle families are likely to be opposed to taxing capital gains.)* Why? *(Students may suggest that gains on assets are similar to income from wages, and so should be taxed in a similar fashion. The students may note that large capital gains indicate a greater ability to pay taxes. Finally, some students may suggest that by NOT taxing capital gains they are encouraging households to buy stocks and other assets that may yield capital gains in the future.)*

16. Ask the groups how they came to an agreement on a tax law. Also ask them to describe the behaviors they witnessed during their deliberations. For example:

• Did you hold a vote on your proposal(s)? *(Some groups may have, others may not have.)* If the students voted, ask if they required a majority vote or a unanimous vote. *(If any of the groups failed to come up with a tax plan, it was likely because they could not come up with a tax plan that received unanimous consent, given that any tax law that was passed required the signature of each member of the group.)*

• If the students did not formally vote, was everything done by consensus? *(Again, answers will vary.)* Did one person in the group tend to act as a dictator? *(Perhaps.)*

- Introduce the term ***log-rolling***; define it as a way of exchanging favors, especially in politics: lawmakers who are engaged in logrolling vote for one another's proposed legislation. They say, in effect, "If you vote for the law I want, I'll vote for the law you want. That way we'll both get what we want." Did the students witness any log-rolling on votes? *(This is likely to have happened. The cards are designed so that families with children and families with capital gains cannot, by themselves, pass a large tax credit for children or a low capital gains tax rate. However, if families with children or capital gains get together, they may be able to propose policies that are favorable to them and that will also be supported by the majority of the families in the group.)*

- Did any of the groups fail to come to an agreement? *(Perhaps.)* Why? *(Some might not have been able to get a unanimous vote; others might not have arrived at any proposal on which to vote; others may have finished the work and voted, only to have someone balk at signing the law.)*

17. Poll the "relatives" across the groups and ask them what they paid in taxes. For example, ask the member of the Chan family from each country to report the taxes he or she paid. In each case, show how the "winner" (the family member who paid the lowest amount of taxes) benefited from the particular tax law passed in his or her country by comparing rates and tax credits on Visual 11.3. Award a prize to each winner, if promised.

18. Close the lesson by noting that the U.S. tax system is very complicated. It includes federal payroll taxes (Social Security and Medicare taxes) that are partly proportional and partly regressive. The federal income tax is progressive in structure, although deductions and separate rates for capital gains can make it less so. State sales taxes, as well

as federal excise taxes (on gasoline, for example), tend to be regressive since people with lower incomes tend to spend a larger share of their incomes on goods and services. A complete understanding of taxation in the United States would take many years of study and personal experience. This lesson has introduced certain principles to serve as a basis for further learning.

CLOSURE

Summarize the following points:

- People have different opinions about how the government should tax its citizens.

- A group may use many different methods to reach a decision.

- Depending on how a country decides to tax its citizens, the tax system may be progressive, proportional, or regressive.

ASSESSMENT

Multiple-choice Questions

1. A flat tax is one that taxes all income at a constant percentage rate. A flat tax is

    A. regressive.

    B. progressive.

    C. proportional.

    D. progressive at first, then regressive.

2. Use the federal income tax table below to answer the following questions. Suppose your household earns $32,100 in 2008. Because of deductions and exemptions, assume that the taxable income for your household is $16,050. For your household, the average tax on household income is _____. The marginal tax rate for another dollar earned in taxable income is _____.

    A. 5%, 15%

    B. 5%, 25%

    C. 10%, 15%

    D. 10%, 25%

The table below is from the 2008 federal income tax table.

Schedule Y-1—If your filing status is **Married filing jointly** or **Qualifying widow(er)**

If your taxable income is:		The tax is:	of the amount over—
Over—	But not over—		
$0	$16,050	·········· 10%	$0
16,050	65,100	$1,605.00 + 15%	16,050
65,100	131,450	8,962.50 + 25%	65,100
131,450	200,300	25,550.00 + 28%	131,450
200,300	357,700	44,828.00 + 33%	200,300
357,700	··········	96,770.00 + 35%	357,700

Constructed-Response Questions

1. Suppose the state where you live decided to increase its income tax rates in order to lower its sales tax. Would the tax system for your state become more progressive or more regressive because of this change? Explain your answer.

   (Sales taxes are generally regressive. By replacing a regressive tax with an income tax, which is likely to be proportional or progressive, the tax system will become more progressive.)

2. Given the 2008 U.S. federal tax schedule shown above, is the U.S. federal tax system progressive, regressive, or proportional? Explain. *(It is progressive, since the marginal rate increases with income. The marginal rate [as of 2009] starts at 10% and moves to 15%, 25%, 28%, 33%, with a top marginal rate of 35%.)*

Visual 11.1
Quotations

The Congress shall have power to lay and collect taxes, duties, imposts and excises to pay the debts and provide for the common defense and general welfare of the United States.

—United States Constitution, Article 1, Section 8

Taxes are the price we pay for civilization.

—Oliver Wendell Holmes, Jr. (Inscription carved above the entrance to the Internal Revenue Service building in Washington, D.C.)

To force a man to pay for the violation of his own liberty is indeed an addition of insult to injury.

—Benjamin Tucker (1890)

Not one cent should be raised unless it is in accord with the law.

—Napoleon Bonaparte (circa 1800)

VISUAL 11.2
TAX SIMULATION ILLUSTRATION

Example:

The group agrees to rates of 5% for the first $25,000 of wage income, 10% for the next $25,000, and 5% for all wage income above $50,000. The group decides to tax capital gains at 10% and to give a child tax credit of $250 per child.

How these rates impact a hypothetical household:

If a household earns $30,000 in wage income, has no capital gains, and has no children, then the household would pay:

5% x $25,000 (5% on first $25,000)	=	$1,250
10% x $5,000 (10% on remaining $5,000)	=	$ 500
Total Tax		$1,750

VISUAL 11.2, CONTINUED

TAX SIMULATION ILLUSTRATION

How much total tax revenue this tax will collect in the country:

The group would fill in the table as follows. This tax plan does not earn enough tax revenue, so tax rates need to be higher.

Tax Law

Tax Bracket	Total Wage Income in Tax Bracket	Tax Rate	Tax Revenue
$0 to $25,000	$110,000	5%	**$5,500**
$25,000 to $50,000	$70,000	10%	**+ $7,000**
$50,000 and Above	$70,000	5%	**+ $3,500**
Sum of Tax Revenues listed above			**= $16,000**
Capital Gains Tax: $25,000 x __**10**__ %			**+ $2,500**
Subtract Amount of Child Tax Credits: $ ___**250**___ X 4 =			**- $1,000**
Total Tax Revenue			**= $17,500**

VISUAL 11.3

GROUP RESULTS: TAX RATES

Tax Laws Passed	Country	Country	Country	Country	Country
$0 to $25,000	%	%	%	%	%
$25,000 to $50,000	%	%	%	%	%
$50,000 and above	%	%	%	%	%
Capital Gains	%	%	%	%	%
Child Tax Credit					
Total Tax Revenue					

VISUAL 11.4

HOW DO WE DESCRIBE TAXES?

A Progressive Tax:

Households with higher incomes pay a larger share of their income in tax than households with lower incomes. For an income tax, this usually implies that the marginal tax rate increases as income increases.

A Proportional Tax:

All households pay the same share of their income in tax. For an income tax, this means that the marginal tax rate is constant.

A Regressive Tax:

Households with higher incomes pay a smaller share of their incomes in tax than households with lower incomes. For an income tax, this usually implies that the marginal tax rate decreases as income increases.

ACTIVITY 11.1
STUDENT ROLE-PLAYING CARDS

The Abbots

Your household wage income is $10,000 a year. Your family has three children. Since your family has no investments, you have no capital gains income.

The Bosmans

Your household wage income is $25,000 a year. You have no children. Since your family has no investments, you have no capital gains income.

The Chans

Your household wage income is $45,000 a year. Your family has no children. Since your family has no investments, you have no capital gains income.

The Dasguptas

Your household wage income is $70,000 a year. Your family has one child. In addition to this income, your investments have earned you $5,000 in capital gains.

The Engles

Your household wage income is $100,000 a year. In addition to this income, your investments have earned you $20,000 in capital gains. Your family has no children.

Activity 11.2
Tax Law Simulation

Directions: Your group lives in a country with five families. Each person in your group represents one of the families. Each person in the group has received a card that describes his or her family. Family representatives should not show their card to others in the group.

Your group must decide what the tax structure is going to be for your country. The country has a total taxable wage income of $250,000. In addition, households earned $25,000 in capital gains. The country's government needs to raise $50,000 for defense, schools, roads, and government salaries. Your group must raise enough ($50,000) in tax revenue to fund the government budget.

It is up to your group to write the tax law. Everyone in your group should participate in deciding what the tax rates in the country should be. When debating how the country should tax its citizens, each person should remember the circumstances of his or her own family, as described on the cards. While family representatives do not have to show their cards to anyone in the group, people in the group may want to introduce themselves to other group members and exchange information about their situations.

Your group will be judged successful if it comes up with a tax scheme that yields $50,000 in tax revenue. A family representative will be viewed as successful if (1) his or her group comes up with a tax scheme that generates $50,000 and (2) his or her family pays less tax than those families with the same background in other groups in the class.

The Revenue Service in your country has put together the following information.

Tax Bracket	Total Wage Income in Tax Bracket	Tax Rate (in %)	Tax Revenue
$0 to $25,000	$110,000		
$25,000 to $50,000	$70,000		+
$50,000 and Above	$70,000		+
Sum of Tax Revenues Listed Above			=
Capital Gains Tax:	$25,000 x _____ %		+
Subtract Amount of Child Tax Credits:	$ _____ X 4 =		-
Total Tax Revenue			=

ACTIVITY 11.2, CONTINUED

TAX LAW SIMULATION

Your group must decide what percentage rate to charge in each tax bracket. The table is read in the following manner:

- The first bracket asks what percentage you wish to tax on the first $25,000 of household income.

- The second bracket asks what percentage you wish to tax on the NEXT $25,000 of household income.

- The third bracket asks what percentage you wish to tax on household income OVER $50,000.

Example:

If your group chooses rates of 5% for the first $25,000 of income, 10% for the next $25,000, and 5% for all income above $50,000, then a household making $30,000 in wage income would pay a total tax of:

5% x $25,000 (5% on first $25,000)	=	$1,250
10% x $5,000 (10% on remaining $5,000)	=	$ 500
Total Tax		$1,750

The table above gives the total taxable income in each tax bracket for the country, so your group can calculate how much tax revenue is earned in the whole country. A tax law with rates of 5% on the first $25,000, 10% on the second $25,000, and 5% on the amount over $50,000 would earn:

5% x $110,000	=	$5,500
10% x $70,000	=	$7,000
5% x $70,000	=	$3,500
Total Tax Revenue		$16,000

Activity 11.2, continued

Tax Law Simulation

In addition to taxing income, your group may also decide to levy a tax on capital gains, which is income a household earns when an asset (such as a stock or property) appreciates in value.

Finally, your group may also elect to give a tax credit for each child living in the country. There are four children in the country. You must subtract the credited amount from your tax collections in calculating tax revenue.

Suppose your group decides to provide a tax credit of $250 per child and decides to charge a 10% capital gains tax in addition to the taxes on wages listed above. This would total up as follows:

$25,000 x 10%   = $2,500

in additional tax revenue from capital gains

$250 per child x 4 children   = $1,000 in credits

Total Tax Revenue with the child tax credit and capital gains tax and tax rates described above:

$16,000 + $2,500 - $1,000   = $17,500

After your group has decided on a tax law and made sure that the law will raise $50,000 in revenue, fill in the table in Activity 11.3 for your country. Each person must sign for the law to be enacted.

Be sure to name your country and enter it on the tax law form!

ACTIVITY 11.3

TAX LAW FOR COUNTRY OF _____

The following shall be the tax rates for the country:

Tax Bracket	Wage Income in Tax Bracket	Tax Rate	Tax Revenue
$0 to $25,000	$110,000		
$25,000 to $50,000	$70,000		+
$50,000 and Above	$70,000		+
Sum of Tax Revenues listed above			=
Capital Gains Tax: $25,000 x _____ %			+
Subtract Amount of Child Tax Credits: $ _____ X 4 =			-
Total Tax Revenue			=

Signed:

_____   _____

_____   _____

_____   _____

Activity 11.4
Tax Forms

Abbots: $10,000 Wage Income

Tax Bracket	Your Wage Income in Each Tax Bracket	Tax Rate (in %)	Taxes on Income
$0 to $25,000	$10,000		
$25,000 to $50,000	$ 0		
$50,000 and Above	$ 0		
Sum of the Taxes Listed Above			=
Capital Gains Tax: $0 x _____ %			+ 0
Subtract Amount of Child Tax Credit: $ _____ x 3			-
Total Tax			=

Total Income (including capital gains) = $10,000

Average Tax Rate = (Total Tax/Total Income) x 100 = _____%

Marginal Tax Rate = If you earned one more dollar, what percent would you pay of that additional dollar in tax = _____%

ACTIVITY 11.4, CONTINUED

TAX FORMS

Bosmans: $25,000 Wage Income

Tax Bracket	Your Wage Income in Each Tax Bracket	Tax Rate (in %)	Taxes on Income
$0 to $25,000	$25,000		
$25,000 to $50,000	$ 0		
$50,000 and Above	$ 0		
Sum of the Taxes Listed Above			=
Capital Gains Tax: $0 x _____ %			+ 0
Subtract Amount of Child Tax Credit: $ _____ x 0			- 0
Total Tax			=

Total Income (including capital gains) = $25,000

Average Tax = (Total Tax / Total Income) x 100 = _____%

Marginal Tax Rate = If you earned one more dollar, what percent would you pay of that additional dollar in tax = _____%

Activity 11.4, continued
Tax Forms

Chans: $45,000 Wage Income

Tax Bracket	Your Wage Income in Each Tax Bracket	Tax Rate (in %)	Taxes on Income
$0 to $25,000	$25,000		
$25,000 to $50,000	$20,000		
$50,000 and Above	$ 0		
Sum of the Taxes Listed Above			=
Capital Gains Tax: $0 x _____ %			+ 0
Subtract Amount of Child Tax Credit: $ _____ x 0			- 0
Total Tax			=

Total Income (including capital gains) = $45,000

Average Tax = (Total Tax / Total Income) x 100 = _____%

Marginal Tax Rate = If you earned one more dollar, what percent would you pay of that additional dollar in tax = _____%

ACTIVITY 11.4, CONTINUED

TAX FORMS

Dasguptas: $70,000 Wage Income

Tax Bracket	Your Wage Income in Each Tax Bracket	Tax Rate (in %)	Taxes on Income
$0 to $25,000	$25,000		
$25,000 to $50,000	$25,000		
$50,000 and Above	$20,000		
Sum of the Taxes Listed Above			=
Capital Gains Tax: $5,000 x _____ %			+
Subtract Amount of Child Tax Credit: $ _____ x 1			-
Total Tax			=

Total Income (including capital gains) = $75,000

Average Tax = (Total Tax / Total Income) x 100 = _____%

Marginal Tax Rate = If you earned one more dollar, what percent would you pay of that additional dollar in tax = _____%

Activity 11.4, continued

Tax Forms

Engles: $100,000 Wage Income

Tax Bracket	Your Wage Income in Each Tax Bracket	Tax Rate (in %)	Taxes on Income
$0 to $25,000	$25,000		
$25,000 to $50,000	$25,000		
$50,000 and Above	$50,000		
Sum of the Taxes Listed Above			=
Capital Gains Tax: $20,000 x _____ %			+
Subtract Amount of Child Tax Credit: $ _____ x 0			- 0
Total Tax			=

Total Income (including capital gains) = $120,000

Average Tax = (Total Tax / Total Income) x 100 = _____%

Marginal Tax Rate = If you earned one more dollar, what percent would you pay of that additional dollar in tax = _____%

FOCUS: UNDERSTANDING ECONOMICS IN CIVICS AND GOVERNMENT © COUNCIL FOR ECONOMIC EDUCATION, NEW YORK, NY

LESSON 12

FEDERALISM

LESSON 12
FEDERALISM

INTRODUCTION

The American founders deeply distrusted the concentration of power in government, especially at the national level. They created the Bill of Rights to serve as a bulwark against government intrusion into the lives of citizens. The founders also believed that the individual states should share sovereign authority with the national government. Even after the failed experiment of the Articles of Confederation, the founders inserted clauses into the U.S. Constitution intended to ensure the dispersion of power and the authority of the individual states.

One aspect of power dispersion is the familiar notion of *checks and balances*, with the tri-partite division of the government into the legislative, executive, and judicial branches, each with various powers to oversee the others. Another is the idea of *federalism*, according to which some powers reside at the national level while others are reserved for the individual states.

So great was the concern about a powerful central government that some of America's founders insisted on the adoption of the first ten amendments to the Constitution, otherwise known as the Bill of Rights. These amendments established the inviolable rights of American citizens; they also explicitly addressed the doctrine of federalism, especially in the Tenth Amendment:

> **The powers not delegated to the United States by the Constitution, nor prohibited by it to the States, are reserved to the States respectively, or to the people.**

Despite the Tenth Amendment, however, the national government has found ways to shape public policy in areas that seem not to be "delegated to the United States by the Constitution." Today, for example, the United States has a uniform drinking age, even though the Twenty-First Amendment (1933) repealed prohibition and *apparently* made regulation of the use of alcohol a state matter.

How did the uniform drinking age come about? The national government used an incentive to encourage the states to raise the drinking age to 21. Using its "spending powers" under Article 1, Section 8 of the Constitution, Congress told the states that the national government would withhold five percent of a state's federal highway funds if the state did not pass legislation to raise the drinking age to 21. In *South Dakota v. Dole* (1987), the U.S. Supreme Court held (7-2) that Congress may attach conditions to the states' voluntary acceptance of federal money, and that the actions of Congress in this case were "not so coercive as to pass the point at which pressure turns into compulsion."

A more recent example in which federal funding is used as an incentive to shape state policy is a federal law known as the No Child Left Behind (NCLB) Act (2001). This federal law specifies certain accountability measures to be used by state officials in efforts to improve teaching and learning in primary and secondary public schools. The states are not required to adopt the NCLB provisions, but states failing to adopt them would forgo federal financial support. All states have elected to receive federal funding under NCLB, thus accepting the conditions it specifies. At the same time, NCLB has generated resentment among some educators and state officials. In *Connecticut v. Spellings* (2006), for example, the State of Connecticut sued the U.S. Department of Education over NCLB, claiming, in part, that the penalties for non-compliance with NCLB violate the Tenth Amendment.

LESSON DESCRIPTION

Using a role-play activity about NCLB, students investigate the concept of federalism and the use of incentives by Congress to get states to follow national government priorities.

CONCEPTS

- Federalism

- Incentives

OBJECTIVES

Students will be able to:

1. Identify the major reasons for the American federal system.

2. Analyze Congressional uses of incentives to encourage states to adopt programs that conform to national priorities.

CONTENT STANDARDS

Economics (CEE Standards)

- People respond predictably to positive and negative incentives. (Standard 4)

Civics and Government (NSCG Standards, Grades 9-12)

- Concepts of *constitution*. Purposes and uses of constitutions. (Standards I.C.1 and 2)

- Confederal, federal, and unitary systems. (Standard I.D.2)

- The American idea of constitutional government. (Standard II.A.1)

TIME REQUIRED

60 minutes

MATERIALS

- A transparency of Visuals 12.1 and 12.2.

- A copy for each student of Activities 12.1 and 12.2.

- A copy for each student of the U.S. Constitution

PROCEDURE

1. Ask the students: How many of you have had to take mandatory math tests since you started school? How about English and reading? Do you think you take enough tests? Why do you suppose you are tested so often? *(Discuss responses briefly.)*

2. Explain that school testing programs aren't simply made up by teachers and principals. They reflect, in part, legal requirements that are binding on the schools. Some of these requirements derive from a federal law known as the No Child Left Behind Act (NCLB). Write *No Child Left Behind Act (NCLB)* on the board.

3. Explain briefly the major goals of the NCLB Act:

   - educational excellence;

   - closing the achievement gap between rich and poor and between Anglos and minorities.

   Note that in proposing the NCLB Act, President Bush stated: "Districts and schools that improve achievement will be rewarded. Failure will be sanctioned." http://www.cew.wisc.edu/ewl/resource/nochildleftbehind.pdf (p.2)

4. Explain that this lesson will address Federalism and the approach to accountability that is built into the NCLB Act.

5. Distribute Activity 12.1 and preview the questions students should be ready to answer at the conclusion of the lesson.

6. Ask the students: Which level of government has the legal authority to decide educational policy? *(Answers will vary, but you are likely to get answers that include federal, state, and local governments).* After some discussion, tell the students that they can look in the Constitution for a definitive answer. Have the students look for references to education in Article 1, Section 8, which lists the powers of the U.S. Congress. When they don't find any reference to education there, have them read the Tenth Amendment to the Constitution.

7. Display Visual 12.1. Briefly explain the idea of federalism: It implies that government power should be dispersed through shared sovereignty; that the power of the national government should be limited to the powers enumerated in the

Constitution; and that government should
be kept close to the people.

8. Pose the question again: Which level of
government has the legal authority to
decide educational policy? When at least
some students have responded that
authority for education policy seems to
rest with the states, ask: Then why would
the states go along with a law like NCLB?
After all, that law gives the federal government a great deal of power to decide
matters of education policy. (Discuss
responses briefly.)

9. Display Visual 12.2. Explain that the
Handy Dandy Guide to Economics may
help to explain the states' responses to the
NCLB. Ask: Which item in the Handy
Dandy Guide is most useful in explaining
why the states have gone along with the
NCLB? (*Item 3: "People respond to incentives in predictable ways."*) Tell the class
that they will conduct a role-play exercise
to illustrate the idea of incentives as it is
related to the NCLB.

10. Distribute a copy of Activity 12.2 to each
student. Place three chairs at the front of
the room. Tell the students that they will
be observing a Supreme Court hearing in
which Supreme Court Justices will
question attorneys. For the purposes of
this activity, there will be three Supreme
Court Justices instead of nine. Select
three students to play the roles of the
Chief Justice and Associate Justices 1 and
2, and have them stand aside. Select one
student to play the role of Supreme Court
Marshal and another to play the role of
Attorney for the Plaintiff.

11. Have the actors quickly familiarize
themselves with their parts and cues.
Meanwhile, make sure the rest of the class
is jotting down answers to the first four
questions on the Lesson Notes and
Questions in Activity 12.1.

12. Tell the Justices that the Chief will sit in
the middle, and make sure that the
Marshal knows how to pronounce "Oyez."
Identify yourself as the narrator; read the

opening sentences to the class and begin
the play.

13. Discuss the play briefly, as appropriate.
Divide the class into pairs and ask each
pair of students to write down answers to
the questions on Debriefing the Play in
Activity 12.1. After the pairs have had
time to work, conduct a general discussion
of the students' answers. Ask:

• Under what authority does the federal
government offer funding for the states
to participate in NCLB? (*Under the
authority of Congress as outlined in the
enumerated powers in the general
welfare clause of the U.S. Constitution.
This is found in Article 1, Section 8,
Clause 1.*)

• Why would states agree to participate?
(*They are provided with an economic
incentive to do so. If they do not participate, they will lose portions of federal
funding for education.*)

• Do you think the NCLB Act violates
the principles of federalism? Why or
why not? (*Answers will vary, but students who think it does not violate the
principles of federalism will argue that
the states retain their right to establish
their own educational policy, and that
it is constitutional for Congress to
spend funds on education in order to
promote the general welfare. Students
who think that the NCLB Act violates
the principle of federalism may argue
that the conditions for accepting
funding are so coercive that the
pressure applied on states amounts
to compulsion.*)

CLOSURE

Return to Activity 12.1. Ask:

• Can incentives be both positive and
negative? (*Yes.*)

• Is it predictable that all 50 states would
agree to participate in NCLB? (*Yes. To opt
out of NCLB would prove very costly.*)

• Point out that the use of incentives by

Congress is very common. In legislation subsequently sanctioned by the Supreme Court (*South Dakota v. Dole*, 1987), Congress effectively established a national drinking age by making grants for federal highway funds contingent on a state's adopting a minimum age of twenty-one for the purchase or possession of alcoholic beverages.

- Conclude by asking the class: Under our federal system, when do incentives become coercive? (*Answers will vary based on subjective views of students.*)

ASSESSMENT
Multiple-Choice Questions

1. All of the following are reasons for having our federal system of government except:

    A. Our federal system brings government closer to the people.

    B. Our federal system disperses govern ment power.

    C. Our federal system allows every thing to be the same across all states.

    D. Our federal system limits the federal government to enumerated powers.

2. Congress expected the states to join the NCLB Act primarily because

    A. the NCLB Act is a really good idea.

    B. the people voted for it.

    C. it had unanimous support from both political parties.

    D. people respond to incentives in predictable ways.

3. Part of the complaint in the *Connecticut v. Spellings* case alleged that the NCLB Act violated

    A. the Tenth Amendment.

    B. the First Amendment.

    C. executive privilege.

    D. the Federal Education Act of 2004.

Constructed-Response Questions

1. Explain how Congress uses incentives to get the states to comply with national priorities.

    (*Congress offers funds to the states and establishes conditions for the use of those funds, thus creating incentives for states to comply with the intent of Congress.*)

2. Based on the information presented in this lesson, write your own court decision for the case of *Connecticut v. Spellings*.

    (*The argument turns on judgments about the point at which the penalties imposed for noncompliance with the NCLB Act become so coercive that the law becomes compulsory.*)

VISUAL 12.1

THE TENTH AMENDMENT AND THE CONCEPT OF FEDERALISM

- The Tenth Amendment to the U.S. Constitution:

  The powers not delegated to the United States by the Constitution, nor prohibited by it to the States, are reserved to the States respectively, or to the people.

- Core ideas of Federalism:

  1. dispersion of government power through shared sovereignty;

  2. limiting federal powers to those enumerated in the Constitution;

  3. Keeping government close to the people.

VISUAL 12.2

HANDY DANDY GUIDE TO ECONOMICS

1. People Choose.

2. All Choices Involve Costs.

3. People Respond to Incentives In Predictable Ways.

4. Economic Systems Influence Individual Choices and Incentives.

5. Voluntary Trade Creates Wealth.

6. The Consequences of Choices Lie in the Future.

ACTIVITY 12.1
LESSON NOTES AND QUESTIONS

Which level of government has the authority to decide educational policy?

What is Federalism?

Why would States want to go along with an educational policy such as NCLB?

Which item on the Handy Dandy Guide to Economics is most useful in explaining why the states have gone along with NCLB?

Debriefing the Play

Under what authority does the federal government offer funding for the states to participate in NCLB?

Why would states agree to participate?

Do you think NCLB violates the principles of federalism? Why or why not?

Can incentives be both positive and negative? How?

Is it predictable that all 50 states would agree to participate in NCLB?

Under our federal system, when do incentives become coercive?

ACTIVITY 12.2

THE SUPREME COURT HEARS A CASE

Narrator: This play is based on a case titled *Connecticut v. Spellings*. It is called this because the State of Connecticut is the *plaintiff*, meaning the person or group bringing the legal action. *Spellings* is the name of the defendant, in this case Margaret Spellings, who was Secretary of the U.S. Department of Education at the time this case began.

One part of Connecticut's case is based on the Tenth Amendment. The State of Connecticut claims that the No Child Left Behind Act (NCLB) has many requirements, but does not provide enough funds from the federal government to meet these requirements. But, if Connecticut decides *not* to participate in NCLB, it will lose lots of federal education money that is not related to NCLB. And the threat of that loss, Connecticut argues, is coercive and constitutes a violation of the Tenth Amendment.

In 2008, the case was dismissed by the U.S. District Court, District of Connecticut. But, what if the District Court's decision is appealed to the U.S. Supreme Court?

All stand: The Court arrives.

Supreme Court Marshal: The Honorable, the Chief Justice, and the Associate Justices of the Supreme Court of the United States. Oyez! Oyez! Oyez! All persons having business before the Honorable, the Supreme Court of the United States, are admonished to draw near and give their attention, for the Court is now sitting. God save the United States and this Honorable Court!

The Justices sit. Everyone else sits.

Chief Justice: We are here today to hear oral arguments in the case of *Connecticut v. Spellings*. We will hear arguments concerning paragraph 192 of the complaint.

Attorney for the Plaintiff: Thank you Mrs. [or Mr.] Chief Justice, and may it please the court. We contend that the provisions of the No Child Left Behind (NCLB) Act violate the sovereign powers of the states as provided by the Tenth Amendment of the Constitution, which states that "The powers not delegated to the United States by the Constitution, nor prohibited by it to the States, are reserved to the States respectively, or to the people."

Associate Justice 1: Let's be clear about something from the beginning. Spending for education is nowhere found in the enumerated powers of Congress. Is it your argument that education is a state function and that NCLB therefore violates the Tenth Amendment?

ACTIVITY 12.2, CONTINUED

THE SUPREME COURT HEARS A CASE

Associate Justice 2: Because, Article 1, Section 8, Clause 1 allows Congress to spend to promote the general welfare. Do you agree that spending for education falls within the scope of its enumerated powers under the general welfare clause?

Attorney for the Plaintiff: We agree that this is a proper function of Congress. So, that is not our concern relative to the Tenth Amendment. Rather, it is with the conditions....

Associate Justice 2: Your state willingly accepted funding for NCLB, is that not the case?

Chief Justice: Because, this is a proper incentive for states to comply with what Congress deems necessary under its enumerated powers.

Attorney for the Plaintiff: Yes, however the conditions attached by the Secretary of Education are....

Associate Justice 1: This Court has long held that Congress may attach conditions to its grants to the states. Congress offers the incentive of funding—with conditions. States can refuse the funding if they don't like the conditions.

Attorney for the Plaintiff: We contend that the way Secretary of Education Spellings has put NCLB into action goes beyond offering incentives. It...

Associate Justice 1: In what way?

Attorney for the Plaintiff: We contend in paragraph 192 of our complaint that the rules the Secretary has created to put NCLB into effect are too rigid and arbitrary. And the penalties for not complying with these rules are so harsh and unrelated to the conditions upon which Connecticut accepted the funds that they violate the Tenth Amendment.

Associate Justice 1: I repeat: In what way?

Attorney for the Plaintiff: In paragraph 67 of the complaint we point out that the consequences of opting out of the NCLB Act apparently are not limited to losing funds related to NCLB. The State of Utah formally posed the question of opting out of the requirements of the NCLB Act to the U.S. Department of Education (USDOE). In 2004, the USDOE responded that not only would Utah lose its NCLB funds, but it also would forfeit nearly twice that much in other funds. Unrelated pro-

ACTIVITY 12.2, CONTINUED
THE SUPREME COURT HEARS A CASE

grams such as the special education funds under the Individuals with Disabilities Education Act, and preschool programs for handicapped children, would be negatively affected.

Chief Justice: Various laws, including NCLB, give the Secretary of Education broad powers to make sure states meet the goals intended in the law.

Attorney for the Plaintiff: True, but in *South Dakota v. Dole*, South Dakota contested a federal law providing that 5 percent of federal highway funds would be withheld from states that didn't adopt the minimum drinking age of 21. The majority court opinion stated that the conditions for accepting funding could not be "so coercive as to pass the point at which pressure turns into compulsion."

Associate Justice 2: But South Dakota lost that case. The majority of the court decided that the threat of withholding 5 percent of federal highway funds was a proper incentive, not compulsion.

Attorney for the Plaintiff: True. But *South Dakota v. Dole* established the principle that withholding money could possibly be more than an incentive—it could be compulsion. We think the threat of lost funding for *other* education programs if we opt out of NCLB is compulsion and therefore violates the sovereignty of the State of Connecticut protected by the Tenth Amendment.

Associate Justice 2: Hmmm. How much funding would be lost in Connecticut?

Attorney for the Plaintiff: Connecticut could lose as much as 5 percent of statewide education spending and 15 percent in the most economically disadvantaged school districts.

Chief Justice: Thank you for your argument before the Court. The case is submitted. The Court will now retire.

Supreme Court Marshal: All rise.

GOVERNMENT FAILURE: USING PUBLIC CHOICE THEORY TO ANALYZE POLITICAL DECISIONS

LESSON 13

GOVERNMENT FAILURE: USING PUBLIC CHOICE THEORY TO ANALYZE POLITICAL DECISIONS[1]

INTRODUCTION

Several economists have won the Nobel Prize in economics for their analyses of decisions that voters and government officials make about taxation and public spending. One relatively new field in which these economists are working is known as public choice theory. A basic premise of public choice theory is that decision makers in the political marketplace are motivated primarily by self-interest. Elected officials, for example, do the things they do out of concern for their own reelection, their salaries, their reputation, and the power, and/or patronage they are able to wield.

It follows from this premise that politicians and government officials may support policies that are economically unwise if it is in their interest to do so. Pursuit of self-interest in these cases may cause a *government failure*—that is, a government intervention that causes a less efficient allocation of goods and resources than would have occured without that intervention. Government failure also occurs when the costs of a public policy clearly outweigh its benefits.

Some government programs are designed to produce widespread benefits. National defense, for example, yields benefits to a large number of people and spreads the costs over a large number of taxpayers. Other government programs benefit special interests. These programs (farm subsidy programs, for example) result in benefits for a few parties, with costs that are borne by many taxpayers. When the benefits of such programs are concentrated in a small group, this *special interest group*

will have a strong incentive to try to influence legislators in order to hold onto those benefits. In the legislative bargaining that ensues, elected representatives may be willing to vote for programs or policies that do not benefit their own constituents if, in return, other representatives will return the favor. According to public choice economists, this practice of *log-rolling,* or the trading of votes among legislators, is one important explanation for government failure.

LESSON DESCRIPTION

The students are introduced to the basics of public choice analysis by reference to two examples of government failure. They participate in mock elections and analyze the impact of special interest groups on legislators. They examine the costs of voting and assess those costs as disincentives that might discourage people from obtaining information before voting, or from voting at all. Finally, they examine the concept of log-rolling by role-playing U.S. senators who are considering whether or not to support a particular bill.

CONCEPTS

- Cost-benefit analysis
- Government failure
- Log-rolling
- Rational ignorance
- Special interest group effects

OBJECTIVES

Students will be able to:

[1] This lesson is based in part on the following sources: J. Dick, J. Blais, and P. Moore, *Focus on Economics: Civics and Government* (New York: National Council on Economic Education, 1996), Lesson 13; M. Watts, S. McCorkle, and B. Meszaros, *Focus: High School Economics* (New York: National Council on Economic Education, 2005), Lesson 13.

1. Define and provide examples of *government failure.*

2. Define *log-rolling.*

3. Explain why policies that cause government failures might continue to be used.

CONTENT STANDARDS
Economics (CEE Standards)

- There is an economic role for government in a market economy whenever the benefits of a government policy outweigh its costs. Governments often provide for national defense, address environmental concerns, define and protect property rights, and attempt to make markets more competitive. Most government policies also redistribute income. (Standard 16)

- Costs of government policies sometimes exceed benefits. This may occur because of incentives facing voters, government officials, and government employees, because of actions by special interest groups that can impose costs on the general public, or because social goals other than economic efficiency are being pursued. (Standard 17)

Civics and Government (NSCG Standards, Grades 9-12)

- Students should be able to evaluate, take, and defend positions on issues regarding the purposes, organization, and functions of the institutions of the national government. (Standard III.B.1)

- Students should be able to evaluate, take, and defend positions on issues regarding the major responsibilities of the national government for domestic and foreign policy. (Standard III. B.2)

- Students should be able to evaluate, take, and defend positions about the formation and implementation of public policy. (Standard III.D.6)

TIME REQUIRED
45 minutes

MATERIALS
- A transparency of Visuals 13.1, 13.2, 13.3, 13.4, 13.5
- A copy for each student of Activity 13.1
- Paper to be used as blank ballots in Activity 13.2
- A ballot box to be used in Activity 13.2
- Role-playing cards from Activity 13.3 to be printed, cut out, and distributed as outlined in the lesson procedures.

PROCEDURE
1. Tell the students that the purpose of this lesson is to use economic analysis—specifically, a branch of economics known as public choice theory—to examine the behavior of voters and the representatives they elect.

2. Distribute Activity 13.1. Have the students read the two fictionalized articles and complete the data chart that follows.

3. Progressively reveal the answers to the data chart exercise in Activity 13.1 by displaying Visual 13.1 as the students discuss their responses in class. Be certain to stress the costs of these two programs as well as the benefits. In addition, stress the unintended consequences of each program, and underscore the point that some costs lie in the future. Tell the students that cost-benefit analysis of this sort can help to explain why policies are often undertaken when costs are delayed until the future. An understanding of such behavior can help make us better decision-makers and more informed citizens.

4. Ask the students why Congress and the President would support policies for which the costs appear to outweigh the benefits. (*Accept a variety of answers at this point.*)

5. Display Visual 13.2. Explain the concept of ***government failure.*** Government failures occur when the costs of a government policy exceed the benefits, or when a government policy yields less in net benefits than a market solution would have yielded.

Explain the difference between government failures and **market failures** (air pollution, for example, may reflect a market failure caused by transactions in which costs "spill over" to people not involved in the transactions in question).

6. Why would members of Congress vote for policies that lead to government failure? Consider the case of a long-serving Senator from California who proposes a bill that would require additional safety features on all new automobiles produced in the United States. This policy would result in higher prices for all automobiles, and many people would question whether the extra safety benefits justify the additional costs. Senators from Ohio, Michigan, and Indiana (where U.S. auto production is concentrated) are opposed to the bill, but it eventually passes into law. What would lead this long-serving elected official—and the rest of the Senate—to vote for a bill that will increase the price of cars? Or, to take a different example (see Activity 13.1), why would an elected representative vote for a bill—such as the Energy Policy Act of 2005—that increases the price of food? (*Accept a variety of answers at this point.*)

7. Explain that while most elected officials try to serve their constituents, not all constituents are interested in the laws and policies their elected officials support. But most officials are interested in staying in office, and in order to get reelected they need to convince a majority of voters to vote for them. Thus, the Senator from California may know that her constituents are concerned about auto safety. Many of her constituents will pay higher prices for their cars if the new safety regulation is enacted, and some will object; but few will be affected enough to vote against the Senator for that reason alone. The California Senator might have also voted for the Energy Policy Act (perhaps proposed by the Senator from Indiana, where much corn is grown)—even though it means higher prices for food in the

Senator's state—if the other Senators will agree to vote for her bill. Few votes are likely to be lost by a Senator who votes for the Energy Policy Act, because the higher cost of food is so widely distributed across millions of U.S. families.

8. Display Visual 13.3 and briefly discuss the three main reasons for government failure.

9. Tell the students that you will now use three mock elections to illustrate three reasons for government failure (rational ignorance, special interest groups, and log-rolling) and why such failures—i.e., programs that cost more than they yield in benefits—can happen, even in a democratic system.

10. Divide the class evenly into five groups. (If the class is not divisible by five, assign some students to work outside the groups, assisting with vote tallies or making payments to the class.) Pass out the appropriate slip from Activity 13.2 to each group.

11. Explain the ground rules for the first two elections. The students will be voting for one of two programs, both of which would have some benefit (if passed) to the class at-large. But in these elections the students should not be guided by any concern for the class at-large. Instead, they should vote for one program or the other strictly on the basis of their own self-interest. In this activity, *self-interest* refers to the direct benefits a program would deliver to a given student (measured in dollars) if that program passed. The students should vote for the program that provides them the greatest individual benefit (as measured in dollars on Visual 13.4).

Election 1

12. Display Visual 13.4 and ask the students to look at the individual benefits associated with each program. Conduct the first election by asking which project (A or B) each student will vote for. To simulate a real election, distribute blank ballots to each student. Ask the students to mark their ballots, fold them in half, and bring

them to the front of the room. (An old shoe box with a slot cut in the top can serve as a ballot box.) Count (or have student assistants count) the votes and record the election results for the class to observe. Once the election has been completed, display Visual 13.4 again and fill in the chart, totaling up the benefits associated with each program. (Note: if there are five students in each group, total benefits [number of students x benefits per student] for Program A = 11,000; total benefits for Program B = 10,000.)

13. Ask the students:

- If Project A is approved, what would the total benefits to the class be? *(This will depend on how many students there are in each group; but, for example, if there are five students in each group, the total benefits would be $11,000.)*

- If Project B is approved, what would the total benefits to the class be? *(This will depend on how many students there are in each group; but, for example, if there are five students in each group, the total benefits would be $10,000.)*

- Why did Project A win the election? *(When all the students vote according to their self-interest, students in groups 3, 4, and 5 are better off if Project A wins.)*

- Did the results of this election lead to the greatest overall benefit for the class? *(Yes. Assuming there are five students in each group, the total overall benefit should be $11,000. If Project B had been approved, the overall benefit would have been only $10,000.)*

Election 2

14. Tell the students that sometimes elections do not result in the greatest overall benefit. Display Visual 13.4 again. Ask the students to vote again for either Project A or Project B, in their groups, by a show of hands. Record the votes (note that these should correspond with the results of Election 1), but first explain that you will

use a special rule this time for tallying the votes. Since groups 1 and 2 spent a lot of time and money lobbying for their project, you are going to allow each of their votes to count twice in tallying up the final vote totals. Then do the tally. Which project won this time? *(Project B.)* Which Project would have resulted in the greatest overall benefit? *(Assuming there are five students in each group, the overall benefit for Project A would be $11,000; the overall benefit for Project B would be $10,000.)* In this case, the project chosen is inefficient, since the total benefit of choosing the alternative (Project A) would be higher than the benefits yielded by Project B. In this case, lobbying pressures by special interest groups helped produce a socially undesirable outcome, which produces economic inefficiency.

15. Remind the students that, of course, people's votes don't count twice in real elections, unless someone is cheating. Still, this activity shows how a minority of voters could achieve an outcome that is not preferred by the majority. Lobbyists and special interest groups (who stand to gain much) often advocate for programs that benefit only a few (e.g., only three percent of Americans are engaged in agriculture, but agricultural subsidies are often passed by Congress).

Election 3

16. Draw attention to the fact that these first two elections had voter-participation rates of 100 percent. Tell the students that the highest voter-participation rate in presidential elections over the past 50 years has been only about 64 percent. Public choice economists explain this low rate by what they refer to as voters' ***rational ignorance.*** How could ignorance be rational? Given the time it takes to vote, the costs associated with becoming an informed voter (spending time reading newspapers or listening to debates, for example), and the likelihood that one's vote will not matter—since it is only one of thousands (or millions) of votes cast in

an election—many people decide it is more costly to vote than to abstain. Thus, these voters' decisions to remain uninformed reflect a rational cost-benefit analysis.

17. Tell the students that before the third election, you are going to charge each voter $500. This is not a poll tax; rather, it represents the "real cost" of voting. In this case, the real cost is the opportunity cost associated with the time and money it takes to vote (missed work, money for gas, daycare costs, etc.) as well as the time needed to become an informed voter (watching debates, reading campaign literature, surfing the Internet, etc.).

18. Ask the students to look closely at their information sheets and to stand up if they are going to vote. Distribute ballots to those standing. Ask them to mark their ballots, fold them in half, and bring them to the front of the room. Count (or have student assistants count) the votes and record the election results. Display Visual 13.4 again and discuss the results.

19. Few members of groups 3 and 4 should have voted this time, since they cannot be better off by voting (and may be worse off if Plan B passes). Some students in groups 1 and 2 may have decided to vote if they thought that Project B had a chance of winning (in which case, their net gain would be $500 for each student). Group 5 students also are likely to have voted only if they thought that Project A would pass, although (depending on how many students in groups 1 and 2 vote) they may end up being worse off if Project B is voted in. This activity illustrates peoples' rational ignorance in choosing, sometimes, not to vote. The costs of voting may seem to be greater than any potential benefits.

20. Discuss these results.

- Which project was approved? *(If Project B was approved, it was because voters had more information about the real cost of voting, relative to expected benefits; the information about costs may have led to fewer people to vote,*

changing the outcome from Election 1. If Project A was approved, it was most certainly a result of very low voter turnout.)

- Did Election 3 result in the greatest overall benefit? *(Not if Project B was approved.)*

21. Remind the students that voters incur real costs—in time and money—when they choose to vote. These costs have the same sort of impact as the $500 charged in this mock election—leading fewer people to vote.

22. Ask the students to reconvene as a whole class. Tell them that you will examine one more cause of government failure. It is known as **log-rolling.**

23. Assign the students to groups of three. Distribute a different one of the three role-playing cards from Activity 13.3 to each student in each group. Ask each student to read his or her card to the other students in the group.

24. Display Visual 13.5. Tell the students they will be voting on each of the two bills described on their cards. Tell them they should vote for a program only if the benefits to their constituents are greater than the costs. Have each group conduct a vote on each of the two programs.

25. Direct students to the questions on Visual 13.5:

- Which of these programs is economically efficient (i.e., yielding benefits that exceed costs)? *(Neither one.)*

- If this vote occurs in a key subcommittee of the Senate, does either bill move out of that committee? *(Both programs will be defeated if Senators vote according to what is best for their constituents. That is because, for each bill, the costs are greater than the benefits for two out of three Senators.)*

- If you were the Southwestern Senator, what could you do to try to get one of the other Senators to vote for the

Medicare increase? *(The Southwestern Senator might approach the Midwestern Senator and offer to vote for the dairy subsidy if, and only if, the Midwestern Senator voted for the Medicare increase. Or the Southwestern Senator might propose the same deal with the Eastern Senator.)*

- What role does the Eastern Senator play in this process? *(The Eastern Senator has a swing vote that can help determine whether either program is approved. If the other two senators are ineffective at achieving a log-rolling result, the Eastern Senator will have a lot of influence over the final legislative outcome.)*

26. Tell the students that such log-rolling could lead to both bills being sent along to the Senate, despite the fact that neither one is economically efficient. Such deal-making goes on all of the time, with elected representatives trading off their votes on projects that do not benefit their constituents in order to get votes for projects that do.

CLOSURE

1. Briefly review the key points of the lesson (government failure, rational ignorance, special interest effect, log-rolling). Remind the students that many factors can lead to government failure, but that, for the most part, government failures can be traced back to the fact that people (voters, elected officials, etc.) tend to act in their own self-interest. Certainly there are times when government programs address the general public interest. Often enough, however, the factors addressed in this lesson can lead to inefficiencies in government policies and programs.

2. Introduce the following case:

- In 2006, the San Jose (CA) Earthquakes of Major League Soccer announced a plan to build a new soccer stadium. One option was to have the

stadium funded primarily by the city residents, through a tax increase. Projects of this sort have become common. Many large American cities have built stadiums to keep (or to win) professional sports franchises, arguing that the increased revenue and high profile that comes with having a professional sports team is worth the cost of building a stadium.

- Ask the students to analyze this case, using their knowledge of public choice economics. To facilitate the discussion, use some or all of the following questions:

A. Who benefits from the decision to use tax money to pay for the stadium? *(The users of the stadium—the team, the players, the owners, the soccer fans, the businesses surrounding the new stadium, those employed to build the stadium, etc.)*

B. Are the benefits concentrated among relatively few people in the city or are they widespread? *(They are most likely concentrated in the hands of relatively few individuals.)*

C. What are the costs of using tax money to pay for the stadium? *(Taxpayers who have no interest in professional soccer are forced to help pay for the stadium through taxation. Therefore, many people bearing the costs of the policy will receive no benefits from it.)*

D. Are the costs spread out over many people in the city? *(Yes.)*

E. Do you think most taxpayers will be interested in this issue? Is it likely to spark a taxpayers' revolt? *(Answers will vary. Many publicly funded stadiums have been built despite vocal opposition from taxpayers.)*

ASSESSMENT

Multiple-Choice Questions

1. Three key reasons for government failure are

   A. log-rolling, rational ignorance, opportunity cost.

   B. **log-rolling, special interest group effects, rational ignorance.**

   C. log-rolling, opportunity cost, special interest group effects.

   D. log-rolling, opportunity cost, deceptive advertising.

2. Government failure is characterized by which of these conditions?

   A. The cost of a government program outweighs the benefits the program yields.

   B. A government program allocates resources less efficiently than a market solution would.

   C. A government program is put in place because elected officials and voters are pursuing their own self-interest.

   D. **All of the above.**

Constructed-Response Question

In 1971, the U.S. Congress established the "for profit" National Railroad Passenger Corporation (Amtrak). Amtrak has since become the nation's only passenger rail system. Over the last 35 years, however, Amtrak has failed to turn a profit and has been funded primarily with $25 billion in taxpayer subsidies. While Amtrak carried more than 33 million passenger trips in 2005, estimates indicate that more than 80 percent of Amtrak riders rode trains in the high-traffic corridors between New York City and Washington, D.C. Other estimates indicate that Amtrak accounts for only one percent of all the miles traveled in the United States, and that travel on Amtrak costs (including the government subsidies) twice as much as travel by plane or bus.

Using your knowledge of public choice economics, analyze this information about Amtrak and answer the following questions:

- Is Amtrak an example of government failure? Be specific. *(Answers will vary, but should include the point that subsidies of $25 billion have been required to support Amtrak.)*

- Why would Congress allocate tax money to fund Amtrak? *(The benefits are highly concentrated among relatively few people who are likely to have a very strong voice in promoting the continuation of existing policy.)*

- Who benefits from Amtrak? Does Amtrak benefit people who don't ride the trains? *(The benefits go largely to travelers in high-traffic corridors on the east coast. Those who use other modes of travel—air, bus, subways, automobiles—experience less congestion as a result of the existence of Amtrak.)*

- Why haven't more taxpayers complained about this use of their tax dollars? *(The cost of subsidizing Amtrak is relatively small for each individual taxpayer; therefore, even those who are opposed to these subsidies have little incentive to voice their opposition or launch an opposition movement.)*

VISUAL 13.1

NEWSPAPER ACCOUNTS

	"Thousands March on Mexico…"	**"Steel Tariffs…"**
Main topic	• U.S. policy on Ethanol(E)85 drives up corn prices • Tortilla price increases in Mexico spark protests	• Tariffs imposed on imports of foreign steel • Costs of products in which steel is an important input likely to rise
Policy	• Energy Policy Act of 2005 requires 7.5 billion gallons of renewable fuel by 2012 • 51 cent per-gallon subsidy for processing corn into ethanol	• 8% to 30% tariff on imported steel • Enacted to prevent "dumping" of low-priced steel
Benefits of policy	• Some reduction of foreign oil use • Corn price increase benefits corn farmers	• Prices paid to U.S. steel firms increased • Steel jobs "saved"
Costs of policy	• Increased prices on all goods made with corn • Impact felt by poor consumers of corn-based tortillas	• Cost per job saved ($1.18 million) • Increased costs for all things made with steel (construction, cars, etc.)

VISUAL 13.2

MARKET FAILURE VS. GOVERNMENT FAILURE

Market Failure

A *market failure* occurs when markets are not working optimally. The result of such failure will be economic inefficiency. In other words, the market will fail to allocate scarce resources in a way that serves the general public interest. In cases of market failure, government intervention may be used to protect the public's interest.

Government Failure

A *government failure* occurs (1) when government intervention causes scarce resources to be allocated less efficiently than they other-wise would have been allocated, or (2) when the costs of the government intervention exceed the benefits. Government failures may become entrenched, preventing policy makers from adopting more efficient market-based solutions to the problems in question.

Costs (taxes, increased prices, etc.) of government programs or policies

Benefits of government intervention (e.g., program, policy, etc.)

VISUAL 13.3

THREE MAIN REASONS WHY GOVERNMENT FAILURES OCCUR

1. **Rational Ignorance:**

   Voters may think that it is not worthwhile to take the time and trouble needed to become well informed about issues or candidates at stake in an election. Their vote is not likely to make a difference in an election, anyway, they may believe, so it probably does not matter how they vote, or whether they vote at all. It therefore seems rational to avoid the costs of becoming well informed. Legislators may make a similar decision by declining to take the trouble to learn about the issues at stake in legislative proceedings.

2. **Special Interest Group Effects:**

   Legislators often vote for policies that do not benefit their constituents but do benefit well-organized special interest groups. For example, trade associations may lobby elected representatives to enact tax breaks for the industry that the associations represent.

3. **Log-rolling:**

   Log-rolling is the process by which legislators trade votes. Legislator Kazmarek might vote for a bill that does not benefit her constituency—if Legislator Gonzalas agrees to vote for Kazmarek's bill in return.

VISUAL 13.4

THE COSTS AND BENEFITS OF VOTING

Group	# of students	Project A		Project B	
		Benefits per student	Total Group Benefits	Benefits per student	Total Group Benefits
1		$100		$1,000	
2		$100		$1,000	
3		$500		$0	
4		$500		$0	
5		$1,000		$0	
Total					

1. If Project A is approved, what are the total benefits to the class?

2. If Project B is approved, what are the total benefits to the class?

VISUAL 13.5
"YOU VOTE FOR MY BILL..."

	(Dollar values in millions)			
	Dairy Subsidy		Medicare Increase	
	Benefits to Constituents	Costs to Constituents	Benefits to Constituents	Costs to Constituents
Eastern Senator	$5	$20	$5	$20
Midwestern Senator	40	20	5	20
Southwestern Senator	5	20	40	20

VISUAL 13.5, CONTINUED

"YOU VOTE FOR MY BILL..."

1. Which of these bills is economically efficient (i.e., the benefits to constituents exceed the costs)?

2. Which bill will get out of the subcommittee with majority approval?

3. If you were the Southwestern Senator, what could you do to convince one of the other Senators to vote for the Medicare increase?

4. What role does the Eastern Senator play in this process?

ACTIVITY 13.1

NEWSPAPER ACCOUNTS

Directions: Read each of the fictional newspaper articles below (they are based on real newspaper reports). When you have finished reading each article, complete the appropriate sections of the data chart that follows.

Newspaper Article 1: Thousands March on Mexico City[2]

February 2007

Inter-Agency News Service

Recently more than 100,000 residents joined a protest march through the streets of Mexico City. What were they protesting? A new government policy? The U.S. presence in Iraq? No. They were protesting the rising price of tortillas.

Tortillas, the flat-bread made from corn, has long been a staple of the Mexican diet, especially for poorer Mexicans. When tortilla prices more than doubled in January 2007, many Mexicans took to the streets in protest. Many of them blamed one particular United States government policy for the massive price increase.

U.S. Policy in Renewable Fuels

In an attempt to address growing concerns over reliance on foreign oil and global warming, the U.S. Congress passed the Energy Policy Act of 2005. One part of the Act specified a Renewable Fuels Standard (RFS), which requires the United States to produce 7.5 billion gallons of renewable fuel by 2012. The most popular renewable fuel, by far, has been Ethanol85 (E85). E85 is made in the United States by distilling corn into ethyl alcohol. In order to entice gasoline producers to produce more E85, the RFS included a 51 cent per gallon subsidy. The corn market has responded—the United States Department of Agriculture (USDA) estimated that 20 percent of the U.S. corn crop went to ethanol production in 2006, and that this surpassed the amount of corn exported from the United States. Many critics contend that the U. S. Congress and other policymakers failed to consider the law of unintended consequences when it adopted the RFS.

---

[2] Sources: C. Carter and H. Miller, "Hidden costs of corn-based ethanol," *Christian Science Monitor,* May 21, 2007 (accessed at http://www.csmonitor.com/2007/0521/p09s02-coop.html on July 27, 2007); BBC News, "Mexicans stage tortilla protest," *BBC News online,* February 1, 2007 (accessed at http://news.bbc.co.uk/2/hi/americas/6319093.stm on July 27, 2007); Institute for Agriculture and Trade Policy (December 2006), *Staying home: How ethanol will change U.S. corn exports (*accessed at http://www.agobservatory.org/library.cfm?refid=96658 on July 27, 2007).

ACTIVITY 13.1, CONTINUED

NEWSPAPER ACCOUNTS

U.S. Corn Farmers and the Corn Market

Until recently, more than 60 percent of the U.S. corn crop went to feed livestock. Thus, thousands of food items contain byproducts of corn (e.g., anything made from these animals or with corn syrup). Because of increased demand for corn from ethanol producers, the price of corn doubled from $2.00 per bushel in 2005 to $4.00 per bushel in 2006. Because corn is an important input in so many products, the prices consumers pay for these products increased.

The USDA predicts that as demand for ethanol increases, the additional corn needed for its production will be diverted from the export market.

Mexican Consumers

Corn farmers continue to respond to the incentives (i.e., subsidies) of the RFS program and to divert corn from food to fuel production. If this means less corn going to Mexican tortilla production, the impact on consumers of corn tortillas could be huge. Many observers, in Mexico and the United States, wonder whether the overall costs of the RFS (increased food prices, government subsidies that must be paid for by higher taxes) outweigh the benefits (marginally decreased dependence on oil, the use of a renewable fuel source, etc.). When the costs of government policies exceed the benefits, economists call the result a *government failure*. But residents of Mexico City aren't concerned with what to call it. They just know that the cost of tortillas grows higher each day.

Newspaper Article 2: President George W. Bush Imposes Tariffs on Imported Steel[3]

October 18, 2003

International Independent Press

Washington

On March 5, 2002, President Bush imposed tariffs of 8 percent to 30 percent on several types of steel that are imported into the United States. He did this in an effort to help the U.S. steel industry, claiming that the tariffs were needed to protect the industry from foreign steel that had been "dumped" in the United States at very low prices.

---

[3] Sources: *USA Today* (March 2002), "Bush Imposes Steel Tariffs" (accessed at http://www.usatoday.com/money/general/2002/03/05/bush-steel.htm on July 23, 2007); "Visclosky Asks Tariffs Be Kept in Place for Long Steel Products" (July 2003; accessed at http://www.house.gov/visclosky/archive/itc030724.html on July 30, 2007); P. Visclosky, "Perspective: Inside Indiana Business" (accessed at http://www.insideindianabusiness.com/authors.asp?D=127, June 3, 2009); "Pat's Problem," *Investor's Business Daily,* February 22, 1996 (accessed at http://www.ncpa.org/pd/trade/tradeb.html on July 30, 2007); A. Blinder, *Hard Heads, Soft Hearts* (Reading, MA: Addison-Wesley, 1987); World Trade Organization (2007), "10 Benefits of the WTO Trading System" (accessed at http://www.wto.org/english/thewto_e/whatis_e/10ben_e/10b00_e.htm on July 30, 2007).

ACTIVITY 13.1, CONTINUED

NEWSPAPER ACCOUNTS

Congressman Pete Visclosky represents a steel-producing district in Indiana. He is a strong supporter of the tariffs. The tariffs, he has stated, "are doing the job they were intended to do, but that job is only partly done [and] I will keep fighting to keep these safeguards in place, for the sake of good-paying steelworker jobs and the families those jobs support."

Many observers criticized these tariffs as violating free trade agreements and as imposing hidden costs on the American consumer. Visclosky, in testimony before Congress, noted that the tariffs have led to higher prices for steel products. "Steel bar prices in June 2003 were 9.4 percent higher than in March 2002, the month in which the President announced his decision."

Economist Alan Blinder has written about the hidden costs (e.g., higher prices, less competition, etc.) of invoking tariffs to "save jobs." He cites several well-known studies that estimate the average, inflation-adjusted cost of using tariffs to save manufacturing jobs at $661,500 (in 2005 dollars) per job saved—with steel jobs costing as much as $1.18 million (in 2005 dollars) per job saved.

Such protectionism is costly because it leads to increased prices on key inputs such as steel, thereby causing the costs of production for many goods to increase (because the domestic steel used in production is more expensive). This ultimately leads to increased prices of finished goods and services, and a higher cost of living.

Manufacturing is not the only industry to seek out such protection, however. In one famous example, the World Trade Organization estimated that the $350 billion in agricultural subsidies paid annually by consumers and governments in rich countries is enough to "fly their 41 million dairy cows first class around the world one and a half times."

Why don't citizens protest such costly governmental policies? Alan Blinder says the reason is that protectionism's "allure stems not from the economics of national interest, but from the politics of special interest." Blinder says that concentrated and highly visible gains for a small minority (for example, steel workers) can be gained through policies that impose small, almost invisible costs on the majority (i.e., consumers generally). But Blinder is very clear when he concludes that the costs (no matter how small to the individual consumer) of such protectionism are significantly greater than any benefits.

ACTIVITY 13.1, CONTINUED

Data Chart

	"Thousands March on Mexico…"	"Steel Tariffs…"
Main topic		
Policy		
Benefits of policy		
Costs of policy		

ACTIVITY 13.2
STUDENT INFORMATION SHEET FOR ELECTIONS 1 AND 3

Group 1

    If Project A is approved, you will receive $100

    If Project B is approved, you will receive $1,000

Group 2

    If Project A is approved, you will receive $100

    If Project B is approved, you will receive $1,000

Group 3

    If Project A is approved, you will receive $500

    If Project B is approved, you will receive $0

Group 4

    If Project A is approved, you will receive $500

    If Project B is approved, you will receive $0

Group 5

    If Project A is approved, you will receive $1,000

    If Project B is approved, you will receive $0

ACTIVITY 13.3
ROLE-PLAYING CARDS

You are playing the Southwestern Senator

Your state is located in the Southwest, where the leading industries are tourism and citrus products. The average age of your constituents is well above the national average because many people move to your state to retire and get away from the cold northern winters. In an attempt to win reelection, you have promised you will do every thing you can to raise the standard of living of your state's elderly retired residents.

Program 1: Dairy Subsidy

Through this program, dairy farmers who sell milk below the prices set by the Federal government will receive payments equal to the difference. While total subsidy payments will equal $1 billion next year, dairy farms in your state expect to receive only about $5 million. Taxes to pay for the subsidy will cost your state $20 million dollars.

Program 2: Increased Medicare Coverage for Prescription Drugs

If this legislation passes, overall benefits to Medicare patients will increase by $500 million. Because your state has a large elderly population, your residents will receive a total of $40 million in these benefits. Taxes to pay for the increase will cost your state $20 million dollars.

You are playing the Midwestern Senator

Your state is located in the Midwest, where the leading industries are dairy and agriculture. The average age of your constituents is about the national average. In an attempt to win reelection, you have promised you will do everything you can to raise the standard of living of your state's dairy-farm owners.

Program 1: Dairy Subsidy

Through this program, dairy farmers who sell milk below the prices set by the Federal government will receive payments equal to the difference. While total subsidy payments will equal $1 billion next year, dairy farms in your state expect to receive only about $40 million. Taxes to pay for the subsidy will cost your state $20 million dollars.

Program 2: Increased Medicare Coverage for Prescription Drugs

If this legislation passes, overall benefits to Medicare patients will increase by $500 million. Because your state does not have a very large elderly population, your residents will receive only $5 million in these benefits. Taxes to pay for the increase will cost your state $20 million.

ACTIVITY 13.3, CONTINUED
ROLE-PLAYING CARDS

You are playing the Eastern Senator

Your state is located in the East, where the leading industries are manufacturing, fishing, tourism, and some agriculture. The average age of your constituents is about the national average. In an attempt to win reelection, you have promised you will do everything you can to encourage the growth of high-tech industries in your state.

Program 1: Dairy Subsidy

Through this program dairy farmers who sell milk below the prices set by the Federal government will receive payments equal to the difference. While total subsidy payments will equal $1 billion next year, dairy farms in your state expect to receive only about $5 million. Taxes to pay for the subsidy will cost your state $20 million.

Program 2: Increased Medicare Coverage for Prescription Drugs

If this legislation passes, overall benefits to Medicare patients will increase by $500 million. Because your state does not have a very large elderly population, your residents will receive only $5 million in these benefits. Taxes to pay for the increase will cost your state $20 million.

FOCUS: UNDERSTANDING ECONOMICS IN CIVICS AND GOVERNMENT © COUNCIL FOR ECONOMIC EDUCATION, NEW YORK, NY

LESSON 14

ECONOMIC SANCTIONS AND U.S. FOREIGN POLICY

LESSON 14
ECONOMIC SANCTIONS AND U.S. FOREIGN POLICY

INTRODUCTION

Economic sanctions are economic penalties imposed by one country (the sender) on another country (the target) for punishment or to express displeasure with actions taken by the target nation. Often, such sanctions are used as part of one nation's foreign policy and are imposed in an attempt to influence another nation's policies. Economic sanctions include tariffs, trade barriers, import duties, embargoes, import or export quotas, and the cutting off of foreign aid.

Sanctions have been used throughout history. During the Peloponnesian War, Pericles, in order to secure the return of sacred land taken by the Megarians, issued a decree banning all trade with the Megarians, and the ban eventually strangled the Megarian economy. Far more recently, the United States has used economic sanctions in support of its overall foreign policy. Some examples include the United States trade embargo against Cuba (1962-present), aimed at toppling the regime of Fidel Castro, and sanctions imposed on the Soviet Union in the mid-1970s in an attempt to improve Soviet treatment of Russian Jews. Also, the United Nations imposed economic sanctions against Iraq prior to the invasion of 2003.

Economic sanctions have been used to destabilize governments, disrupt military action, and bring about major policy changes. One example of success in the use of sanctions is the economic boycott that eventually led, in 1991, to the end of apartheid policies in South Africa.

But sanctions are not always successful. One analysis shows, in fact, that only about one third of economic sanctions have been successful.[1] In any given case, the likelihood of success is a function of the relative size of the target country, the strength of the countries' trade relationship, and the kind of policy changes the target is expected to undertake. Major policy shifts (e.g., troop withdrawals) are rarely brought about by economic sanctions.

Finally, economic sanctions have costs. When mutually beneficial exchange between nations is interrupted (through trade embargoes or other trade barriers), both sides bear costs. For the target nation, this means not getting certain goods or aid payments. The nation that imposes the sanction also bears costs, often in terms of lost trade revenue and higher prices for goods normally imported from the target nation.

LESSON DESCRIPTION

The students analyze cases in which the United States has imposed economic sanctions on other countries. They examine the characteristics of successful economic sanctions and apply their knowledge to predict the likelihood of the success of U.S. economic sanctions in three countries.

CONCEPTS

- Barriers to trade
- Economic sanctions
- Exports
- Imports
- Regulation
- Role of government
- Trade

---

[1] Gary Hufbauer, Diane T. Berliner, and Kimberly A. Elliot, *Economic Sanctions Reconsidered, 2d Ed.* (Washington, D.C.: Institute for International Economics, 1990).

OBJECTIVES

Students will be able to:

1. Define and provide examples of economic sanctions from recent U.S. history.

2. Explain how economic sanctions have been part of U.S. foreign policy.

3. Analyze factors that make sanctions more or less effective.

4. Predict in which of three scenarios U.S. economic sanctions will be successful.

CONTENT STANDARDS

Economics (CEE Standards)

- There is an economic role for government in a market economy whenever the benefits of a government policy outweigh its costs. Governments often provide for national defense, address environmental concerns, define and protect property rights, and attempt to make markets more competitive. Most government policies also redistribute income. (Standard 16)

- Costs of government policies sometimes exceed benefits. This may occur because of incentives facing voters, government officials, and government employees, because of actions by special interest groups that can impose costs on the general public, or because social goals other than economic efficiency are being pursued. (Standard 17)

Civics and Government (NSCG Standards, Grades 9-12)

- Students should be able to evaluate, take, and defend positions about how United States foreign policy is made and the means by which it is carried out. (Standard IV.B.2)

- Students should be able to evaluate, take, and defend positions on foreign policy issues in light of American national interests, values, and principles. (Standard IV.B.3)

TIME REQUIRED

45 minutes

MATERIALS

- A transparency of Visuals 14.1, 14.2, 14.3, and 14.4

- A copy for each student of Activity 14.1 and 14.2

PROCEDURE

1. Display Visual 14.1. Ask the students to read each headline as it is revealed. Ask the students: What do these headlines, spanning nearly seven years, have in common? (*They all deal with foreign nations and they all describe economic sanctions.*)

2. Ask the students: Have you heard of the term *economic sanction*? If they have, ask them to offer a tentative definition of it.

3. Tell the students that not all sanctions are applied in far-off places. In fact, it is possible that some of them have been on the receiving end of a personal form of economic sanction. Ask:

   - How many of you have had your allowance cut, or have lost access to the family automobile, or have had your cell phone or landline phone privileges cut? (*Answers will vary, but chances are that students can think of some occasion on which their behavior was sanctioned.*)

   - Why do you think your parents or others would impose these sanctions on you? (*To curtail certain behaviors, or as punishment, or to achieve a particular result, etc.*) Explain that nations often act like their parents, imposing economic sanctions on other nations in an effort to achieve some desired goal.

4. Display Visual 14.2 and briefly review Parts 1 and 2 with the students. Make certain that the students can distinguish between sender nations and target nations.

5. Refer again to cases in which parents might have imposed sanctions of some sort on students. Ask: Why do you think your parents chose the specific sanctions of

cutting your allowance, restricting use
of the family car, taking away phone
privileges, etc? (*These sanctions touch on
privileges that serve as strong incentives
for teens. Taking such privileges away, or
restricting them, could be very effective as
punishments for breaking curfew, misusing
the family car, etc. The sanctions might
prevent something from happening again,
or they might encourage better decision
making.*)

6. Remind the students that people (and
nations) often respond to economic incentives in predictable ways. Because of this,
economic sanctions have been part of the
foreign policy of nations since the time of
Pericles (432 BC). Review with students
Part 3 of Visual 14.2 ("History of Economic
Sanctions") and discuss some of the recent,
notable sanctions imposed by the United
States. Point out that, as of 2007, the
United States maintained ongoing economic sanctions against 13 target nations
and regions. Ask: Do you recall any background information about why these sanctions were imposed by the United States?
(E.g., *North Korea—nuclear weapons
development; Sudan—Darfur region.*)

7. Distribute Activity 14.1. Have the students
read the two case studies and complete the
summary activity. When the students
have completed their work, discuss each
case. Here are some sample responses:

Cuba

a. *Cuba*

b. *1960- present*

c. *Bans on all trade with Cuba; travel
bans*

d. *"Promote peaceful transition to democracy and respect for human rights in
Cuba…"*

Burma/Myanmar

a. *Burma/ Myanmar*

b. *1988-present*

c. *No arms sales and no U.S. foreign aid
except humanitarian assistance*

d. *"…encourage a transition to democratic
rule and greater respect for human
rights…"*

8. Display Visual 14.3, Part 1. Reveal the
quotation from economist Jeffery Sachs.
Read Sachs's claim with the students and
ask whether any evidence from the two
case studies supports his claim (*In both
cases, the sanctions have been in place for
a long time [Cuba, for over 45 years;
Burma/Myanmar, for more than 20
years]—the long time periods implying that
the sanctions have not had the desired
impact.*)

9. Reveal Part 2 of Visual 14.3 and discuss
the results of the research done by
Hufbauer, Schott, and Elliot (1990).
Emphasize the point that, over the 75-year
period studied, only one third of the sanctions were deemed successful.

10. Also emphasize the point that not all sanctions are alike. The research summarized
in Part 2 identifies certain characteristics
of economic sanctions that are more likely
than others to prove successful.

11. Distribute Activity 14.2. Direct the students to complete Part 1 of this activity.
They should circle the statements that
identify characteristics likely to increase
the effectiveness of economic sanctions.
After the students have finished, reveal
the answers. (*Statements 1, 3, 5, 6, 11.*)

12. Review this portion of Activity 14.2 by
discussing examples of statements that
identify characteristics of successful
sanctions:

• The sender nation seeks minor changes
in the target nation's policies. (*Minor
policy changes such as drug enforcement or travel restrictions.*)

• The sender has a strong economy; the
target has a weak economy. (*If a target's GDP per capita is small relative to
the sender, then the target is more likely*

to adopt desired policies.)

- The target and the sender have a close trade relationship. (*Targets that rely on the sender for a large proportion of trade are more likely to be influenced by the sanctions.*)

- The sender is a big country relative to the target. (*If the target is a very small nation, the implied threat of sanction from a large nation may be enough to bring about policy changes.*)

- The target and the sender have a history of trade. (*Long-time trading partners are more likely to compromise with one another.*)

- The target is a "friend" of the sender. (*If the target and sender have strong diplomatic relations, then the sanctions can spark negotiations that lead to desirable outcomes for the sender.*)

13. Introduce the case study activity presented in Part 2 of Activity 14.2. Tell the students that they will analyze three real cases of U.S. economic sanctions. In each case, they will try to predict whether or not the sanctions in question will be effective, based on the characteristics discussed in Visual 14.3 and the first part of Activity 14.2. Ask the students to complete Part 2 of Activity 14.2 on their own. When they have finished their work, create groups of three or four students. Allow five minutes for each group to discuss its analysis and arrive at a consensus prediction for each case. Poll the groups and briefly discuss the results. (*Students should note that in each of the three cases a number of characteristics are not met. Therefore, questions remain as to whether any of these three sanctions programs will be effective in meeting the stated policy goals. Sample responses are given below.*)

	Syria	*Iran*	*North Korea*
Goals of the sanction: seek minor changes in policy?	*Score:* 0 *Rationale: End of military intervention is not minor.*	*Score:* 0 *Rationale:* *End state- sponsored terrorism and end nuclear program are major policy issues.*	*Score:* 0 *Rationale:* *Stop development of nuclear weapons and support human rights are major policy issues.*
Target has a weak economy relative to the U.S.?	*Score:* 3 *Rationale:* *Very low per capita GDP.*	*Score:* 1 *Rationale:* *Low per capita GDP.*	*Score:* 5 *Rationale:* *Extremely low per capita GDP.*
U.S. has a close trade relationship with target?	*Score:* 1 *Rationale:* *U.S. trade with Syria is $438 million.*	*Score:* 0 *Rationale:* *U.S. has very small share of trade with Iran.*	*Score:* 0 *Rationale:* *U.S. trade with North Korea is basically non-existent.*

	Syria	*Iran*	*North Korea*
Target has a small population relative to the U.S.?	*Score:* 5 *Rationale:* Small population.	*Score:* 3 *Rationale:* Small to moderate-sized population.	*Score:* 5 *Rationale:* Small population.
The target is a "friend" of the U.S.?	*Score:* 0 *Rationale:* Not a friend.	*Score:* 0 *Rationale:* Not a friend.	*Score:* 0 *Rationale:* Not a friend.
TOTAL SCORE	**9**	**4**	**10**
Prediction: *(Likely to succeed,* *Uncertain,* *Unlikely to succeed)*	*Unlikely*	*Unlikely*	*Unlikely*

CLOSURE

1. Review the definition of *economic sanctions* with the students. Ask them to recall several notable examples of U.S. economic sanctions (*e.g., regarding Cuba, South Africa, etc.*). Ask: If sanctions are effective only about one third of the time—and you have doubts about their effectiveness in the three case studies examined—why does the United States continue to use them? (*Among other things, there may be political reasons to adopt sanctions; U.S. citizens may be willing to tolerate the lack of success of economic sanctions in order to achieve a feeling of having done the right thing.*)

2. Display Visual 14.4. Ask: What are the "other goals of economic sanctions" mentioned here?

   (*Asserting national resolve; upholding international norms.*)

3. Given the overall analysis of sanctions presented in this lesson, do you think that economic sanctions should continue to be used as components of U.S. foreign policy? (*Answers will vary.*)

ASSESSMENT
Multiple-Choice Questions

1. Which of the following conditions makes economic sanctions more likely to be effective?

   A. The sender nation and the target nation have populations of about the same size.

   B. The target nation has never engaged in trade with the sender nation before.

   C. The target is not friendly with the sender.

   D. The sender and the target have a close trade relationship.

2. Which of the following is NOT a recognized goal for which economic sanctions can be effective?

   A. Destabilize the target nation.

   B. Disrupt a major military action by the target nation.

   C. Change minor policies of target nation.

   D. Demonstrate sender's national resolve.

3. According to research, economic sanctions are effective at meeting the stated goals of the sender about

   A. one half of the time.

   B. one third of the time.

   C. ten percent of the time.

   D. almost always.

Constructed-Response Question

Gabon President Omar Bongo (1935 -) once stated, "Economic sanctions rarely achieve the desired results." Based on what you have learned about economic sanctions, do you agree with Bongo? Why or why not? Should economic sanctions continue to be used in the conduct of U.S. foreign policy? Why or why not? (*While success in the use of sanctions is not a rarity, economic sanctions achieve their desired results only in about one case out of three. There are both benefits and costs associated with economic sanctions, and many of these benefits are related to non-economic goals. Therefore, whether or not economic sanctions should be part of U.S. foreign policy is a highly subjective question.*)

VISUAL 14.1
HEADLINES RELATED TO ECONOMIC SANCTIONS

Sudan: U.S. Sanctions to Have Little Fiscal Impact

(N.Y. Times, May 30, 2007)

Bush Tightens Sanctions on Sudan Over Darfur

(N.Y. Times, May 30, 2007)

Time to End Sanctions - Iraq's Young Have Suffered
Enough

(Milwaukee Journal Sentinel, August 20, 2000)

Bush Puts Economic Sanctions on Syria – Says It
Seeks Weapons of Mass Destruction

(Philadelphia Inquirer, May 12, 2004)

Bush Urges End to Iraq Sanctions: He Calls on UN to
Drop Curbs From 1991

(International Herald Tribune, April 17, 2003)

Report Written for United Nations Says Economic
Sanctions Don't Work and Are Often Illegal

(St. Louis Post-Dispatch, August 16, 2000)

Iraq Sanctions Complicate Terrorism Fight

(The [S.C]. State, April 15, 2002)

VISUAL 14.2

ECONOMIC SANCTIONS

Part 1: Definition

Economic sanctions are trade restrictions or other financial restrictions used by one country to punish another country, or to force another country to change its policies, or to show displeasure with another country's policies.

- The *Sender Nation* applies the sanctions.
- The *Target Nation* receives the sanctions.

Part 2: Goals of Economic Sanctions

- Change a target nation's policy in some way
- Destabilize the target nation
- Disrupt a minor military action by the target nation (e.g., amassing troops on another nation's borders)
- Impair the military potential of the target nation

Part 3: The History of Economic Sanctions

- Economic sanctions date from the time of Pericles (432 BC)
- Notable U.S. sanctions:
    - U.S. sanctions against Cuba (1960 – present)
    - U.S. boycott of Panamanian goods (1987-1990) to force Panamanian dictator Manuel Noriega out of power
    - U.S. sanctions against South Africa (1962-1994) to end South Africa's apartheid racial policy
    - U.S. sanctions against China to foster human rights (1989)

VISUAL 14.2, CONTINUED
ECONOMIC SANCTIONS

The U.S. (as of 2007) applies sanctions against 13 nations or regions:

The Balkans

Belarus

Burma

Cote d'Ivoire (Ivory Coast)

Cuba

The Democratic Republic of the Congo

Iran

Iraq

The former Liberian Regime of Charles Taylor

North Korea

Sudan

Syria

Zimbabwe

Visual 14.3

When Sanctions Don't Work...

Part 1: Symbols or Effective Tools?

"[S]anctions are mainly a symbolic stand for justice. But they are not symbolic in their effects. They are economically destructive and only occasionally politically productive. America's misguided sanctions against Myanmar, for example, have done nothing in the past year to resolve the country's political and economic crisis.... Sanctions should be lifted because they do not work."

> —Economist Jeffrey D. Sachs (*Financial Times*, 28 July 2004, p. 17)

Part 2: What Can We Learn from Research?

In 1990, three scholars (Hufbauer, Schott, and Elliott) reported a study of 116 cases of economic sanctions used in support of foreign policy goals from 1914-1990. Their findings can be summarized as follows:

- Sanctions were effective only 1/3 of the time.

- Sanctions were more likely to be effective when:

  - The sender nation seeks minor changes in the target nation's policies.

  - The sender has a strong economy; the target has a weak economy.

  - The target and the sender have a close trade relationship.

  - The sender is a big country relative to the target.

  - The target and the sender have a history of trade.

  - The target is a "friend" of the sender.

VISUAL 14.4
GAO REPORT ON ECONOMIC SANCTIONS[2]

In 1992, the U.S. General Accounting Office (GAO) produced a report for Congress. Among the GAO's conclusions were the following:

Other goals of sanctions, such as demonstrating national resolve or punishing misbehavior of the target to uphold international norms…may be more crucial than the stated primary goal. These [other] goals may in fact be motivating factors for imposing economic sanctions. And, sanctions are often better at fulfilling these other goals.

For example, the publicly perceived primary purpose of U.S. sanctions in 1980 against the Soviet Union was to compel Soviet withdrawal from Afghanistan. Yet, evidence indicates that President Jimmy Carter believed the more realistic and important objectives of sanctions were showing resolve and deterring Soviet incursions into Iran, Pakistan, or the Persian Gulf, which he considered strategically more important (pp. 3-4).

[2] Source: United States General Accounting Office. Economic Sanctions: Effectiveness as Tools of Foreign Policy. Washington, DC: GAO, 1992. Accessed at http://archive.gao.gov/t2pbat6/146166.pdf on June 1, 2007.

ACTIVITY 14.1
Case Studies in Economic Sanctions

Directions: Read the following two case studies of economic sanctions and complete the summary section that follows. Pay close attention to why the sanctions were imposed on the target nations.

Cuba[3]

The time is February 1960, and Cuba and the Soviet Union sign a trade agreement in which the Soviet Union agrees to buy sugar and other items from Cuba and to supply Cuba with crude oil. President Dwight D. Eisenhower cancels most of the Cuban sugar quota to be imported into the United States. Cuba retaliates by expropriating (taking) all U.S. property, valued at about $1 billion, in Cuba, and outlaws the import of U.S. products. In February 1962, the United States bans virtually all imports from Cuba.

U. S. sanctions against Cuba continue, and in March 1999, Alan Larson, U.S. Assistant Secretary of State, states: "Our policy is to promote a peaceful transition to democracy and respect for human rights in Cuba in four ways: (1) pressure on the government through economic sanctions and the measures delineated in the 1996 Libertad Act; (2) reaching out to and supporting the Cuban people to encourage development of independent civil society; (3) cooperation with the Cuban government on interests of direct concern, particularly to maintain migration in safe, orderly, and legal channels; and (4) forging a multilateral effort to press for democratic change, respect for human rights, and development of independent civil society." (USIS, 11 March 1999)

Summarize this case study by completing the requested information:

a. **Who (target nation):**

b. **When:**

[3] Case studies developed from the Peterson Institute for International Economics; accessed at http://www.petersoninstitute.org/research/topics/sanctions/casestudy.cfm on May 30, 2007.

ACTIVITY 14.1, CONTINUED
CASE STUDIES IN ECONOMIC SANCTIONS

c. What (type of sanctions):

d. Why (goal of the sanctions):

Burma/Myanmar

In August 1988, thousands of demonstrators marched through Rangoon (the capital city of Burma) and other Burmese cities, demanding removal of the current government, establishment of a multiparty political system, and free elections. The government suppressed the marchers. Estimates were that, in Rangoon alone, at least 3,000 people were killed by security forces firing on unarmed demonstrators. In August 1988, the U.S. Senate unanimously passed a resolution condemning the Burmese government for its brutality and calling for restoration of democracy. In September 1988, Washington suspended all arms sales and foreign assistance except humanitarian aid to Burma. These sanctions have continued up through 2007. A report from the U.S. Department of State concluded that:

> "In coordination with the European Union and other states, the United States has maintained sanctions on Burma. These include an arms embargo, a ban on new investment, and other measures. Our goal in applying these sanctions is to encourage a transition to democratic rule and greater respect for human rights. Should there be significant progress towards those goals as a result of dialogue between Aung San Suu Kyi and the military government, then the United States would look seriously at measures to support this process of constructive change. Continued absence of positive change would force the U.S. to look at the possibility of increased sanctions in conjunction with the international community."

Source: Department of State Report "Conditions in Burma and U.S. Policy Towards Burma for the period September 28, 2002-March 27, 2003," cited in "Case Studies in Sanctions and Terrorism," accessed on February 5, 2009, at http://www.iie.com/research/topics/sanctions/myanmar2.cfm.

Activity 14.1, continued

Case Studies in Economic Sanctions

Summarize this case study by completing the requested information:

a. **Who (target nation):**

b. **When:**

c. **What (type of sanctions):**

d. **Why (goal of the sanctions):**

ACTIVITY 14.2

SANCTIONS AREN'T ALWAYS EFFECTIVE

Sanctions do not always achieve their desired effect. Research suggests that economic sanctions are effective only about one third of the time. Under certain conditions, however, it becomes more likely that sanctions will achieve the desired effect.

Part 1

Directions: Five of the following eleven statements identify conditions that increase the likelihood that sanctions will be effective. Circle the five statements that identify conditions likely to increase the effectiveness of sanctions.[4]

1. The sender nation seeks minor changes in the target nation's policies.

2. The target and the sender are about the same size.

3. The target has a weak economy.

4. The sender seeks major changes in the target's policies.

5. The target and the sender have a close trade relationship.

6. The sender is a big country relative to the target.

7. The target has a strong economy.

8. The target is not a "friend" of the sender.

9. The target and the sender have little history of trade.

10. The sender is small relative to the target.

11. The target is a "friend" of the sender.

[4] This activity is based on S. L. Miller, "The use of economic sanctions." In S.L. Miller, ed., *Economics and National Security* (Columbus, OH: Mershon Center, 1992).

ACTIVITY 14.2, CONTINUED

SANCTIONS AREN'T ALWAYS EFFECTIVE

Part 2

Directions: The chart below provides information about key characteristics of three nations against which the United States maintains ongoing economic sanctions. You will assess these sanctions, applying your knowledge of conditions that are likely to make sanctions successful. Review all the information for each case. Complete the blank data-retrieval chart by rating each sanction according to the five conditions that make success more likely. Use a 0 – 5 scale. A score of 0 means that this case fails to meet this condition (e.g., if the target is not at all friendly with the United States, you would assign a score of 0 in the category titled "the target is a 'friend' of the U.S."). A score of 5 would mean that the condition is clearly met. A score between 0 and 5 implies that the condition is partially met. Write a brief rationale for each score you assign. Finally, total the scores for each case and make a prediction whether or not each sanction is likely to achieve its stated goals. (Hint: a total score of 0 means success is not very likely; a score of 25 implies a good

Target	Type of Sanction[5]	Goal of Sanction	2006 GDP/capita, in dollars (U.S. GDP/capita: $43,500)[6]	Population (2006 U.S. population: 300,000,000)	2006 Trade with U.S. (Total trade for target, 2006)[7]	Relationship with the U.S.
Syria	Freeze on Syrian assets in the U.S.; end to all U.S. exports apart from humanitarian items.	Stop Syrian occupation of Lebanon; stop attempting to acquire weapons of mass destruction and missiles; stop training and harboring terrorists.	$4,000	19,314,747	$438,100,000 (total trade: $13,600,000,000)	U.S.-Syrian relations have been marred by longstanding disagreements over regional and international policy. Since 1970, diplomatic relations have often been strained as result of the Arab-Israeli conflict.

[5] Source: U.S. Treasury Sanctions Program Summaries: http://www.treas.gov/offices/enforcement/ofac/programs/syria/syria.shtml. Accessed May 31, 2007.

[6] Source: CIA World Factbook: https://www.cia.gov/library/publications/the-world-factbook/index.html. Accessed May 31, 2007.

[7] Source: U.S. Census Bureau Foreign Trade Statistics: http://www.census.gov/foreign-trade/www/index.html. Accessed May 31, 2007.

ACTIVITY 14.2, CONTINUED

SANCTIONS AREN'T ALWAYS EFFECTIVE

Target	Type of Sanction	Goal of Sanction	2006 GDP/capita, in dollars (U.S. GDP/capita: $43,500)	Population (2006 U.S. population: 300,000,000)	2006 Trade with U.S. (Total trade for target, 2006)	Relationship with the U.S.
Iran	Since 1987, unilateral embargo of all Iranian goods; virtually all trade activities with Iran prohibited.	Eliminate nuclear weapons development program; stop sponsorship and funding of terrorism; promote human rights.	$8,900	65,300,000	$242,000,000 (total trade: $108,000,000,000)	Iranian-U.S. relations have been strained since a group of Iranian students seized the U.S. Embassy (and took hostages) in Tehran in 1979. During 1980-88, Iran fought a bloody war with Iraq (which was supported by the U.S.). Iran has been designated a state sponsor of terrorism and remains subject to U.S. economic sanctions and export controls.
North Korea	All trade with, and financial aid to, North Korea has been restricted since 1950.	Stop development of nuclear weapons; stop sponsoring terrorism; support human rights.	$1,800	23,300,00	$5,000,000 (total trade: $3,060,000,000)	In 1950, the U.S. supported South Korea in the Korean War, and relations between North Korea and the U.S. have been strained since then. In 2002 President Bush named North Korea as part of the "Axis of Evil." North Korea does not have diplomatic representation in the U.S. (i.e., no embassy).

ACTIVITY 14.2, CONTINUED

SANCTIONS AREN'T ALWAYS EFFECTIVE

Data-Retrieval Chart:

Analyzing Economic Sanctions

Condition	Syria	Iran	North Korea
Goals of the sanction: seek minor changes in policy?	Score: Rationale:	Score: Rationale:	Score: Rationale:
Target has a weak economy relative to the U.S.?	Score: Rationale:	Score: Rationale:	Score: Rationale:
U.S. has a close trade relationship with target?	Score: Rationale:	Score: Rationale:	Score: Rationale:
Target has a small population relative to the U.S.?	Score: Rationale:	Score: Rationale:	Score: Rationale:
The target is a "friend" of the U.S.?	Score: Rationale:	Score: Rationale:	Score: Rationale:
TOTAL SCORE			

Prediction:
    (Likely to succeed,
    Uncertain,
    Unlikely to succeed)			

Lesson 15

The Judiciary and Eminent Domain: The Case of *Kelo v. City of New London*

THE JUDICIARY AND EMINENT DOMAIN: THE CASE OF *KELO V. CITY OF NEW LONDON*

INTRODUCTION

Property rights and their enforcement are fundamental to the operation of a market economy. Private property rights are protected by the Fifth Amendment to the U.S. Constitution in its "due process of law" clause. However, the "takings" clause of the Fifth Amendment also provides the basis for *eminent domain*. Eminent domain is the power of government to take private land for public use. Traditionally, eminent domain has made it possible for local governments to acquire private land for public projects like road construction, bridges, and parks.

In the case of *Kelo v. City of New London (2005),* the U.S. Supreme Court ruled that private property could be taken for the use of a private company. This ruling has been very controversial. Justice John Paul Stevens wrote the opinion for the majority. He argued that the City of New London acted in accordance with the "takings" clause of the Fifth Amendment and that the city was exercising its traditional right of eminent domain. Justice Sandra Day O'Connor dissented from the majority opinion. Given the Court's ruling in *Kelo*, she wrote, "Nothing is to prevent the State from replacing any Motel 6 with a Ritz-Carlton, any home with a shopping mall, or any farm with a factory." Did the U.S. Supreme Court rule correctly in a case involving a fundamental economic freedom?

LESSON DESCRIPTION

The students learn about the importance of private property rights and the enforcement of those rights. They are introduced to the concept of eminent domain and its grounding in the Fifth Amendment to the U.S. Constitution. To explore issues of property rights, the students play roles in a simulated U.S. Supreme Court press conference attended by Justice Stevens and Justice O'Connor.

They then make their own judgments about the Supreme Court's ruling in *Kelo*.

CONCEPTS

- Due process of law
- Property rights
- Role of government
- Takings clause

Objectives

Students will be able to:

1. Explain the economic provisions of the U.S. Constitution contained in the Fifth Amendment.

2. Explain the reasoning of the Supreme Court in the Case of *Kelo v. City of New London.*

3. Evaluate the majority opinion in *Kelo*.

CONTENT STANDARDS
Economics (CEE Standards)

- Voluntary exchange occurs only when all participating parties expect to gain. This is true for trade among individuals or organizations within a nation, and among individuals or organizations in different nations. (Standard 5)

- Institutions evolve in market economies to help individuals and groups accomplish their goals. Banks, labor unions, corporations, legal systems, and not-for-profit organizations are examples of important institutions. A different kind of institution, clearly defined and well enforced property rights, is essential to a market economy. (Standard 10)

- There is an economic role for government to play in a market economy whenever the benefits of a government policy outweigh its costs. Governments often provide for national defense, address environmental concerns, define and protect property rights, and attempt to make markets more competitive. Most government policies also redistribute income. (Standard 16)

- Costs of government policies sometimes exceed benefits. This may occur because of incentives facing voters, government officials, and government employees, because of actions by special interest groups that can impose costs on the general public, or because social goals other than economic efficiency are being pursued. (Standard 17)

Civics and Government (NSCG Standards, Grades 9-12)

- The relationship of limited government to political and economic freedom. (Standard I.B.4)

- Concepts of *constitution*. (Standard I.C.1)

TIME REQUIRED

45 minutes

MATERIALS

- A transparency of Visuals 15.1 and 15.2.

- A copy for each student of Activity 15.1.

PROCEDURE

1. Tell the class that the purpose of this lesson is to analyze an important Supreme Court case that brings into sharp focus an issue regarding economic freedom. The class will be asked to consider under what circumstances a local government may acquire land from private owners.

2. Display Visual 15.1. Discuss the points it presents. Then pose the following questions to the class:

   - In a market economy, who owns most of the property?

   (In a market economy, most property is owned by individuals and businesses.)

- What is private property ownership?

  (Private ownership means that people and businesses are free to benefit from the ownership of their property. They can obtain, use, and transfer property as they see fit, according to applicable laws.)

- What are some key advantages of private ownership of property?

  (Property rights encourage investment and care of property.)

- Why is enforcement of private ownership so important?

  (Private owners need to have confidence that their rights will be protected or they will have less incentive to make productive uses of their property.)

3. Display Visual 15.2. Ask the students to identify the "due process of law" clause in the Fifth Amendment to the U.S. Constitution. Clarify its meaning as necessary. *(This clause provides for the protection of private property rights. It states that government bodies may not take property away from property owners except by following legal requirements ["due process of law"].)*

4. Ask the students to identify the "takings" clause. Clarify its meaning as necessary. *(This clause [found in the last sentence of Visual 15.2] authorizes governments to take private property for public use, provided that they pay for the property they take ["just compensation"].)*

5. Distribute a copy of Activity 15.1 to each student. Explain to the students that they will be participating in a first-ever press conference held by Supreme Court Justices after a ruling. Ask the students to read the Directions and the Background Memo on Activity 15.1. Then assign students to play the roles of Justice Stevens, Justice O'Connor, the Supreme Court Director of Communications, and three reporters. Ask the designated students to read the transcript of the press conference to the

class. Then discuss the substance of the case:

- What was the redevelopment plan proposed by New London officials?

  (Officials wanted to develop 90 acres of waterfront land, on which many people owned homes, for construction of office buildings, new housing, a marina, and other facilities near a research center being built by a large pharmaceutical company.)

- Who objected to the plan?

  (While most home owners agreed and sold their property for redevelopment, 15 of them did not. They wanted to keep their property. They took their case to the courts.)

- What did the U.S. Supreme Court rule in the case of *Kelo v. City of New London*?

  (The Court ruled in favor of the City of New London. It said that the city was acting within its legal power of eminent domain when it required that the 15 reluctant homeowners sell.)

- What reasons did Justice Stevens state in explaining the Court's ruling?

  (Justice Stevens interpreted the "public use" statement in the Fifth Amendment to include not only such traditional public projects as parks, bridges, and highways, but also economic development carried out by private developers.)

- What reasons did Justice O'Connor give in opposing the Court's ruling?

  (Justice O'Connor argued that a government body cannot take land from one private owner and give it to another private owner, even with fair compensation, without violating the Fifth Amendment to the Constitution.)

- Should political officials be able to take property from some private owners and transfer it to other private owners if they think that doing so will promote the public good? Explain your answer.

(Accept a variety of responses. Relevant points to bring up include the following: On the one hand, private ownership of property is a fundamental right in a market economy. Private property rights provide an incentive for people to save, invest, and care for property. On the other hand, local governments have the authority to exercise eminent domain when they feel it is in the interest of the community to do so. The exercise of eminent domain for "public use" of property is protected by the Fifth Amendment.)

CLOSURE

Review the lesson by posing the following questions:

- What part of the Fifth Amendment protects private property rights? What part protects eminent domain?

  (The "due process of law" clause in the Fifth Amendment to the U.S Constitution protects private property rights. The "takings" clause authorizes governments to take private property for public use, provided that they pay for what they take.)

- What was the key issue in the case of *Kelo v. the City of New London*?

  (Eminent domain is the ability of government to take private land for public use. Traditionally, eminent domain makes it possible for local governments to acquire private land for public projects like road construction, bridges, and parks. In such cases, there is no transfer of ownership to other private owners. In Kelo v. City of New London, however, the court ruled that it was proper for private property to be taken and given over to other private owners for new uses deemed to be in the public interest.)

ASSESSMENT
Multiple-Choice Questions

1. Which part of the Fifth Amendment to the

U.S. Constitution authorizes the use of eminent domain?

A. The "takings" clause

B. The "leavings" clause

C. The "domain" clause

D. The Pfizer clause

2. In the case of *Kelo v. City of New London*, the U.S. Supreme Court ruled that

   A. the property ownership rights of the 15 home owners outweighed the eminent domain powers of the local government.

   B. the "due process of law" clause in the Fifth Amendment protected the home owners who had taken the case to court.

   C. taking private property to foster economic development satisfied the "public use" requirement in the Fifth Amendment.

   D. the statute of limitations had run out on the New London home owners' appeal to the courts.

Constructed-Response Questions

1. In 2001, city officials in New Rochelle, New York, announced plans to develop a 308,000 square foot Ikea furniture store. City officials wanted to use eminent domain to clear the 16 acres of land needed for the new store. Clearing the area would mean condemning much of the City Park neighborhood, razing 26 local businesses employing 400 people, and razing two churches and the homes of 160 residents. Ikea contended that the new store would generate $4.2 million in local sales and property taxes, as well as 350 jobs. Opponents argued that the plan was an abuse of the power of eminent domain and a violation of the Fifth Amendment to the U.S. Constitution. If this case had made it to the U.S. Supreme Court after the Court ruled on *Kelo v. New London,* how do you think the Court would have ruled?

(Background information: Ikea ultimately abandoned its plan after community groups launched a campaign against it. But suppose New Rochelle and Ikea had pressed the case: Would the Kelo *ruling have permitted the use of eminent domain? Some students might argue that the public purpose recognized in* Kelo *[taking privately owned homes to clear the way for new, private development] seems very similar to the purpose at stake in the Ikea case. Because of that similarity, the Court might have ruled for New Rochelle and Ikea, permitting the use of eminent domain. Other students might suggest a way to distinguish this case from* Kelo, *perhaps arguing that the proposed "taking" here does not meet the "public purpose" requirement since no significant public purpose would be served by the construction of one new big-box store. More background: Some well informed students might know that the membership of the Supreme Court has changed since the ruling in* Kelo, *and it is therefore possible, though unlikely, that the Court would reverse its earlier ruling.)*

2. What is an alternative to the use of eminent domain when potential business owners and city officials wish to acquire private property for new development? What are the advantages of the alternative?

(In most cases in which a developer wishes to gain ownership of private property in order to put it to new uses, the developer will negotiate with the property owners to see if an agreement can be reached for purchase of the property in question. In such cases, developers must offer to pay a price that will be acceptable to the property owners, and the sales that follow are therefore voluntary. No agreement, no sale. The exercise of eminent domain also involves compensation for property taken; but when a government body is determined to exercise eminent domain, the property owners cannot decline to sell. The transactions that follow may therefore seem forced, generating resentment and even political backlash against the developers and the public officials involved.)

VISUAL 15.1

WHY ARE PROPERTY OWNERS' RIGHTS IMPORTANT?

- In a market economy, most resources are owned by individuals and businesses, not by government.

- Private ownership means that people and businesses are able to obtain, use, and transfer property as they see fit, according to applicable laws.

- Private ownership provides incentives for people to take care of their property because, with proper care, it can gain in value, benefitting its owner.

- If private property could be taken from owners without their consent, the threat of loss would discourage people from investing in their property—their homes and businesses—or caring for it.

- Private owners need to have confidence that their rights will be protected by the courts or they will have less incentive to make productive use of their property.

- Despite the importance of private ownership, governments are permitted under certain circumstances, according to specified legal procedures, to acquire privately owned land for a public use.

VISUAL 15.2
THE FIFTH AMENDMENT TO THE U.S CONSTITUTION

The text of the Fifth Amendment:

No person shall be held to answer for a capital, or otherwise infamous crime, unless on a presentment or indictment of a grand jury, except in cases arising in the land or naval forces, or in the militia, when in actual service in time of war or public danger; nor shall any person be subject for the same offense to be twice put in jeopardy of life or limb; nor shall any person be compelled in any criminal case to be a witness against himself, ***nor be deprived of life, liberty, or property, without due process of law; nor shall private property be taken for public use, without just compensation*** [emphasis added].

ACTIVITY 15.1
SUPREME COURT CASE OF *KELO V. CITY OF NEW LONDON,* CONNECTICUT

Directions: The following is a hypothetical press conference held after the U.S Supreme Court ruling in the case of *Kelo v. the City of New London, Connecticut* (2005). The justices attending the press conference are Justice John Paul Stevens, who wrote the opinion for the majority in *Kelo*, and Justice Sandra Day O'Connor, who wrote a dissenting opinion. The Director of Communications for the U.S. Supreme Court will moderate the meeting, and three reporters will pose questions. Read the **Background Memo for Reporters**. After your class has gone over the **Press Conference Transcript**, respond to the questions that follow.

Background Memo for Reporters

This case focuses on the legal concept of eminent domain. *Eminent domain* means "superior ownership." It refers to the power of government to take privately owned land for public use.

The community of New London, Connecticut, with a population of about 24,000, was hurt in 1996 when the Naval Undersea Warfare Center, an employer of more than 1,500 people in the area, was closed.

City leaders responded with a redevelopment plan to help get the community back on its feet. They wanted to develop 90 acres of waterfront land for construction of new office buildings, upscale housing, a marina, and other facilities near a $300 million research center being built by Pfizer, a large pharmaceutical company. The plan was expected to generate hundreds of jobs and well over $500,000 in additional tax revenues.

Most property owners in the area slated for redevelopment agreed to the city's offer to purchase their homes, and their homes were torn down. However, 15 home owners, holding 1.5 acres, refused to go along. Some had lived in the area for many years. Others had just remodeled their homes. These homeowners challenged the takeover effort in court. The Connecticut Supreme Court upheld the city's plan. The homeowners appealed, and the case ultimately landed in the U.S. Supreme Court.

U.S. Supreme Court Press Conference Transcript June 23, 2005

Supreme Court Director of Communications: Thanks, everyone, for coming to the first-ever press conference held by the U.S. Supreme Court following a court ruling.

Before we begin, let me give some background to the Supreme Court case of *Kelo v. City of New London, Connecticut.*

In a 5-4 decision today, June 23, 2005, the U.S. Supreme Court ruled that local governments may force property owners to sell their property in order to make way for private economic development when local government officials believe that such development would benefit the public. Local governments, according to this decision, could take such actions even if the property is not rundown and even if the success of the new development is not certain.

Reporter 1: Justice Stevens, can you tell us the basis for your ruling?

Justice Stevens: Of course. I wrote the opinion for the majority on the Court. We cited other court cases in which the "public use" clause in the Fifth Amendment has been interpreted to include

ACTIVITY 15.1, CONTINUED
SUPREME COURT CASE OF *KELO V. CITY OF NEW LONDON*, CONNECTICUT

not only such traditional public projects as parks, bridges, and highways, but also slum clearance. We concluded that a "public purpose" such as creating jobs in a depressed city is constitutional and satisfies the requirements of the Fifth Amendment.

Reporter 2: Justice O'Connor, is that how you see it?

Justice O'Connor: With all due respect to my colleagues on the Court, I must respectfully but emphatically disagree. I agree with the opponents of this ruling who argued that using the power of government to forcibly take land from one private owner and give it to another private owner, even with fair compensation, violates the Fifth Amendment to the Constitution.

Reporter 3: What say you, Justice Stevens?

Justice Stevens: While I dislike disagreeing with my esteemed colleague, Justice O'Connor, I think that she and her colleagues in the minority in this case are not correct. I believe that the Court should not second-guess local governments when the question is whether a given course of action serves a public purpose. Promoting economic development is a traditional and long-accepted function of local government.

Reporter 1: Justice O'Connor? Do you have a response?

Justice O'Connor: I wrote in the dissenting opinion that this ruling by the majority favors the most powerful and influential people in society, leaving small property owners little recourse. This is not what the Founders intended in writing the Fifth Amendment. I wrote the following: the "specter of condemnation hangs over all property. Nothing is to prevent the State from replacing any Motel 6 with a Ritz-Carlton, any home with a shopping mall, or any farm with a factory." This is an abuse of eminent domain by local government.

Reporter 2: Justice Stevens, Justice O'Connor makes an important point. And many Americans, I believe, would tend to agree with her.

Justice Stevens: The Supreme Court is not influenced by public opinion polls. We do our best to interpret documentary evidence in the context of earlier rulings. This decision affirms the right of state and local governments seeking to use eminent domain for urban revitalization, a legitimate public purpose. Absent such efforts, many city centers have decayed.

Supreme Court Director of Communications: I see that our time is nearly up. We have time for only one more question.

Reporter 3: Justice O'Connor, do you have any additional thoughts?

Justice O'Connor: I am sympathetic to the problems facing city leaders who wish to improve blighted areas. Nonetheless, these leaders have to work within the rules of private property ownership. If they wish to acquire private land and use it for what are essentially private purposes, they must do it the old-fashioned way. They should provide the land owners with persuasive offers to sell voluntarily, or they should look elsewhere.

ACTIVITY 15.1, CONTINUED
SUPREME COURT CASE OF *KELO V. CITY OF NEW LONDON*, CONNECTICUT

Questions for Discussion

1. What was the redevelopment plan proposed by New London officials?

2. Who objected to the plan?

3. What did the U.S. Supreme Court rule in the case of *Kelo v. City of New London*?

4. What reasons did Justice Stevens give in explaining the Court's ruling?

5. What reasons did Justice O'Connor give in opposing the court's ruling?

6. Should political officials be able to take property from some private owners and transfer it to others if they think that doing so will promote the public good? Explain your answer.

LESSON 16

ECONOMIC FREEDOM IN CHINA AND INDIA

Lesson 16
Economic Freedom in China and India

INTRODUCTION

Political and economic freedoms are basic human rights. Students generally appreciate the importance of political freedoms, especially freedom of speech and assembly. Economic freedom is less well understood, despite its enormous importance. Across several nations, economic freedom correlates with per capita income. Higher levels of economic freedom go hand in hand with higher per capita incomes. Higher per capita incomes are, in turn, associated with longer life expectancies, higher literacy rates, and lower infant mortality rates.

In order to make correlations of this sort, it is necessary to have valid and reliable measures of economic freedom. This lesson makes use of two such measures. The first measure, developed largely as a result of the work of Milton Friedman, is based on annual reports known as *Economic Freedom of the World* (developed and published by the Fraser Institute). The second measure is the *Index of Economic Freedom*, published by the Heritage Foundation and the *Wall Street Journal*. By reference to these measures and by reference to statistics published by Freedom House (www.freedomhouse.org), an organization that has measured political freedom since 1941, this lesson tracks changes in political and economic freedom in two of the world's fastest-growing economies, India and China.

LESSON DESCRIPTION

The students examine a table and two graphs to identify trends in political freedom worldwide, particularly in China and India. They are introduced to the concept of economic freedom, and they discuss examples of the concept. They discuss a graph that shows the positive relationship between high levels of economic freedom and high levels of per capita income. They work in groups to predict which economies might have higher levels of economic freedom and per capita income.

Finally, they examine graphs to identify recent changes in levels of economic freedom in China and India.

CONCEPTS

- Economic freedom
- GDP
- Per capita income
- Political freedom

OBJECTIVES

Students will be able to:

1. Distinguish between political freedom and economic freedom.

2. Identify measures of political and economic freedom.

3. Describe the relationship between economic freedom and per capita income.

4. Compare levels of economic and political freedom in India and China.

CONTENT STANDARDS
Economics (CEE Standards)

- Institutions evolve in market economies to help individuals and groups accomplish their goals. Banks, labor unions, corporations, legal systems, and not-for-profit organizations are examples of important institutions. A different kind of institution, clearly defined and well enforced property rights, is essential to a market economy. (Standard 10)

- There is an economic role for government to play in a market economy whenever the benefits of a government policy outweigh its costs. Governments often provide for national defense, address environmental concerns, define and protect property rights, and attempt to make markets more competitive. Most government policies also redistribute income. (Standard 16)

- Costs of government policies sometimes exceed benefits. This may occur because of incentives facing voters, government officials, and government employees, because of actions by special interest groups that can impose costs on the general public, or because social goals other than economic efficiency are being pursued. (Standard 17)

Civics and Government (NSCG Standards, Grades 9-12)

- Limited and unlimited governments (Standard I.B.1)

- The rule of law (Standard I.B.2)

- Civil society and governments (Standard I.B.3)

- The relationship of limited government to political and economic freedom. (Standard I.B.4)

TIME REQUIRED

60 minutes

MATERIALS

- A transparency of Visuals 16.1, 16.2, 16.3, 16.4, 16.5, 16.6., 16.7, and 16.8

- A copy for each student of Activity 16.1

- You may wish to visit www.freedomhouse.org to learn more about rankings of political freedom. The two economic freedom indexes used in this lesson are Economic Freedom of the World, produced by the Fraser Institute (www.fraserinstitute.ca/economicfreedom/index), and the Index of Economic Freedom (www.heritage.org/research/features/index/), produced by the Heritage Foundation. These websites are useful sources for classroom instruction.

PROCEDURE

1. Tell the class that the purpose of this lesson is to develop an understanding of political and economic freedom around the world. The students will learn how economic freedom is associated with per capita income. This lesson will also highlight levels of political and economic freedom in China and India, two of the world's fastest-growing economies.

2. Your students are probably familiar with the concept of political freedom. Display Visual 16.1. It shows a list of political freedoms compiled by an organization called Freedom House, an international, non-governmental organization, based in the United States, that measures levels of political freedom around the world. Explain that the Freedom House definition of *freedom* is heavily influenced by the Universal Declaration of Human Rights, adopted by the United Nations General Assembly in 1948. Briefly discuss the political freedoms listed on Visual 16.1; in discussion, ask the students to provide examples of those freedoms.

3. Display Visual 16.2. It summarizes measures of political freedom for several countries, 1976-2006. Ask: What are the trends referred to in the Visual's title?

(Political freedom is increasingly widespread. Since 1976, the number of countries classified as free *has grown from 42 to 90. The number of countries classified as* not free *has declined from 68 to 45.)*

4. Display Visual 16.3. It summarizes information about political rights and civil liberties in China, India, and the United States. Explain that Freedom House measures freedom according to two broad categories: political rights and civil liberties. Political rights enable people to participate freely in the political process (through the right to vote, compete for public office, and elect representatives). Civil liberties allow for freedom of expression and belief, freedom of association, access to an equitable rule of law, and social and economic freedoms. Ask: How do the United States, China, and India compare in terms of political rights and civil liberties?

(The United States and India have relatively high levels of political rights and civil liberties. Political rights in China are almost nonexistent, and civil liberties are ranked

very low.)

5. Students may not be familiar with the concept of economic freedom. To introduce the concept, display Visual 16.4. Discuss the types of economic freedom it lists, including the right to own private property and freedom of exchange. Invite the students to add additional examples of economic freedoms, and restrictions on economic freedom. Write their comments into the far right column on Visual 16.4.

6. Display Visual 16.5. This visual lists the characteristics of economic freedom used in the indexes produced by the Fraser Institute and the Heritage Foundation. Briefly discuss these characteristics with the students.

7. Display Visual 16.6. The data displayed here are provided by the Index of Economic Freedom prepared by the Heritage Foundation and the *Wall Street Journal*. Explain that this graph displays the relationship between per capita Gross Domestic Product (GDP) and levels of economic freedom. Remind the students that *GDP* refers to the total market value of final goods and services produced within the borders of a nation during a given period of time. You may wish to note that since the value of production ultimately accrues to the factors of production, GDP can also be thought of as an income measure. *Per capita income* means total income divided by the total population. Ask: What is the relationship between economic freedom and per capita GDP?

(In economies in which economic freedoms are repressed, people have lower levels of per capita income. In economies that are economically free, people have higher levels of per capita income. Economic freedom is positively associated with per capita income levels.)

8. Distribute Activity 16.1. Explain to the students that they should read the information about the four economies and place each country into one of the following categories of economic freedom:

Repressed, Mostly Unfree, Mostly Free, Free. Then ask: Using what you know about the relationship between economic freedom and per capita GDP, make predictions about the level of per capita GDP you believe each country might attain. Then based on their predictions, the students should rank the four countries from highest to lowest levels of per capita GDP. Tell them to rank the economy that has the **highest level** of per capita GDP as **4**, the **next highest** as **3**, and so forth. Divide the class into groups; direct them to read the information and do the rankings. Discuss the results. Ask: Which economies did you tend to rank higher? Lower?

(The students will provide a variety of answers. Some might suggest that Economy A and D will rank high for economic freedom and have high levels of per capita GDP, since they seem to have well developed market systems. Economies B and C appear to be emerging from non-market systems and thus may lag in economic freedom and in per capita GDP.)

9. Display Visual 16.7 and reveal the names of the economies, their categories of economic freedom, and their levels of per capita GDP. Ask:

   - Which economies have the highest per capita GDP?

     (Hong Kong and the United States.)

   - Which economies have lower levels of per capita GDP?

     (China, at $7,700, is well below Hong Kong and the United States, but its per capita GDP is nearly twice that of India. India has a per capita GDP of $3,800.)

10. Display Visual 16.8. This graph shows levels of economic freedom according to the Economic Freedom of the World index. This index is of special interest because it is based on measurements over a longer time period than those of the Index of Economic Freedom. Discuss Visual 16.8. Ask:

- Remember Visual 16.7. Which nation—China or India—has a higher level of per capita GDP?

  (China outperforms India in per capita GDP.)

- Returning to Visual 16.8: which nation—China or India—currently has a higher level of economic freedom?

  (India outperforms China in economic freedom.)

- How have levels of economic freedom changed in China and India?

  (In 1985, both economies were at the same level. At that time, the government in each country exercised strong control over the economy. In subsequent years, China and India have made considerable progress in moving toward economic freedom. However, India's progress toward economic freedom has been greater since the early 1990s.)

- Why do you suppose Hong Kong is included for comparison?

  (Hong Kong is now part of China. It shares many cultural characteristics with China. The comparison shows that high levels of economic freedom can be accomplished in this common cultural setting. Students should also note that Hong Kong's higher per capita GDP [$37,300 in 2006] is associated with Hong Kong's higher level of economic freedom.)

CLOSURE

Review the lesson by posing the following questions:

- What are some examples of political freedom?

  (Ability to participate freely in the political process, right to vote freely in legitimate elections, freedom of expression and belief, freedom of assembly, access to an equitable rule of law.)

- What are some examples of economic freedom?

  (Limited economic role of government, private property rights, freedom to choose jobs, openness to international trade, etc.)

- Compare China to India in respect to political freedom.

  (India has high levels of political freedom and civil liberty. Political rights in China are almost nonexistent, and civil rights are ranked only somewhat higher.)

- What is the relationship between economic freedom and per capita GDP?

  (In economies that are economically repressed, per capita GDP tends to be low. In economies that enjoy greater economic freedom, per capita GDP tends to be higher. Economic freedom is positively associated with per capita GDP.)

- How have levels of economic freedom changed in China and India recently?

  (In 1985, both economies had relatively low levels of economic freedom. Since 1985, China and India have made considerable progress in expanding economic freedom. However, India's progress has in this respect been greater than China's.)

ASSESSMENT
Multiple-Choice Questions

1. Which one of the following statements is true?

   A. Lower levels of economic freedom are associated with higher levels of per capita GDP.

   B. Higher levels of economic freedom are associated with lower levels of per capita GDP.

   C. Higher levels of economic freedom are associated with higher barriers to international trade.

   D. Higher levels of economic freedom are associated with higher levels of per capita GDP.

2. Since 1985, how have levels of economic freedom changed in China and India?

   A. Both nations started at the same point, but economic freedom in both countries has declined.

   B. Both nations started at the same point, but economic freedom in both countries has increased.

   C. China started out at a lower level of economic freedom than India, but it has now achieved levels of economic freedom greater than those in India.

   D. The level of economic freedom in China and India has been unchanged.

Constructed-Response Questions

1. Using data from Freedom House, the Fraser Institute, and the Heritage Foundation, compare China and India in respect to political and economic freedom.

(Freedom House defines political freedom by reference to political rights and civil liberties. Political rights enable people to participate freely in the political process through the right to vote, to compete for public office, and to elect accountable representatives. Civil liberties allow for freedom of expression and belief, freedom of association, rule of law, and individual autonomy. By these measures, India has relatively high levels of political freedom and civil liberty. Political rights in China are almost nonexistent, and civil liberties ranked only slightly better.

The Fraser Institute created the Economic Freedom of the World Index; later, the Heritage Foundation and the Wall Street Journal *created a measure called the Index of Economic Freedom. Both indexes measure basics of economic freedom including limited economic role of government, the rule of law, secure rights to own private property, low inflation, and openness to international trade.*

In 1985, India and China had low levels of economic freedom. Since then, both countries have moved toward higher levels of economic freedom. However, India's progress has been greater than China's.)

2. How do Hong Kong, the United States, China, and India differ in respect to political and economic freedom?

(Hong Kong and the United States both experience a level of political freedom that is considered "free," while India and China are "mostly unfree." While the gap between the United States / Hong Kong and India / China has narrowed since 1985, the level of economic freedom remains higher in the United States and Hong Kong.)

VISUAL 16.1
WHAT ARE POLITICAL FREEDOMS?

Citizens in politically free nations should be able to do the following:

- Participate freely in the political process.

- Vote freely in legitimate elections.

- Elect representatives who will be accountable to them.

- Exercise freedom of expression and belief.

- Assemble and associate freely.

- Have access to an established, equitable system of rule of law.

- Have social and economic freedoms including equal access to economic opportunities and the right to hold private property.

Source: www.freedomhouse.org.

VISUAL 16.2
GLOBAL TRENDS IN POLITICAL FREEDOM

Year	Free Countries	Partly Free Countries	Not Free Countries
1976	42 (26 percent)	49 (31 percent)	68 (43 percent)
1986	57 (34 percent)	57 (34 percent)	53 (32 percent)
1996	79 (41 percent)	59 (31 percent)	53 (28 percent)
2006	90 (47 percent)	58 (30 percent)	45 (23 percent)

Source: www.freedomhouse.org.

VISUAL 16.3

AGGREGATE SCORES FOR POLITICAL FREEDOM IN CHINA, INDIA, AND THE UNITED STATES: POLITICAL RIGHTS AND CIVIL LIBERTIES

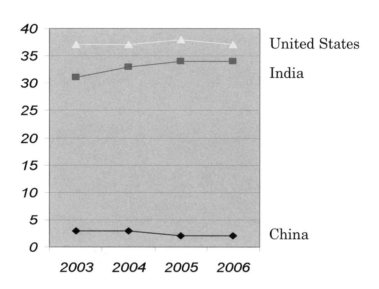

Source: www.freedomhouse.org.

VISUAL 16.3, CONTINUED

AGGREGATE SCORES FOR POLITICAL FREEDOM IN CHINA, INDIA, AND THE UNITED STATES: POLITICAL RIGHTS AND CIVIL LIBERTIES

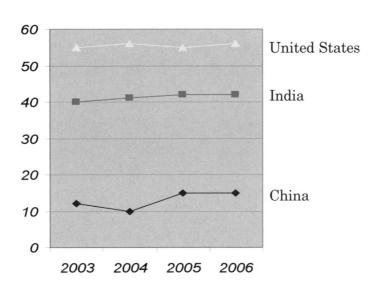

Source: www.freedomhouse.org.

Visual 16.4
Examples of Economic Freedom

Types of Economic Freedom	Examples of Economic Freedom	Examples of Restrictions on Economic Freedom	New Examples of Economic Freedom and/or Restrictions
Freedom for individuals to own property, use property as they wish, and keep any benefits that accrue from property ownership	Buy a house, farm, or business of your choice. Benefit (or not) from increased value or profits associated with ownership	Property taxes, zoning restrictions	
Freedom to make voluntary exchanges	Owners of clothing stores may purchase clothing made in other nations and offer it for sale	Tariffs, import quotas, price controls	
Freedom for individuals to use their income as they wish	Buy a car of your choice	Certain goods and services may not be legally purchased.	
Freedom for individuals to choose their jobs	Choose your own major in college; apply for any job you are interested in, anywhere	Occupational licensing, job-market discrimination	

VISUAL 16.5
COMPARING MEASURES OF ECONOMIC FREEDOM

1. **Economic Freedom of the World**
   (Produced annually by the Fraser Institute: see www.fraserinstitute.org.)

   - Size of Government: Expenditures, Taxes, and Enterprises

   - Legal Structure and Security of Property Rights

   - Access to Sound Money

   - Freedom to Trade Internationally

   - Regulation of Credit, Labor, and Business

2. **Index of Economic Freedom**
   (Produced annually by the Heritage Foundation and the *Wall Street Journal:* see www.heritage.org.)

   - Business Freedom

   - Trade Freedom

   - Monetary Freedom

   - Freedom from Government

   - Fiscal Freedom

   - Property Rights

   - Investment Freedom

   - Financial Freedom

   - Freedom from Corruption

   - Labor Freedom

VISUAL 16.6

ECONOMIC FREEDOM AND PER CAPITA INCOME

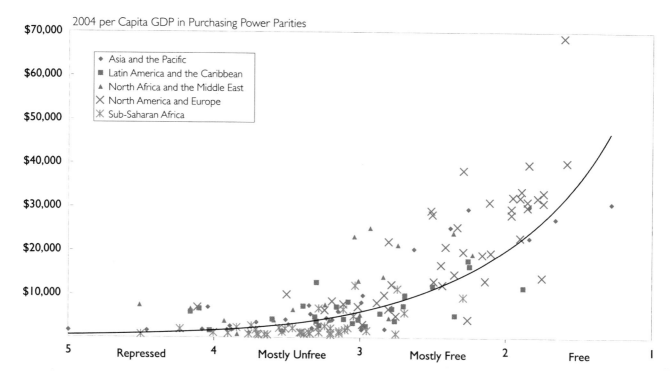

2004 per Capita GDP in Purchasing Power Parities

2006 Index of Economic Freedom

Sources: World Bank, *World Development Indicators Online*, available by subscription at *www.worldbank.org/data;* Central Intelligence Agency, *The World Factbook 2005*, available at *www.old.gov/cia/publications/factbook/index.html,* for the following countries: Bahamas, Bahrain, Barbados, Burma, Cuba, Equatorial Guinea, Irag, Kuwait, North Korea, Libya. Qatar, Surinam, Taiwan, United Arab Emirates, Zimbabwe; Marc A. Miles, Kim R. Holmes, and Mary Anastasia O'Grady, *2006 Index of Economic Freedom* (Washington, D.C.: The Heritage Foundation and Dow Jones & Company, Inc., 2006), at *www.heritage.org/index.*

VISUAL 16.7
PREDICTING LEVELS OF ECONOMIC FREEDOM AND PER CAPITA GDP

Economy A

Hong Kong

Free

Per capita GDP = $37,300 (2006 estimate)

Economy B

China

Mostly Unfree

Per capita GDP = $7,700 (2006 estimate)

Economy C

India

Mostly Unfree

Per capita GDP = $3,800 (2006 estimate)

Economy D

United States

Free

Per capita GDP = $43,500 (2006 estimate)

Visual 16.8

Economic Freedom in China, Hong Kong, India, and the United States

Economic Freedom of the World Index

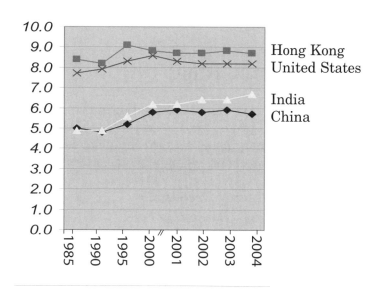

Source: Fraser Institute, Economic Freedom of the World.

ACTIVITY 16.1
PREDICTING LEVELS OF ECONOMIC FREEDOM AND INCOME

Directions: Read about each of the four economies below. Discuss the information with others in your group. Try to determine a level of economic freedom for each economy; place each economy into one of the following categories: **Repressed, Mostly Unfree, Mostly Free,** or **Free**. Note that not all of these rankings will be used and that a given ranking may be used more than once. Then predict a level of per capita GDP for each economy; rank the **highest** per capita GDP economy as **4**, the **next highest** as **3**, and so forth. Be ready to discuss your answers.

Economy A   **Category of Economic Freedom = _____**

                       Ranking of Per Capita GDP = _____

This country has a market economy that is highly engaged in international trade. It has a vast amount of imports and exports including re-exports to and from third countries. It has a rapidly growing service industry and is now emerging as a world financial center.   Many new businesses are launched on its stock exchange. It is experiencing a boom in tourism.

Economy B   **Category of Economic Freedom = _____**

                       Ranking of Per Capita GDP = _____

This country once had a centrally planned economic system, largely closed to international trade. It has now changed.   It has a rapidly growing private sector and is a major player in the global economy. Collectivized farms have been phased out. Price controls have been removed. Managers of state enterprises are allowed to make local decisions and retain some of the benefits that follow when they perform their jobs effectively. The economy has developed stock markets and some rapidly growing non-state enterprises, and it participates increasingly in foreign trade and investment.

Economy C   **Category of Economic Freedom = _____**

                       Ranking of Per Capita GDP = _____

This country uses traditional village farming, modern agriculture, handicrafts, and a wide range of modern industries and services.   It has a well-educated workforce. Services are the major source of this economy's economic growth. It has become a major exporter of software services and software workers. The government has reduced controls on foreign trade and investment. Increases in foreign investment have been permitted in a few key areas, such as telecommunications. Over the past few years, several government-owned industries have been turned over to private owners. However, high tariffs remain in place in some sectors of the economy, including agriculture.

Economy D   **Category of Economic Freedom = _____**

                       Ranking of Per Capita GDP = _____

In this country, most economic decisions are made by private individuals and business firms. National and state governments buy their goods and services predominantly from the private marketplace. Business firms enjoy broad measures of freedom in decisions they make about building new plants, laying off workers, and developing new products.   This economy is among the world's leaders in production of computers and medical, aerospace, and military equipment. Substantial gains in labor productivity have contributed to this economy's economic growth.

LESSON 17

MAKING TRADE-OFFS IN POLICY DECISIONS: THE PATRIOT ACT

LESSON 17
MAKING TRADE-OFFS IN POLICY DECISIONS: THE PATRIOT ACT

INTRODUCTION

All societies have fundamental goals aligned to the values held by their people. Economic goals in the United States include economic growth, economic freedom, and economic security. An essential skill in economic reasoning is to weigh the outcomes of proposed policy alternatives in terms of these fundamental goals. All government policy decisions involve trade-offs: the results of a given choice require giving up some increment of one or more desired goals in order to gain some increment of another goal. For example, policymakers might adopt a policy in which some increase in economic growth is gained at the expense of some degree of equity.

Sometimes people differ about policy actions because they disagree about the expected consequences of their choices. One person may think, for whatever reason, that a policy under consideration will not yield a particular outcome, while others think that it will. Perhaps more likely, the disagreement will be one about the relative impact of the policy on economic goals. Thus, one person might think that a policy will greatly improve environmental quality at a small cost in forgone economic growth, while another might think that the environmental improvement will be small and come at a great cost in reduced economic growth. Moreover, people can value economic goals differently. One who values equity much more than efficiency might support a policy that makes small improvements in equity even at a great cost in economic efficiency.

Thinking in terms of trade-offs is important because it often clarifies the nature of our disagreements. In a given case, are we disagreeing about the likely results of a decision, or about how we value the results, or both? Both kinds of disagreement arose in the United States after 2001 in controversy over a federal law known as the Patriot Act.

LESSON DESCRIPTION

Using a case study approach, the students weigh certain trade-offs associated with the Patriot Act. The class decides whether the trade-off of civil liberties for improved security is a good one. In addition, students consider how incentives might affect the behavior of government officials under the provisions of the Patriot Act.

CONCEPTS

- Civil liberties
- Security
- Trade-offs
- Incentives

OBJECTIVES

Students will be able to:

1. Evaluate policy trade-offs by reference to goals.

2. Discuss and evaluate different views of the Patriot Act.

3. Identify the mixed incentives for government authorities to follow guidelines in fully reporting out the various parts of the Patriot Act.

CONTENT STANDARDS
Economics (CEE Standards)

- Effective decision making requires comparing the additional costs of alternatives with the additional benefits. Most choices involve doing a little more or a little less of something; few choices are all-or-nothing decisions. (Standard 2)

- Costs of government policies sometimes exceed benefits. This may occur because of incentives facing voters, government officials, and government employees, because of actions by special interest groups that can impose costs on the general public, or because social goals other than economic efficiency are being pursued. (Standard 17)

Civics and Government (NSCG Standards, Grades 9-12)

- Fundamental values and principles. (Standard II.D.3)

- Conflicts among values and principles in American political and social life. (Standard II.D.4)

TIME REQUIRED

100 minutes

MATERIALS

- A transparency of Visuals 17.1, 17.2, 17.3, and 17.4

- A copy of Activities 17.1, 17.2, and 17.3, each handed out to one third of the class.

PROCEDURE

1. Tell the students that this lesson will focus on various elements of a federal law about which some of them may have heard. Ask the students whether they are familiar with the Uniting and Strengthening America by Providing Appropriate Tools Required to Intercept and Obstruct Terrorism Act of 2001. (*It is unlikely that any students will have heard of this law.*) Then ask the students whether they have heard of the Patriot Act. (*Some students may have heard of this.*) Tell the students that the Patriot Act is the familiar name of the Uniting and Strengthening America by Providing Appropriate Tools Required to Intercept and Obstruct Terrorism Act of 2001. Ask: Can any of you tell me what this act is about?

2. After you have given students a chance to respond, summarize the Patriot Act briefly. The Act expands the definition of *terrorism* to include domestic acts of terrorism. Also, it gives U.S. officials increased authority to do the following:

    - to search telephone, electronic, and other personal records;

    - to gather foreign intelligence within the United States;

    - to detain and deport immigrants who are suspected of being involved in terrorist activities;

    - to regulate financial transactions.

3. Explain that the Patriot Act was controversial when it was first introduced in Congress, and it continues to be controversial. In 2006, when Congress was considering reauthorizing the Act, *USA Today* conducted a poll to find out how Americans felt about changing the Act. To show the poll results, display Visual 17.1. Ask the students to interpret the data.

4. Tell the class that Congress made some changes in the Act upon reauthorizing it; then the revised Patriot Act was signed into law by President Bush on March 9, 2006. However, it remains controversial. Display Visual 17.2 and ask the students to note the concerns expressed by the League of Women Voters.

    (*Does not protect civil liberties; insufficient checks and balances—e.g., judicial review; and insufficient safeguards against indiscriminate searches.*)

    Draw special attention to the underlined portions of the statement.

5. Explain that not everyone agrees with the League's assessment. To illustrate the disagreements, display Visual 17.3. This Visual contains an excerpt from a *Washington Times* article that appeared in October 2006. Ask the class to list some of the provisions of the Act that the writer felt were "overdue and prudent."

    (*Updating wiretap authority for the era of the Internet, allowing roving wiretaps not fixed to one phone or location, breaking down barriers between the FBI and CIA, requiring that banks report suspicious money transfers, and so forth.*)

    Again, draw attention to the underlined portion of the statement.

6. Ask the students to take stock of the two statements (Visuals 17.2 and 17.3): Overall, what goals are in conflict here? (*Civil liberties and security.*) Using the underlined portions, work with the students to help them see that some observers believe that the Patriot Act goes too far in promoting security at the expense of civil liberties, while others think that a reasonable balance has been achieved. Note that much of the concern centers on the Fourth Amendment to the U.S. Constitution. Here is the text of the Fourth Amendment:

    > ***The right of the people to be secure in their persons, houses, papers, and effects, against unreasonable searches and seizures, shall not be violated, and no Warrants shall issue, but upon probable cause, supported by Oath or affirmation, and particularly describing the place to be searched, and the persons or things to be seized.***

7. Introduce the concept of *trade-offs,* using Visual 17.4. Ask the students: What trade-off is implicit in the Patriot Act? (*People in the United States should give up some civil liberties in exchange for more security.*) Using Visual 17.4, make sure the students understand that in the case of trade-offs it is very important to determine the *size* of the gains and losses at stake. *How much* in the way of civil liberties must be given up? *How great* will the gain in national security be? Explain that the class will try to make such a determination in this lesson. Doing so will not be a simple matter. The information needed to make such a determination is itself subject to interpretation. Opponents of the Patriot Act will try to emphasize the civil liberties threat and minimize the national security value. Proponents will do the opposite. It is, therefore, important to be mindful of the point of view of sources.

8. Explain that the class will work in groups to assess the Patriot Act. There will be a

National Security Letter Working Group (NSL), a Section 215 Working Group (215), and a Patriot Act Effectiveness Working Group (EWG). And, because the Act is quite long and complex, the class will concentrate only on certain aspects of it, with one working group (or two, depending on class size) focused on each aspect: The NSL and 215 groups will evaluate the seriousness of the threat to civil liberties posed by their respective provisions of the Patriot Act. The EWG group will assess how valuable the Patriot Act has been in promoting security.

9. Organize the class and distribute copies of Activities 17.1, 17.2, and 17.3 to the appropriate groups. Because the readings are lengthy, the groups will need plenty of time to work. There may be disagreements within groups about what to report. This is useful since it helps to illustrate disagreements where trade-offs are involved. You might wish to allow for majority and minority reports.

10. Have the groups report to the class. Be sure that each group presents an overall assessment supported by evidence.

CLOSURE

Conduct a class discussion of the overall assessment of the trade-off involved in the Patriot Act. Solicit opinions from students about whether, on balance, they support the trade-off of reduced civil liberties for greater security. Draw attention to the possibility that some students may value the goals differently. You might wish to conduct a class vote.

Ask the class to consider the effect of incentives on the behavior of government officials. For example, consider an FBI agent who believes, based on experience and instincts, that she or he is "on to something" in an investigation, but might not have much proof—yet. What incentive might this agent have to violate the civil liberties protections in the Patriot Act? Are the possible consequences of such a violation strong enough to prevent abuse?

In concluding the lesson, remind the students that the class did not examine the entire Act, and that events in the future could provide more evidence of threats to civil liberties or of the Act's effectiveness that could change their opinions.

ASSESSMENT

Multiple-Choice Questions

1. When a choice requires giving up something linked to one or more desired goals in order to gain something linked to other goals, we call that

   A. public policy.

   B. a trade-off.

   C. a "no-win" situation.

   D. a dilemma.

2. NSLs are

   A. a possible threat to civil liberties.

   B. statistics on national security legislation.

   C. FBI letters to Congress.

   D. a possible threat to national security.

3. The Patriot Act expanded the FBI's powers to gain information through an order from the FISA court under

   A. the Fourth Amendment.

   B. writs of habeas corpus.

   C. Section 104.

   D. Section 215.

Constructed-Response Questions

1. Describe a government law or policy (other than the Patriot Act) that involves a trade-off. Identify the goals that are in conflict.

   (*Answers will vary, but may include such things as policies that promote environmental quality but cause reduced economic growth; policies that lead to a more equal distribution of income by increasing tax rates on higher-income earners; policies*

that expand Social Security or Medicare by increasing taxes on current wage earners, and so forth.)

2. Explain why information about the likely consequences of proposed policies is important when making a decision that involves trade-offs.

   (*Knowing the consequences helps to determine how much of one goal is gained at the expense of another goal.*)

Visual 17.1
USA Today Poll on the Patriot Act

"Based on what you have heard or read about the Patriot Act, do you think all of its provisions should be kept, that it needs minor changes, that it needs major changes, [or that] it needs to be eliminated completely?"*

Keep all provisions	Minor changes	Major changes	Eliminated completely	No opinion
13	50	24	7	7

* Poll conducted January 6-8, 2006. http://www.usatoday.com/news/polls/2006-01-09-poll.htm#patriot. All numbers are percentages of poll respondents and have been rounded.

VISUAL 17.2

LEAGUE PRESSES SENATE TO OPPOSE REAUTHORIZATION OF THE USA PATRIOT ACT

December 15, 2005

Washington, D.C. – The League of Women Voters today urged the U.S. Senate to oppose ... the reauthorization of the USA PATRIOT Act.

"We are very concerned that the conference agreement does not sufficiently protect civil liberties," said Kay J. Maxwell, President of the League of Women Voters of the United States. "It fails to restore the vital checks and balances taken away by the USA PATRIOT Act."

"<u>The bill goes too far</u> and must be stopped," Maxwell said. "It provides for more government secrecy in the name of homeland security and anti-terrorism without the checks and balances needed to protect civil liberties. Medical, banking or library records of Americans can still be obtained by law enforcement without necessary safeguards...," stated Maxwell.

"For the past 85 years, members of the League have been steadfast in their conviction that the need to protect against <u>security threats to America must be balanced with the need to preserve the very liberties</u> that are the foundation of this country. There are fundamental principles that guard our liberty – from independent judicial review of law enforcement actions to prohibitions on indiscriminate searches – that must be preserved," Maxwell said.

Source: http://www.lwv.org/AM/Template.cfm?Section=Individual_Liberties&TEMPLATE=/CM/ContentDisplay.cfm&CONTENTID=4113. Emphasis added.

VISUAL 17.3

NATIONAL SECURITY: LET'S PLAY OUR STRENGTHS

The Washington Times, October 9, 2006
by Michael E. O'Hanlon, *Senior Fellow*, Foreign Policy Studies, Brookings
Institution

"The Patriot Act, <u>whatever its problems in insufficiently guaranteeing</u> <u>civil liberties, on balance has been good legislation</u>. Critics of the administration need to acknowledge that updating wiretap authority for the era of the Internet, allowing roving wiretaps not fixed to one phone or location, breaking down barriers between the FBI and CIA, requiring that banks report suspicious money transfers, requiring visa-waiver countries to have biometric indicators on their passports, prohibiting possession of dangerous biological materials in the absence of good research or medicinal reasons, and similar measures, were overdue and prudent."

Source: http://www.brookings.edu/views/op-ed/ohanlon/20061009.htm. Emphasis added.

VISUAL 17.4

TRADE-OFFS

Most government policy decisions involve a trade-off: a policy choice requires giving up some of one or more desired goals in order to gain some of one or more other goals.

What's the trade-off in the case of the Patriot Act?

Disagreements about trade-offs occur when one person thinks that you give up too much of one or more goals to get more of other goals. Also, people tend to value goals differently.

How do these points apply to assessing the Patriot Act? It is crucial to decide how much more security we are getting in exchange for a loss, in some measure, of civil liberties. If the loss of civil liberties is large while we gain very little in additional security, the Patriot Act might be a bad idea. On the other hand, the Patriot Act might be good policy if we gain a great deal of security at a small cost in civil liberties.

Information about this trade-off is subject to interpretation. Opponents of the Patriot Act will try to emphasize the civil liberties threat and minimize the national security value. Proponents of the Act will do the opposite.

Be mindful of the point of view of sources of disagreement.

ACTIVITY 17.1

NATIONAL SECURITY LETTER (NSL) WORKING GROUP

Before working on this assignment, you should understand the provisions of the Fourth Amendment to the U.S. Constitution. Here is the text of the Fourth Amendment:

> *The right of the people to be secure in their persons, houses, papers, and effects, against unreasonable searches and seizures, shall not be violated, and no Warrants shall issue, but upon probable cause, supported by Oath or affirmation, and particularly describing the place to be searched, and the persons or things to be seized.*

Directions: One area of concern about the Patriot Act has to do with National Security Letters (NSLs). Read the information below. It contains excerpts from the Electronic Policy Information Center's (EPIC) website regarding NSLs, and some additional information from a report of the Office of the Inspector General (OIG), Department of Justice. As you read the information, **your overall goal is to evaluate the seriousness of the threat to civil liberties posed by NSLs.**

The following questions may help to provide focus for your reading.

1. What is an NSL? What information can be obtained?

2. How great an invasion of privacy is FBI access to this information? Does it seem to violate the Fourth Amendment?

3. Are the safeguards against abuse adequate?

   - Do the procedures necessary to obtain NSLs adequately protect civil liberties?

   - How serious are the problems found in the OIG report?

4. Will the FBI do better in following the law and procedures in the future?

   - What incentives are there for the FBI to violate the law?

   - What incentives are there for the FBI to follow the law?

5. How should we interpret the numbers of NSLs? For example: "It doesn't matter. The potential for abuse is enough." or "The growing number is still very small, so it isn't much of a problem."

After considering the information, be prepared to answer these questions and report to the class on how much of an infringement on civil liberties NSLs pose.

Excerpts Quoted from EPIC (Note: EPIC has grave concerns over the Patriot Act)

National Security Letters (NSLs) are an extraordinary search procedure which gives the FBI the power to compel the disclosure of customer records held by banks, telephone companies, Internet Service Providers, and others.

...

ACTIVITY 17.1, CONTINUED

NATIONAL SECURITY LETTER (NSL) WORKING GROUP

What Types of Information Can Be Obtained by NSLs?

- **Telephone and E-mail Records:** "Toll records," a historical record of calls made and received from land lines, cell phones, and other sources, of a specified phone number, as well as billing records associated with that number. E-mail records, including e-mail addresses and screen names associated with the requested account and the e-mail addresses and screen names who have contacted that account.

- **Financial Records:** Financial information, including open and closed checking and savings accounts, from banks, private bankers, credit unions, thrift institutions, brokers and dealers, investment bankers and companies, credit card companies, insurance companies, travel agencies, casinos, and others.

- **Credit Information:** Full credit reports, names and addresses of all financial institutions at which the consumer has maintained an account.

...

Office of the Inspector General (OIG) Report, March 2007

The report detailed significant violations of laws and regulations by the FBI in its use of its national security letter authority.

The FBI is required to report to Congress on the number of NSLs issued; the OIG found that the FBI underreported this number. The OIG review looked at 77 case files containing 293 NSLs from four separate FBI field offices issued in the 2003-2005 period. This review found that there were 17 percent more NSLs in the sample of case files than in FBI reporting databases. Delays in data entry also caused about 4,600 NSLs to not be reported to Congress. The OIG concluded that the FBI database significantly understates the number of NSL requests issued, and that Congress has been misinformed about the scale of the usage of the NSL authority.

The report further stated that violations are supposed to be self-reported by the FBI to the Intelligence Oversight Board. During the three-year period in question, the FBI self-reported 26 violations out of the 140,000 NSLs issued. The OIG, however, found 22 potential violations out of the sample of 293 NSLs it reviewed. The OIG has stated that there is no indication that the 293 NSLs it reviewed are not representative of all of the NSLs issued, thus indicating that the FBI is failing to self-report a very significant number of violations.

...

ACTIVITY 17.1, CONTINUED

NATIONAL SECURITY LETTER (NSL) WORKING GROUP

NSL Statistics

The Inspector General's report detailed the FBI's use of NSLs from 2003 to 2005.

- Total number of NSL requests from 2000 (prior to passage of the Patriot Act): about 8,500.

- Total number of NSL requests from 2003-2005 (after passage of the Patriot Act): 143,074.

...

The USA PATRIOT Act's Impact on NSL Authority

The FBI's NSL authority was significantly expanded by the Patriot Act in the following ways:

- The Act lowered the threshold for situations in which NSLs may be issued. Previously, the FBI could use NSLs to request information only if it had "specific [statable] facts giving reason to believe that the customer or entity whose records are sought is a foreign power or an agent of a foreign power." The Patriot Act eliminated this requirement; now, NSLs may be issued to request information that is merely "relevant to an authorized investigation to protect against international terrorism or clandestine intelligence activities," provided that such an investigation of a U.S. person is not based on activities protected by the First Amendment.

- The Act expanded approval authority beyond senior FBI Headquarters officials. Special Agents in charge of the FBI's 56 field offices may now authorize NSLs.

(http://www.epic.org/privacy/nsl/)

Information Quoted from the OIG Report

To obtain approval for national security letters, FBI case agents must prepare: (1) an electronic communication (EC) seeking approval to issue the letter (approval EC), and (2) the national security letter itself. The approval EC explains the justification for opening or maintaining the investigation and why the information requested by the NSL is relevant to that investigation.

For field division-initiated NSLs, the Supervisory Special Agent of the case agent's squad, the Chief Division Counsel (CDC), and the Assistant Special Agent in Charge are responsible for reviewing the approval EC and NSL prior to approval by the Special Agent in Charge. Division Counsel are required to review the NSLs to ensure their legal sufficiency—specifically, the relevance of the information requested to an authorized security investigation.

The final step in the approval process occurs when the Special Agent in Charge or authorized FBI Headquarters official (the certifying official) certifies that the requested records are relevant to an authorized investigation to protect against international terrorism or clandestine intelligence activities and, with respect to investigation of "U.S. persons," that the investigation is not conducted solely on the basis of activities protected by the First Amendment. After making the required certification, the official initials the approval and signs the national security letter. (p. xiv)

...

ACTIVITY 17.1, CONTINUED

NATIONAL SECURITY LETTER (NSL) WORKING GROUP

Finally, in evaluating the FBI's use of national security letters it is important to note the significant challenges the FBI faced during the period covered by our review and the major organizational changes it was undergoing. It is also important to recognize that in most cases the FBI was seeking to obtain information that it could have obtained properly if it had followed applicable statutes, guidelines, and internal policies. We also did not find any indication that the FBI's misuse of NSL authorities constituted criminal misconduct.

However, as described above, we found that the FBI used NSLs in violation of applicable NSL statutes, Attorney General Guidelines, and internal FBI policies. In addition, we found that the FBI circumvented the [Electronic Communications Privacy Act] NSL statute when it issued over 700 "exigent letters" to obtain telephone billing records and subscriber information from three telephone companies without first issuing NSLs. Moreover, in a few instances, the FBI sought or obtained information to which it was not entitled under NSL authorities.

The OIG issued 10 recommendations to "improve the accuracy of the reporting of the FBI's use of national security letters and ensure the FBI's compliance with requirements governing their use." In a letter dated March 1, 2007, Attorney General Alberto Gonzales directed the Inspector General to report to him in four months on the FBI's "implementation of your recommendations."

(http://www.usdoj.gov/oig/special/s0703b/final.pdf)

For the Class Report:

- What is an NSL?

- How great an invasion of privacy is FBI access to this information? Does it seem to violate the Fourth Amendment?

- Are the safeguards against abuse adequate? Explain.

- Will the FBI do better in following the law and procedures in the future? What are the incentives for doing so?

- How should we interpret the numbers of NSLs?

- Present your overall evaluation of the seriousness of the threat to civil liberties posed by NSLs. Provide evidence for your conclusion.

ACTIVITY 17.2
SECTION 215 WORKING GROUP

Before working on this assignment, you should understand the provisions of the First and Fourth amendments to the U.S. Constitution. Here is the text of the First Amendment:

Congress shall make no law respecting an establishment of religion, or prohibiting the free exercise thereof; or abridging the freedom of speech, or of the press; or the right of the people peaceably to assemble, and to petition the Government for a redress of grievances.

Here is the text of the Fourth Amendment:

The right of the people to be secure in their persons, houses, papers, and effects, against unreasonable searches and seizures, shall not be violated, and no Warrants shall issue, but upon probable cause, supported by Oath or affirmation, and particularly describing the place to be searched, and the persons or things to be seized.

Directions: One specific area of concern about the Patriot Act has to do with Section 215. To learn about Section 215, read the information below. Your overall goal is to evaluate the seriousness of the threat to civil liberties posed by Section 215.

The excerpts you will read are from a report of the Office of the Inspector General (OIG), Department of Justice; they also contain information about changes made in the Patriot Act when Congress reauthorized it in 2006.

The following questions may help to provide focus for your reading:

1. What is Section 215? What information can be obtained?

2. How great an invasion of privacy is FBI access to this information? Does it seem to violate the Fourth Amendment?

3. Some people are concerned that Section 215 allows the FBI to obtain library records, thereby threatening civil liberties under the First Amendment. Is this a reasonable concern? Explain.

4. Are the safeguards against abuse adequate?

   - Is the lowered "threshold" for obtaining information under Section 215 serious?

   - Are the procedures necessary to obtain information under Section 215 adequate?

   - Are the changes made by the reauthorization adequate?

   - How serious are the problems found in the OIG report?

After considering the information, be prepared to report to the class on how much of an infringement on civil liberties Section 215 poses.

ACTIVITY 17.2, CONTINUED
SECTION 215 WORKING GROUP

What is Section 215?

Quoted Excerpts from Office of the Inspector General (OIG) Report, March 9, 2007

Pursuant to Section 215 of the Patriot Act, the FBI may obtain "any tangible things," including books, records, and other items from any business, organization, or entity provided the item or items are for an authorized investigation to protect against international terrorism or clandestine intelligence activities. Section 215 did not create any new investigative authority but instead expanded existing authority found in the Foreign Intelligence Surveillance Act (FISA) of 1978. (p. ii)

FISA requires the FBI to obtain an order from the Foreign Intelligence Surveillance Court (FISA Court)…(p. ii)

Section 215 significantly expanded the scope of the FBI's investigative authority… and lowered the standard of proof…(p. iii)

… the new language does not explicitly limit the type of entity or business that can be compelled by an order. Section 215 … also expanded the categories of documents… (p. iii)

Section 215 lowered the evidentiary threshold to obtain such an order. As a result the number of people whose information could be obtained was expanded because the FBI is no longer required to show that the items being sought pertain to a person whom the FBI is investigating. Instead, the items sought need only be requested "for an authorized investigation conducted in accordance with [applicable law and guidelines] to obtain foreign intelligence information not concerning a United States person or to protect against international terrorism or clandestine intelligence activities. (p. iv)

Other Information from the OIG Report

The first Section 215 request was made in May 2004. From then until September 2005, there were 162 requests, all approved by the FISA court. The court made minor modifications to 4 of these. (p. 77)

The report found two instances of improper use of Section 215 orders. Both errors involved telephone numbers no longer used by the target of the investigation. Both were reported to the President's Intelligence Oversight Board and the FISA Court. (p.78)

(OIG Report source: http://www.usdoj.gov/oig/special/s0703a/final.pdf)

ACTIVITY 17.2, CONTINUED

SECTION 215 WORKING GROUP

Changes Made by the Patriot Act Reauthorization (Excerpts from the Bill of Rights Defense Committee)

- Recipients of Section 215 orders have the right to challenge them in court. However, [the reauthorized Act] places the bar for succeeding in a challenge too high. In order to succeed in a challenge, the third-party holder of records sought must prove that the government acted in bad faith, without the advantage of knowing whether the government is using secret evidence.

- [The Act] gives recipients of court-approved subpoenas for information in terrorist investigations the right to challenge a requirement that they refrain from telling anyone.

- Two new procedural hurdles have been imposed on FBI agents who want to apply for a Section 215 order to search bookstore or library records: they must first obtain the permission of one of three top officials—the director or deputy director of the FBI or the Executive Assistant Director of National Security; they must also present a statement of facts justifying the relevance of their request to a judge in the secret court established by the Foreign Intelligence Surveillance Act (FISA).

- Third parties who receive a Section 215 order will have the right to consult an attorney and the right to challenge the order in the FISA court.

- Automatic, permanent gag orders imposed on everyone who receives a National Security Letter or a Section 215 order may be appealed one year after the order is received.

- The public has gained the right to learn whether Section 215 is being abused: the Inspector General of the Justice Department will conduct a review of the use of Section 215 since 2001 and report publicly whether any abuses have occurred; in addition, the Justice Department must annually report the number of bookstore and library searches that have occurred under Section 215.

- The package clarifies that most libraries are not subject to demands in those letters for information about suspected terrorists. If the library is not an Internet Service Provider, the government will seek the Internet records directly from the ISP rather than seizing the library computer.

Source: http://www.bordc.org/threats/legislation/reauthchanges.php#changes

ACTIVITY 17.2, CONTINUED

SECTION 215 WORKING GROUP

For the Class Report:

- Explain what Section 215 is.

- How great an invasion of privacy is FBI access to this information? Does it seem to violate the Fourth Amendment? Explain.

- Some people are concerned that Section 215 allows the FBI to obtain library records, thereby threatening civil liberties under the First Amendment. Is this a reasonable concern? Explain.

- Are the safeguards against abuse adequate?

- Present your overall evaluation of the seriousness of the threat to civil liberties posed by Section 215. Provide evidence to support your conclusion.

ACTIVITY 17.3
EFFECTIVENESS WORKING GROUP

Your task is to use the information below to assess the effectiveness of National Security Letters (NSLs) and Section 215 in enhancing security. NSLs are used to compel a person, business, organization, etc., to turn over information on telephone and e-mail records, financial records, consumer credit information, etc., to the FBI. Section 215 allows the FBI to seek an order from a special court to obtain records and other information from businesses and other organizations.

Instructions

Using the information below, assess the effectiveness of the NSLs and Section 215. How valuable are these measures for enhancing national security? As you read the information, keep the following questions in mind:

1. How is the information obtained used by the FBI?

2. What evidence is there that these tools have enhanced security?

3. The FBI states that these tools are two of many used in investigating national security threats. Is it reasonable to expect "success stories" based on the use of these methods alone?

4. Will more "results" occur as the FBI increases the use of these methods?

5. Should we accept at face value the statements of agents about the effectiveness of these tools? What incentives are there for the FBI to follow guidelines in fully reporting out the various elements and uses of NSLs and Section 215 orders?

Information

Your task is complicated because there is little information about how the FBI has used the information it has obtained. Opponents of the Patriot Act try to minimize its effectiveness as a tool to enhance security. For example, a *Washington Post* story by Barton Gellman from November 5, 2005, states the following:

> As the Justice Department prepared congressional testimony this year, FBI headquarters searched for examples that would show how expanded surveillance powers made a difference. Michael Mason, who runs the Washington field office and has the rank of assistant FBI director, found no ready answer. "I'd love to have a made-for-Hollywood story, but I don't have one," Mason said. "I am not even sure such an example exists."

> (http://www.washingtonpost.com/wp-dyn/content/article/2005/11/05/AR2005110501366.html)

> In *Reason Magazine*, April 6, 2005, Julian Sanchez wrote about an early FBI report ("Report from the Field") on the use of their Patriot Act powers.

> What's striking is how weak the case for the PATRIOT Act's vital necessity as an anti-terror measure appears even when we focus on the Department of Justice's handpicked examples, as provided in their "Report from the Field."

> (http://www.reason.com/news/show/34019.html)

ACTIVITY 17.3, CONTINUED

EFFECTIVENESS WORKING GROUP

However, in March 2007, more recent public information came from two reports (one each on NSLs and Section 215) from the Office of the Inspector General (OIG) of the Department of Justice. The law requires these reports to present information on the effectiveness of NSLs and Section 215. The information below is drawn from these two reports.

Information Quoted from the OIG Report on NSLs
(http://www.usdoj.gov/oig/special/s0703b/final.pdf)

FBI Headquarters and field personnel told us that they found national security letters to be effective in both counterterrorism and counterintelligence investigations. Many FBI personnel used terms to describe NSLs such as "indispensable" or "our bread and butter."

FBI personnel reported that the principal objectives for using NSLs are to:

- Establish evidence to support Foreign Intelligence Surveillance Act (FISA) applications to the Foreign Intelligence Surveillance Court for electronic surveillance, physical searches, or pen register/trap and trace orders;

- Assess communication or financial links between investigative subjects and others;

- Collect information sufficient to fully develop national security investigations;

- Generate leads for other field divisions, members of Joint Terrorism Task Forces, other federal agencies, or to pass to foreign governments;

- Develop analytical products for distribution within the FBI, other Department components, other federal agencies, and the intelligence community;

- Develop information that is provided to law enforcement authorities for use in criminal proceedings;

- Collect information sufficient to eliminate concerns about investigative subjects and thereby close national security investigations; and

- Corroborate information derived from other investigative techniques.

Information Quoted from the OIG Report on Section 215

(http://www.usdoj.gov/oig/special/s0703a/final.pdf)

We examined how the FBI has used this information in national security investigations. We found that Section 215 orders have been used primarily to exhaust investigative leads, although in some instances the FBI obtained identifying information about suspected agents of a foreign power not previously known to the FBI. However, the evidence showed no instance where the information obtained from a Section 215 order resulted in a major case development, such as the disruption of a terrorist plot. In addition, we found that the FBI disseminated informa-tion...to another intelligence agency in only three instances.... We identified only one instance in which the FBI sought to use information...in a criminal proceeding....[However,] no [Section

ACTIVITY 17.3, CONTINUED

EFFECTIVENESS WORKING GROUP

215] information was used in the grand jury or subsequent proceedings. (p. 78)

....The FBI began using Section 215 authority more widely in 2006. (pp. 78-79)

Agents told us they believe that the kind of intelligence gathering from Section 215 orders was essential for national security investigations. They also stated that the importance of the information is sometimes not known until much later in an investigation when the information is linked to some other piece of intelligence...(p. xxii)

Agents called section 215 authority "critical" and a tool of last resort.... "a specialized tool that has a purpose." ... "The only way to obtain some information."

For the Class Report:

- How is the information obtained used by the FBI?

- What evidence is there that these tools have enhanced security?

- The FBI states that these tools are two among many used in investigating national security threats. Is it reasonable to expect "success stories" based on the use of these methods alone? Explain.

- Will more "results" occur as the FBI increases the use of these methods? Explain.

- Should we accept at face value the statements of agents about the effectiveness of these tools? What incentives are there for the FBI to follow guidelines in fully reporting out the various elements and uses of NSLs and Section 215 orders? Explain.

- Assess the effectiveness of National Security Letters (NSLs) and Section 215 in enhancing security, based on the available information. Be sure to back up your evaluation with evidence.

LESSON 18

ECONOMIC INDICATORS FOR INFORMED CITIZENS

LESSON 18
ECONOMIC INDICATORS FOR INFORMED CITIZENS

INTRODUCTION

On any given day, citizens reading a newspaper or watching a newscast are likely to read or hear reports about the state of the U.S. economy. Often these reports discuss *economic indicators*. An economic indicator is a statistic that indicates something about the current performance of the U.S. economy. The three most commonly reported indicators are *real gross domestic product (GDP), the inflation rate,* and *the unemployment rate.*

Economic indicators serve people in several ways. Investors use economic indicators to make decisions about how to invest. Consumers use economic indicators to make decisions about buying a home. Business owners use economic indicators to make   decisions about how many workers to employ. And citizens may use economic indicators to make decisions about which representatives to vote for and which public policies to support. These and other uses of economic indicators will be important to students as they move toward adult participation in the economy.

LESSON DESCRIPTION

This lesson introduces students to three basic economic indicators: real GDP, the inflation rate, and the unemployment rate. The students work in small groups to develop an economic forecast, using the three basic economic indicators. They participate in a simulation activity involving a fictional economic forecasting firm. The firm has taken on a client who wishes to start a new business and wants to know whether this is a good idea, given the current economic climate. To advise the client, the students produce a report based on research they conduct about the state of the economy, according to the three economic indicators.

CONCEPTS

- Economic forecasting

- Gross domestic product (GDP)

- Inflation

- Unemployment

OBJECTIVES

Students will be able to:

1. Define *real gross domestic product, inflation,* and *unemployment rate.*

2. Locate current data for real gross domestic product, inflation, and the unemployment rate.

3. Examine 12-month trend data for gross domestic product, inflation, and the unemployment rate.

4. Use economic data to produce a report that describes the current state of economic activity and provides an economic forecast to a fictional client.

CONTENT STANDARDS
Economics (CEE Standards)

- A nation's overall levels of income, employment, and prices are determined by the interaction of spending and production decisions made by all households, firms, government agencies, and others in the economy. (Standard 18)

- Unemployment imposes costs on individuals and nations. Unexpected inflation imposes costs on many people and benefits some others because it arbitrarily redistributes purchasing power. Inflation can reduce the rate of growth of national living standards because individuals and organizations use resources to protect themselves against the uncertainty of future prices. (Standard 19)

- Federal government budgetary policy and the Federal Reserve System's monetary policy influence the overall levels of employment, output, and prices. (Standard 20)

Civics and Government (NSCG Standards, Grades 9-12)

- Students should be able to evaluate, take, and defend positions on issues regarding the major responsibilities of the national government for domestic and foreign policy. (Standard III.B.2)

- Students should be able to evaluate, take, and defend positions about the effects of significant economic, technological, and cultural developments in the United States and other nations. (Standard IV.C.3)

TIME REQUIRED

60-90 minutes

MATERIALS

- A transparency of Visuals 18.1 and 18.2

- A copy for each student of Activity 18.1 and 18.2

- Online sources: See Procedure 3 below

PROCEDURE

1. Tell the students that this lesson will focus on some key indicators that are used to measure the health of the nation's economic system. Ask the students if they are familiar with any TV shows set in emergency rooms. Prompt them to think of the important medical information (the vital signs) that emergency room doctors use to determine the health of the patient (e.g., pulse, blood pressure, respiration, etc.). Explain that, much like an emergency room patient, the United States economy has important "vital signs" as well. These vital signs can be thought of as economic indicators.

2. To move toward an introduction of the lesson's main concepts, ask the students whether they have ever heard or read a news story about the "health" of the U.S. economy. If anybody has, ask whether the news item mentioned inflation, unemployment, or gross domestic product. (*Discuss responses briefly*.) Explain that these

concepts refer to three important economic indicators—vital signs that can tell us a great deal about the "health" of the economy. Display and briefly discuss Visual 18.1, explaining that today the students will be learning about all three of these indicators.

3. Introduce the simulation activity: in order to learn about the economic indicators, the students will play the role of a partner in a fictional economic forecasting firm. Distribute Activity 18.1. Note: If you have access to a computer lab, the students should read the most recent EconEdLink Case Studies on the inflation rate, the unemployment rate, and real gross domestic product:

- Case Study: The Inflation Rate
  http://econedlink.org/lessons/index.php?lesson=EM760&page=teacher

- Case Study: The Unemployment Rate
  http://econedlink.org/lessons/index.php?lesson=EM770&page=teacher

- Case Study: Real Gross Domestic Product
  http://econedlink.org/lessons/index.php?lesson=EM775&page=teacher

Students will also need access to current economic data. The following are sources for current economic data:

- White House Economics Briefing Room:
  http://www.whitehouse.gov/fsbr/esbr.html

- Bureau of Labor Statistics:
  http://www.bls.gov/eag/eag.us.htm

- Bureau of Economic Analysis:
  http://www.bea.gov/

- EconEdLink Data Links:
  http://econedlink.org/datalinks/

4. This lesson uses a form of cooperative group learning. Explain to the students that they will be assigned to two groups. First, they will be assigned to a Home Group that represents their economic forecasting firm, Economic Forecasters,

Inc. (or EFI). Each EFI group will have at least three members. The second group is an Expert Group. Within this group the students will learn about one economic indicator, and complete the appropriate Study Guide. Then they will return to their EFI groups to report what they have learned. Each student will have a data retrieval chart (see Table 18.1) in which to enter relevant information. Sample responses to Study Guides:

Study Guide Answers: Unemployment Rate

1. All people without a job are considered unemployed.
   (circle one)   TRUE / (FALSE)

2. The unemployment rate measures__. *(The percentage of the U.S. labor force that is unemployed.)*

3. The unemployment rate is calculated by_____. *(It is calculated by dividing the number of unemployed individuals [U] by the number of people in the labor force, which is the sum of the number of people unemployed [U] and the number of people employed [E]. The result is then multiplied by 100 to turn the unemployment rate into a percentage; unemployment rate = [U / U+E] x 100.)*

4. Calculate the unemployment rate if:
   U = 7,000,000   E = 145,000,000
   _____ *(4.8%)*

5. Costs of an increasing unemployment rate:
   - *Workers do not have the income to support themselves.*
   - *GDP is lower.*
   - *Average standards of living are lower as a result of unemployment.*

5. Three types of unemployment:
   - *Frictional unemployment.*
   - *Structural unemployment.*
   - *Cyclical unemployment.*

7. Current unemployment rate: _____. *(Answer will depend on current information; see www.bls.gov.)*

8. Unemployment rate trend over the last year: _____. *(Answer will depend on current information; see www.bls.gov.)*

Study Guide Answers: Inflation Rate

1. The Consumer Price Index (CPI) is____. *(A measure of the average level of prices paid for goods and services by households.)*

2. The Consumer Price Index measures____. *(The cost of purchasing a fixed market basket of goods and services.)*

3. The inflation rate is calculated by____. *(Determining the percentage change in the CPI from one month to the next or from one year to another.)*

4. Calculate the inflation rate if:
   CPI (September 2007) = 208.5
   CPI (September 2008) = 218.8
   _____ *(4.9%)*

5. Two causes of inflation:
   a. *Demand-pull.*
   b. *Cost-push.*

6. Costs when the inflation rate increases faster than expected:
   a. *People on fixed incomes are worse off.*
   b. *Interest rates increase.*
   c. *Business investment decreases.*
   d. *Purchasing power decreases.*

7. Current (12-month) inflation rate: ____. *(Answer will depend on current information; see www.bls.gov.)*

8. Inflation rate trend over the last three years: _____. *(Answer will depend on current and historical information; see www.bls.gov.)*

Study Guide Answers:
Real Gross Domestic Product (GDP)

1. The gross domestic product (GDP) is____. *(The output of final goods and services produced in the U.S. in one year.)*

2. Real GDP is_____. *(Output adjusted for inflation.)*

3. The components of GDP are:
   _____ *consumer spending.*
   _____ *investment spending.*
   _____ *government purchases of goods and services.*
   _____ *net exports (exports – imports).*

Complete the formula: GDP =   *(C + I + G + Xn [net exports])*

4. GDP is an important measure of the nation's economic health because _____. *(Output is crucial to employment, earnings, income, spending, and other key measures of overall economic well-being.)*

5. Increasing GDP indicates _____. *(Greater output, higher productivity, and / or more employment, higher standard of living, etc.)*

6. Decreasing GDP indicates _____. *(Less output, lower productivity, and / or less employment, lower standard of living, etc.)*

7. Current level and growth rate of real GDP: _____. *(Answer will depend on current information; see www.bea.gov.)*

8. Trend in the growth of real GDP over the last three years: _____. *(Answer will depend on current and historical information; see www.bea.gov.)*

5. Assign the students to their EFI groups. (Note: It is possible that an EFI group may have more than three members if the number of students in the class is not divisible by three). At the same time, assign the students to one of the three Expert Groups (Inflation, Unemployment, real GDP). Note that each EFI group is required to have one expert in each of the three categories of unemployment, inflation, and real GDP. This means that students must be evenly distributed across expert groups. Once these groups have formed, display Visual 18.2. Announce that the groups will now break up into their assigned expert groups.

6. Allow the students 15 minutes to read the description of their indicator, discuss it, and complete the row in Table 18.1 that pertains to their indicator. Note that the students will need access to the Internet in order to complete the section asking for current information and recent trends of their indicator. For sample responses, see Table 18.1.

TABLE 18.1

KEY ECONOMIC INDICATORS

Indicator	Indicator measures?	How calculated?	An **increase** in this indicator means…?	A **decrease** in this indicator means…?	Current data (and trend) for the indicator?
Real GDP	Growth in U.S. output of final goods and services (adjusted for inflation) in a given year.	Sum of all consumption spending, investment spending, and government purchases of goods and services added to net exports (exports –imports).	More output in U.S., more "product" (goods and services) produced; living standards may be higher.	Less output in U.S., less "product" (goods and services) produced; living standards may be lower; potential for recession.	Answers will depend on current information.
Inflation Rate	Percentage change in average level of prices of goods and services purchased by the typical house-hold. The consumer price index (CPI) is the most widely reported measure of the overall price level.	Compares the cost of purchasing a fixed market basket of goods and services to its cost in a previous month or year: {[CPI (Year 2) – CPI (Year 1)] / CPI (Year 1)} x 100	An unexpectedly large increase in inflation can lead to reduced purchasing power; people on fixed incomes without cost-of-living adjust-ments (COLAs) are hurt; interest rates go up.	An unexpectedly large decrease in the rate of inflation can lead to people having more purchasing power than they expected; people on fixed incomes are relatively better off than they expected; interest rates go down.	Answers will depend on current information.
Unemploy-ment Rate	The percentage of the United States labor force that is unemployed.	Labor force = unemployed + employed; unemployment rate = {unemployed / (unemployed + employed)} x 100	Workers do not have the income to support them-selves; GDP is lower; average living standards may be lower.	Workers are better off; GDP is higher; average living standards may be higher.	Answers will depend on current information.

7. Once the students have completed their respective sections of Table 18.1, have them return to their EFI groups; in the EFI groups they should share what they have learned with other members of the group. Each member should then complete the remaining sections of Table 18.1 based on the reports of the other two members.

8. Once students complete Table 18.1, each EFI group will prepare a report written to the fictional client ("Ms. J. Q. Public"). Each group should use the report template provided at the end of Activity 18.2.

CLOSURE

Once the reports have been completed, ask the students to share their recommendations. How many recommended opening the new business? Why?

(Answers will vary, based on the current performance of the economy.)

Quickly review the definitions of each of the economic indicators. Ask the students what the trend was for each indicator. Ask them to explain their recommendations based on these trends.

(E.g., if real GDP has fallen for two quarters, EFI might recommend that Ms. Public be cautious about starting a new business.)

ASSESSMENT

Multiple-Choice Questions

1. Which of the following statements is not true?

   A. Unemployment can lead to financial and family problems.

   B. **Unemployment leads to higher standards of living.**

   C. The labor force includes those who are working or actively looking for work.

   D. Unemployment is associated with less output in the overall economy.

2. If the Consumer Price Index (CPI) for one year was 150 and for the next year it was 157.5, the inflation rate from one year to the next is

   A. **5.0%.**

   B. 7.5%.

   C. 57.5%.

   D. 157.5%.

3. Gross domestic product is calculated by adding together

   A. consumer spending, government spending, and all imports.

   B. consumer spending, government spending, and all investments.

   C. consumer spending, investment spending, and net exports.

   D. **consumer spending, investment spending, government purchases of goods and services, and net exports.**

Constructed-Response Question

Read the following fictional headline:

U.S. output increases for the 10th consecutive quarter

Define the economic indicator used in the headline. Then explain the headline: what does it mean, literally, and what does it suggest about the U.S. economy?

(This headline refers to real GDP. The headline means that the U.S. economy has been experiencing an economic expansion for the past 2½ years. Associated with this expansion, there probably has been an improvement in average living standards, increased spending in various sectors of the economy, and, perhaps, a reduction in the unemployment rate.)

VISUAL 18.1

ECONOMIC INDICATORS: THE VITAL SIGNS OF THE U.S. ECONOMY

Economic Indicator:

A statistic that describes the current performance of the U.S. economy.

Three Main Economic Indicators:

1. **Real Gross Domestic Product (GDP)**

   This indicator measures the output of the final goods and services produced in the U.S. economy in a given time period (typically, one year).

2. **The Inflation Rate**

   This indicator measures how rapidly the overall price level is changing in the U.S. economy.

3. **The Unemployment Rate**

   This indicator measures the percentage of the U.S. labor force that wishes to work, but are currently without jobs.

Visual 18.2

Letter from a Client

From the Desk Of:

J. Q. Public,

CEO

Acme Industries, Inc.

November 19, 2008

The Economic Forecasters, Inc.

123 Any Street

Muncie, Indiana

To Whom It May Concern:

I am the CEO of a successful business. My firm manufactures and distributes many consumer products. I would like to have the company open another factory, but our Board of Directors is concerned that the U. S. economy is too weak to support its expansion. Recent economic reports—especially in the popular media—paint a mixed picture.

Therefore, I would like to hire your firm to produce a report that describes the current state of the U.S. economy and forecasts the performance of the economy over the next 12 months.

I would appreciate a complete report, so please include several charts or graphs that will help me see the trends in the economy. I will then share these results with the Board of Directors.

I look forward to receiving your report.

Sincerely,

Jocelyn Q. Public

Chief Executive Officer

Acme Industries, Inc.

ACTIVITY 18.1

INTRODUCTION TO KEY ECONOMIC INDICATORS

Directions: Read each of the three descriptions below, paying close attention to the economic indicator you have been assigned in your Expert Group. In your Expert Group, work to complete both the Study Guide and Table 18.1 for that indicator. Be prepared to share your findings when you return to your EFI group.

1. The Unemployment Rate[1]

The unemployment rate is the percentage of the United States labor force that is unemployed. It is calculated by dividing the number of unemployed individuals (U) by the sum of the number of people unemployed (U) and the number of people employed (E). This result is then multiplied by 100 to turn the unemployment rate into a percentage:

$$\text{Unemployment Rate} = [U/U+E] \times 100$$

The U.S. labor force equals the number of people who are unemployed added to the number of people who are employed. An individual is counted as *unemployed* if he or she is 16 years old or older and is actively looking for a job, but cannot find one. Students, individuals who choose not to work, and retirees are *not* in the labor force, and therefore not counted in the unemployment rate.

Unemployed workers often do not have sufficient income to support themselves or their families; this can lead to financial challenges, marital problems, and even criminal activity.

State and federal governments provide unemployment compensation (insurance) to some unemployed workers. Because most workers pay the taxes that fund the unemployment compensation, some of the cost of unemployment is spread to employed taxpayers as well.

Increases in unemployment mean that real GDP is lower than it otherwise could be. If more individuals had been employed, the nation's economic output would be higher. Average standards of living are lower as a result of unemployment.

There are ***three types of unemployment,*** each of which describes the particular circumstances of individuals and their employment situations.

- ***Frictional unemployment*** is temporary unemployment arising from the normal job search process: it may include people who are seeking better or more convenient jobs, or those who are graduating from school and just entering the job market.

- ***Structural unemployment*** results from changes in the economy caused by technological progress and long-term shifts in the demand for goods and services. With structural unemployment, some jobs in certain sectors of the economy are eliminated and new jobs are created in faster-growing areas. Persons who are structurally unemployed may lack skills for new types of jobs and may face prolonged periods of unemployment.

- ***Cyclical unemployment*** is unemployment caused by a general downturn in economic activity. This type of unemployment can hit many different industries during a period of overall economic weakness.

[1] Description created using S. Buckles (2006), "A Case Study: The Unemployment Rate," *EconEdLink*. Accessed at http://econedlink.org/lessons/index.cfm?lesson=EM219&page=teacher on April 20, 2007.

ACTIVITY 18.1, CONTINUED

INTRODUCTION TO KEY ECONOMIC INDICATORS

Study Guide: The Unemployment Rate (fill out the Study Guide in your Expert Group; you will share this information with your EFI group).

1. All people without a job are considered unemployed. (circle one)　　TRUE / FALSE

2. The unemployment rate measures_____.

3. The unemployment rate is calculated by_____.

4. Calculate the unemployment rate if:

   U = 7,000,000　　　　E = 145,000,000

   _____.

5. Costs of an increasing unemployment rate:
   -
   -
   -

6. Three types of unemployment:
   -
   -
   -

7. Current unemployment rate:_____.

8. Unemployment rate trend over the last year:_____.

ACTIVITY 18.1, CONTINUED

INTRODUCTION TO KEY ECONOMIC INDICATORS

2. Inflation: The Consumer Price Index (CPI)[2]

Inflation is a rise in the average prices of all goods and services. The consumer price index (CPI) is the most widely reported measure of inflation. The CPI compares the prices of a fixed set of goods and services (called a "market basket of goods and services") to the prices of those same goods and services in a previous month or year. Any increase in the cost of purchasing this market basket of goods and services means an overall increase in the average level of prices paid by consumers, and thus inflation is said to be present.

The inflation rate is calculated by determining the percentage change in the CPI from one month to the next or from one year to another. For example, the CPI for November 2005 was 199.2 The CPI in November 2006 was 201.7. Therefore, the percent change in the CPI was:

$$[(201.7 - 199.2) / 199.2] \times 100 =$$

$$[2.5 / 199.2] \times 100 =$$

$$= 1.3\%$$

The inflation rate from November 2005 to November 2006 was 1.3%. In other words, the average price of the market basket of goods and services rose 1.3% during that one- year period.

Over short periods of time, inflation can be caused by increases in costs or increases in spending. *Demand-pull inflation* occurs when overall increases in demand *pull up* the average level of prices. If spending increases faster than the economy's capacity to produce more goods and services, there will be upward pressure on prices. *Cost-push inflation* is caused by increases in costs of major inputs used throughout the economy. Increases in costs *push up* the average level of prices. For example, throughout much of 2007 and 2008, inflation rates increased largely because of increases in the price of oil. Because oil is an important input for many goods and services, an increase in its price leads to price increases for many other things. In the long run, inflation can also be caused by excessive growth of the money supply.

Costs of Inflation. Inflation that is greater than people expected reduces the purchasing power of money. Because prices rise over time, consumers require a larger income to purchase the goods and services necessary to maintain a constant standard of living. People on fixed incomes such as pensioners or workers without cost-of-living adjustments (COLAs) are especially hurt by unexpected inflation. High inflation makes it difficult for businesses and consumers to predict the future and can discourage long-term saving and investment. High inflation leads to high interest rates. Lenders receive higher interest payments, part of which is compensation for the decrease in the value of the money lent (due to inflation). Borrowers have to pay higher interest rates and lose any advantage they may have from repaying loans with money that is not worth as much as it was prior to the inflation.

[2] Description created using S. Buckles (2006), "A Case Study: The Inflation Rate," *EconEdLink*. Accessed at http://econedlink.org/lessons/index.cfm?lesson=EM222&page=teacher on April 23, 2007.

ACTIVITY 18.1, CONTINUED

INTRODUCTION TO KEY ECONOMIC INDICATORS

Study Guide: The Inflation Rate. Fill out the study guide in your expert group; you will share this information with your EFI group.

1. The Consumer Price Index (CPI) is_____.

2. The Consumer Price Index measures_____._

3. The inflation rate is calculated by_____.

4. Calculate the inflation rate if:

   CPI (September 2007) = 208.5   CPI (September 2008) = 218.8

   _____

5. Two causes of inflation:

   a.

   b.

6. Costs when the inflation rate increases faster than expected:

   a.

   b.

   c.

   d.

7. Current (12-month) inflation rate: _____.

8. Inflation rate trend over the last three years:_____.

ACTIVITY 18.1, CONTINUED

INTRODUCTION TO KEY ECONOMIC INDICATORS

3. Economic Output: Real Gross Domestic Product (GDP)[3]

Real gross domestic product (real **GDP**) is a measure of economic output. It is defined as the market value of final goods and services produced in the United States in a year, adjusted for inflation. Real GDP is total output adjusted for inflation by holding prices constant.

- ***Gross*** measurement includes the total amount of goods and services produced, some of which replace goods that have depreciated or have worn out.

- ***Domestic*** production includes only goods and services produced within the United States.

- Current ***production*** is measured during the year in question.

- It is a measurement of the ***final*** goods and services produced because it does not separately include the value of an intermediate good that is part of a transaction between parties that do not involve the final customer. We count only the final sale.

Changes in real GDP from one year to the next reflect changes in the market value of the output of goods and services holding the prices of goods and services constant. Therefore, any changes in real GDP can only arise from a change in the quantities of goods and services produced. Prices are held constant in constructing real GDP measures. **Real GDP per capita** is the real GDP per person in the economy and is commonly thought of as the best measure of overall economic well-being in a country.

The GDP is calculated by totaling up consumption spending, investment spending, government purchases of goods and services, and spending on U.S. exports. To arrive at the amount actually produced in the United States (that is, U.S. Gross Domestic Product), our spending on imports is subtracted from those other amounts of spending. Thus,

GDP = Consumption spending + investment spending + government purchases of goods and services + (export spending – import spending)

Consumption spending consists of household spending on final goods and services. These purchases can account for 60 to 70 percent of GDP and include goods such as new cars, furniture, food, and clothing; and services such as rent paid on apartments, airplane tickets, legal advice, and entertainment. Services are the largest and fastest growing component of consumption spending.

Investment spending accounts for approximately 15 percent of GDP and can fluctuate a lot over time. It includes the production of tools, equipment, new business structures, machinery, etc., that are used in the production of other goods and services. These items are expected to yield a stream of returns over time, which is why expenditures in this category are referred to as economic

---

[3] Description created using S. Buckles (2006), "A Case Study: Gross Domestic Product," *EconEdLink*. Accessed at http://econedlink.org/lessons/index.cfm?lesson=EM225&page=teacher on April 23, 2007.

Activity 18.1, continued

Introduction to Key Economic Indicators

investment. GDP *does not* include financial investment such as purchases of stocks and bonds The investment category of GDP also includes the building of a new homes or apartments. Inventory changes are also found in investment expenditures.

Government purchases of goods and services includes federal, state, and local government spending on goods and services such as research, roads, defense, schools, and police and fire departments. This spending (approximately 20 percent of GDP) does not include transfer payments such as Social Security, unemployment compensation, and welfare payments, which do not represent production of goods and services. National defense spending now accounts for approximately 5 percent of GDP. State and local government spending on goods and services accounts for about 12 percent of GDP, while federal government purchases of goods and services are about 8 percent of GDP.

Exports are goods and services produced in the United States and purchased by foreigners. Currently exports account for about 10 percent of GDP.

Imports are items produced by foreigners and purchased by U.S. consumers; they account for about 16 percent of GDP.

Net exports (exports minus imports) have consistently been negative over the past three decades and are now about negative 6 percent of GDP.

Real GDP per capita is a measure of the claim on final goods and services of the average member of the U.S. population. This is the best measure of overall material standards of living and is commonly used in making comparisons of living standards across countries and over time.

While there are several measures of overall economic performance (such as inflation, unemployment, personal income, etc.), none is a more important indicator of our economy's health than rates of change in real GDP. When our real GDP increases, we are producing more "product" as a nation, and we are usually better off.

Changes in real GDP are discussed in the press and on the nightly news after every announcement of the latest quarter's newly released or revised data. Any change in the growth of real GDP will be discussed in news reports as an indicator of the health of the national economy.

Real GDP trends are prominently included in discussions of potential slowdowns and economic booms. Economic commentators use decreases in real GDP as indicators of recessions. For example, the most popular (although technically inaccurate) definition of a recession is at least two consecutive quarters of declining real GDP.

ACTIVITY 18.1, CONTINUED

INTRODUCTION TO KEY ECONOMIC INDICATORS

Study Guide: Real Gross Domestic Product (GDP). (Fill out the study guide in your expert group; you will share this information with your EFI group.)

1. The gross domestic product (GDP) is_____.

2. Real GDP is_____.

3. The components of GDP are

   a. _____.
   b. _____.
   c. _____.
   d. _____.

   Complete the formula: GDP =

4. GDP is an important measure of the nation's economic health because

   _____.

5. Increasing GDP indicates

   _____.

6. Decreasing GDP indicates

   _____.

7. Current level and growth rate of real GDP:
   _____.

8. Trend in the growth of real GDP over the last three
   years:_____.

ACTIVITY 18.1, CONTINUED

TABLE 18.1 KEY ECONOMIC INDICATORS

Indicator	Indicator measures?	How calculated?	An <u>increase</u> in this indicator means...?	A <u>decrease</u> in this indicator means...?	Current data (and trend) for the indicator?
Real GDP					
Inflation Rate					
Unemploy-ment Rate					

ACTIVITY 18.2
ECONOMIC FORECAST REPORT

Directions: Use the completed Study Guides and Table 18.1 to develop a report to Ms. J. Q. Public. As a group, come to a consensus about your recommendation. Use the template below to prepare your report.

Economic Forecasters, Inc.

Economic Forecast Report

Prepared for Ms. J. Q. Public

Output of the United States economy, as measured by _____ is currently

_____. The trend in output over the last 12 months has been

_____

_____.

The overall effect of this trend implies that_____

_____.

The average level of prices in the U.S., as measured by

_____, is rising at a current rate of

_____. The trend in the U.S. price level over the last 12

months has been_____.

_____.

The overall effect of this trend implies that_____

_____.

ACTIVITY 18.2, CONTINUED
ECONOMIC FORECAST REPORT

The percentage of the U.S. labor force that wishes to work, but is unable to find a job, as

measured by _____, is currently

_____. The trend in this percentage

over the last 12 months has been_____

_____.

The overall effect of this trend implies that_____

_____.

Given these economic statistics, Economic Forecasters, Inc. (EFI) recommends

_____

_____

_____

_____

_____

_____

_____

Signed,

_____

_____

_____

EFI Economists

LESSON 19

IMMIGRATION

LESSON 19
IMMIGRATION

INTRODUCTION

In the United States, immigration is a controversial and emotionally charged subject. Elected officials face serious difficulties in trying to formulate immigration policy. The difficulties reflect the problem's complexity and a lack of consensus among voters. Even when there has been broad agreement on some goals (e.g., greater control of national borders), there has been conflict over how best to accomplish these goals.

Disagreement is widespread even among experts. One can find enormous differences among experts in their assessments of the impact of immigration, legal and illegal, on the budgets of federal, state, and local governments. Former President George W. Bush's Council of Economic Advisers and the Heritage Foundation, for example, differed markedly in their estimates of the fiscal impact of immigration policy. Nor is it clear what effects immigration has had on wages. Most economists agree that immigration has increased competition for jobs among low-skilled workers, and that this competition has depressed their wages, but estimates of how great the effect has been vary widely.

In one area, however, there is broad agreement: immigrants are responding to incentives and disincentives as they make their decisions. For instance, wage differentials between the United States and Mexico are clearly animating forces, as are job opportunities in the United States, compared to Mexico. The incentives sometimes are great enough to prompt millions of people to leave their families, brave the hardships of an illegal border crossing, and venture into an unfamiliar culture in order to seek a better job at higher pay. It is no wonder that most "reform" proposals pay at least some attention to the incentives and disincentives that have a bearing on immigration.

LESSON DESCRIPTION

The students analyze legal and illegal immigration, creating concept maps to identify the incentives and disincentives that may influence prospective immigrants as they make their decisions.

CONCEPTS

- Immigration (Note: The words *immigration* and *emigration* have very similar meanings. Some usage manuals state that *immigration* should be used to stress a person's *entering into* a new country, while *emigration* should be used to stress a person's *leaving from* a home country. In actual usage, however, the distinction is not consistently observed. This lesson uses *immigration* throughout.)

- Incentives

- Markets

OBJECTIVES

Students will be able to:

1. Predict the impact on immigration of various conditions, events, and policies.

2. Explain how labor market conditions might affect immigration.

CONTENT STANDARDS
Economics (CEE Standards)

- People respond predictably to positive and negative incentives. (Standard 4)

- Prices send signals and provide incentives to buyers and sellers. When supply or demand changes, market prices adjust, affecting incentives. (Standard 8)

Civics and Government (NSCG Standards, Grades 9-12)

- The rule of law. (Standard I.A.2)

- Demographic and environmental developments. (Standard IV.C.4)

TIME REQUIRED

60 minutes

MATERIALS

- A transparency of Visuals 19.1, 19.2., 19.3, 19.4, and 19.5

- A copy for each student of Activity 19.1

- One overhead transparency marker

PROCEDURE

1. Tell the students that the purpose of this lesson is to examine some of the economic issues surrounding immigration. Tell them to take out a sheet of scrap paper for a quick quiz on U.S. immigration trends. Ask the following three questions:

   A. About what percentage of the U.S. population is composed of immigrants?

   B. Has the rate of immigration in recent years been increasing or decreasing?

   C. In recent years most immigrants entering the U.S. have come from which country?

2. Discuss the quiz briefly. Then Display Visual 19.1. Call for a student volunteer to read the information aloud. Ask: Which quiz question is answered by this information? (*Question B.*) What is the answer to the question? *(The immigration rate has been increasing.)*

3. To continue sketching out background information, display Visual 19.2. Discuss the data briefly with the students. Ask: Which quiz questions are answered by this information? (*Questions A and B.*) What are the answers to the questions? (*About 12 percent of the U.S. population is composed of immigrants; the rate of immigration has been increasing.*)

4. Extend the discussion of information from Visual 19.2. Ask:

   - How many immigrants are there in the United States? (About *35.2 million.*)

- What long-term trends are shown in the data?

   (*The immigrant percentage of the population peaked around 1910; then it declined until 1970, when it began to increase again.*)

- What might explain the long-term trends? (*Answers will vary. Students might mention changes in immigration laws, the lure of economic opportunity, the desire to escape political persecution, etc.*)

5. Display Visual 19.3 and have students examine the data. Point out that the number of immigrants is expressed in thousands. Ask: Which quiz question is answered here? (*Question C.*) What is the answer to the question? (*Mexico.*) Extend the discussion by asking:

   - From which of the listed countries do you think people might be political refugees? (*Answers will vary. Students might mention Vietnam, Cuba, Russia, and Iran.*)

   - When do you think Vietnamese immigrants were most likely to arrive? (*The 1960s and 1970s are decades in which Vietnamese immigrants were especially likely to arrive.*)

   - When do you think most Cuban immigrants arrived? (*Since the late 1950s, when the Castro regime came into power in Cuba.*)

6. Explain to the students that the incentives prompting immigrants to leave their homes for a new country must obviously be very powerful. Ask the students to speculate about this: What economic and political incentives might be powerful enough to cause people to immigrate? (*The economic incentives include prospects for earning higher incomes—perhaps enough to send some money back to the home country; gaining economic freedom; gaining better options for education, etc. The political incentives include escaping from political repression, gaining freedom*

of religion, gaining the right to engage in free speech, etc.)

7. What about disincentives? What might cause some people to hold back—to stay home? (*Disincentives might include the cost of traveling to the U.S., the difficulty of obtaining a visa and achieving citizenship, the fear [for illegal immigrants] of being caught, the reluctance to leave one's family behind, etc.)*

8. Display Visual 19.4 and distribute the accompanying activity (Activity 19.1). Show the students how to place ideas on the concept map, using the item that has already been completed. Note that "Low pay in the home country" is an incentive to immigrate to the United States for both legal and illegal immigrants. Point out, however, that some incentives and some disincentives have their effects *conditionally*, depending on the legal status of the immigrants in question. For example, "More U.S. border security" is a disincentive to illegal, not legal, immigrants. Tell the class to feel free to add items to the list.

   (*Possible incentives for both **legal and illegal immigrants** include more job opportunities in the U.S., speaks English, more political freedom in the U.S.— although political freedom may be enjoyed more by legal immigrants. Possible incentives for **legal immigrants only** include increase in U.S. work visas. Possible incentives for **illegal immigrants only** include amnesty for illegal immigrants in the U.S. Disincentives for both **legal and illegal immigrants** include better pay in the home country, ties to a close-knit family, strong cultural ties to home country, bad economic times in the U.S. Disincentives for **illegal immigrants only** include identification policy for U.S. employment, more U.S. border security.)*

9. Divide the class into small groups to begin work. Give the students in one group Visual 19.4 and a marker so that they can show their conclusions to the rest of the class.

10. Ask the group that completed its work on Visual 19.4 to show it to the class. Have these students explain their concept map. Solicit comments and questions from the class. (A sample completed concept map is found in Visual 19.5. There are different ways to create concept maps, so students may come up with acceptable variations of Visual 19.5.)

CLOSURE

Remind the class that in the United States today, the local, state, and national governments are trying to craft new immigration policies. In any policies that emerge, it will be important to pay attention to the incentives and disincentives for immigration, both legal and illegal. Ask: What are some policies that might encourage legal immigration and discourage illegal immigration? (*See the concept map in Activity 19.1, which includes incentives such as offering more visas and disincentives such as requiring identification for employment, increased border security, etc.)*

ASSESSMENT
Multiple-Choice Questions

1. In recent years the largest number of immigrants entering the United States has come from

   A. Russia.

   B. Canada.

   C. Mexico.

   D. China.

2. Since the 1970s, the number of immigrants in the United States, as a percentage of the U.S. population, has

   A. increased.

   B. decreased.

   C. remained constant.

   D. approached 0.

3. Policies to control immigration into the United States must take account of

   A. the stock market.

   B. disincentives only.

   C. incentives only.

   D. incentives and disincentives.

Constructed-Response Questions

1. Imagine that you are a Mexican citizen who is thinking about entering the United States illegally. The U.S. Congress has passed new legislation that provides a guest worker program and a "path to citizenship" for illegal immigrants already in the U.S. How might this legislation affect your decision?

   (The new guest worker program might create an incentive for the prospective immigrant to go through legal channels to enter the U.S. However, the prospective immigrant might also interpret the "path to citizenship" policy as a sort of loophole: a policy that rewards yesterday's illegal immigration may also reward illegal immigration some time in the future. That is, there may be an economic return to being an illegal immigrant, past or future.)

2. Some people have said that the United States can and should do more to boost the Mexican economy. What effect would this have on Mexican immigration into the United States and why?

   (Answers will vary. If new U.S. policies fostered growth in the Mexican economy, real earnings in Mexico would rise, and the potential for improved earnings would make it less desirable for Mexican citizens to immigrate to the United States. Any such policies would have to be well designed; not all forms of foreign assistance work effectively to foster long-run improvements in the recipients' economic condition.)

VISUAL 19.1

RECENT INFORMATION ON IMMIGRANTS TO THE UNITED STATES

- 35.2 million immigrants (legal and illegal) lived in the United States in March 2005. This is the highest number of immigrants ever recorded—two and a half times the 13.5 million immigrants counted during the peak of the last great immigration wave in 1910.

- Between January 2000 and March 2005, 7.9 million new immigrants (legal and illegal) settled in the country, making it the highest five-year period of immigration in American history.

- Nearly half of the post-2000 immigrant arrivals (3.7 million) are estimated to be illegal aliens.

Source: Steven A. Camarota, the Center for Immigration Studies, *Immigrants at Mid-Decade: A Snapshot of America's Foreign-Born Population in 2005.*

VISUAL 19.2

IMMIGRANTS IN THE UNITED STATES:
NUMBER AND PERCENT OF POPULATION, 1900-2005

Immigrants (as of 2005) accounted for 12.1 percent of the total
U.S. population, the highest percentage in eight decades. If
current trends continue, the figure within a decade will
surpass the high of 14.7 percent reached in 1910.

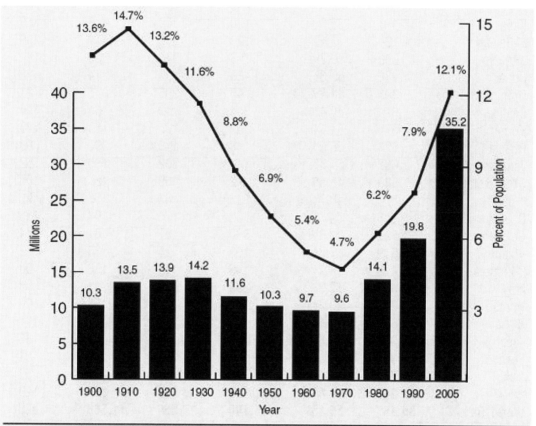

Source: Decenial Census for 1900 to 1990, and Center for Immigration Studies analysis of March 2005 Current
Population Survey.

Source: Steven A. Camarota, Center for Immigration Studies, *Immigrants at
Mid-Decade: A Snapshot of America's Foreign-Born Population in 2005.*

VISUAL 19.3

WHAT ARE THE IMMIGRANTS' HOME COUNTRIES?

As of 2005, Mexico accounted for 31 percent of all immigrants to the United States, with 10.8 million Mexican immigrants living in United States.

Region	Total	Citizenship Rate	Year of Entry*			
			Pre-1980	1980-89	1990-99	2000-05
1. Mexico	10,805	18.8%	1,839	2,262	3,852	2,852
2. China/HK/Taiwan	1,833	54.1%	359	473	646	355
3. Philippines	1,530	61.5%	449	386	431	264
4. India	1,411	33.6%	170	209	573	459
5. El Salvador	1,120	21.4%	123	380	411	206
6. Vietnam	996	60.2%	193	277	362	164
7. Cuba	948	55.8%	435	171	214	128
8. Dominican Rep.	695	41.8%	145	206	223	121
9. Canada	674	42.4%	344	49	165	116
10. Korea	672	51.7%	167	225	153	127
11. Russia	621	56.9%	46	79	397	99
12. Jamaica	607	54.7%	148	202	195	62
13. Great Britain	589	45.8%	272	89	121	107
14. Haiti	570	40.7%	123	163	193	91
15. Guatermala	546	24.7%	72	126	193	155
16. Germany	522	62.8%	380	37	61	44
17. Poland	519	57.0%	168	95	183	72
18. Colombia	479	44.7%	96	135	158	90
19. Italy	391	75.3%	299	31	31	30
20. Honduras	379	23.2%	42	73	158	106
21. Brazil	356	21.1%	35	37	90	194
22. Japan	350	33.3%	121	46	45	138
23. Ecuador	339	35.4%	50	78	120	91
24. Iran	331	62.7%	93	86	93	59
25. Peru	330	38.4%	46	53	102	129
World Total	**35,157**	**35.1%**	**8,100**	**7,569**	**11,563**	**7,925**

Source: Center for Immigration Studies analysis of March 2005 Current Population Survey.
*Indicates the year that immigrants said they came to the United States to stay.

Source: Steven A. Camarota, Center for Immigration Studies, *Immigrants at Mid-Decade: A Snapshot of America's Foreign-Born Population in 2005.*

VISUAL 19.4
CONCEPT MAP

Directions: Below is a grid showing several conditions, policies, and events that might constitute incentives or disincentives for immigration. Your task is to write these items on your concept map, placing each item on the incentives (top) or the disincentives (bottom) half of the map. An item might apply to both legal and illegal immigrants. If so, put it on *both* the left (Legal Immigration) and right (Illegal Immigration) sides of the map. The first condition (Low pay in the home country) has been done for you. It represents an incentive for both legal and illegal immigrants to come to the United States, so it has been placed in the top half (Incentives) and on both sides (Legal and Illegal Immigration). If you think of other items that should also be included on the map, add them.

Low pay in the home country	More job opportunities in the U.S.	More political freedom in the U.S.
Identification policy for U.S. employment	Amnesty for illegal immigrants in the U.S.	Better pay in the home country
More U.S. border security	Close-knit family	Strong cultural ties to the home country
Speaks English	Bad economic times in the U.S.	Increase in U.S. work visas

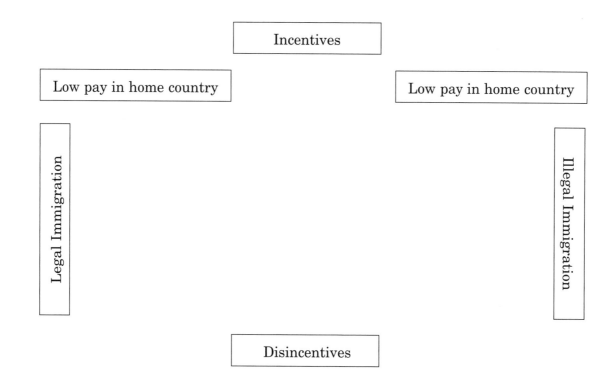

VISUAL 19.5
A COMPLETED CONCEPT MAP

Incentives

Legal Immigration		Illegal Immigration
Low pay in home country		Low pay in home country
Speaks English		Speaks English
More job opportunities in the U.S.		More job opportunities in the U.S.
More political freedom in the U.S.		Amnesty for illegal immigrants in the U.S.
Increase in U.S. work visas		More political freedom in the U.S.
Bad economic times in U.S.		Bad economic times in U.S.
Close-knit family		Close-knit family
Better pay in home country		Identification policy for U.S. employment
Strong cultural ties to home country		More U.S. border security
		Strong cultural ties to home country
		Better pay in home country

Disincentives

ACTIVITY 19.1

CONCEPT MAP

Directions: Below is a grid showing several conditions, policies, and events that might constitute incentives or disincentives for immigration. Your task is to write these items on your concept map, placing each item on the incentives (top) or the disincentives (bottom) half of the map. An item might apply to both legal and illegal immigrants. If so, put it on *both* the left (Legal Immigration) and right (Illegal Immigration) sides of the map. The first condition (Low pay in the home country) has been done for you. It represents an incentive for both legal and illegal immigrants to come to the United States, so it has been placed in the top half (Incentives) and on both sides (Legal and Illegal Immigration). If you think of other items that should also be included on the map, add them.

Low pay in the home country	More job opportunities in the U.S.	More political freedom in the U.S.
Identification policy for U.S. employment	Amnesty for illegal immigrants in the U.S.	Better pay in the home country
More U.S. border security	Close-knit family	Strong cultural ties to the home country
Speaks English	Bad economic times in the U.S.	Increase in U.S. work visas

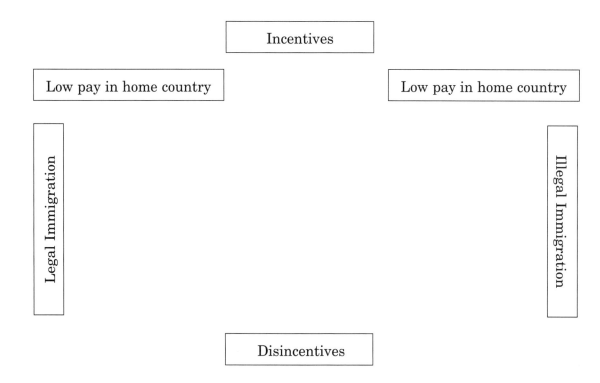

LESSON 20

ECONOMIC FREEDOM AND RIGHTS

LESSON 20
ECONOMIC FREEDOM AND RIGHTS

INTRODUCTION

The United States Constitution guarantees citizens certain personal and political rights. This lesson examines the relationship between these rights and economic rights.

LESSON DESCRIPTION

To get started, the students take note of the economic freedoms and rights they enjoy in the United States today. Then they examine how political and personal rights established by the Constitution may either reinforce or conflict with economic rights and freedoms. Finally, the students examine Franklin Delano Roosevelt's Economic Bill of Rights, presented in his State of the Union address in 1944.

CONCEPTS

- Capitalism
- Economic rights
- Freedom
- Personal rights
- Political rights

OBJECTIVES

Students will be able to:

1. Describe examples of economic rights.

2. Explain how political and personal rights reinforce economic rights.

3. Explain how political and personal rights may conflict with economic rights.

4. Explain how economic deprivation may limit a person's capability to exercise personal and political rights.

CONTENT STANDARDS
Economics (CEE Standards)

- Different methods can be used to allocate goods and services. People, acting individually or collectively through government, must choose which methods to use to allocate different kinds of goods and services. (Standard 3)

- Institutions evolve in market economies to help individuals and groups accomplish their goals. Banks, labor unions, corporations, legal systems, and not-for-profit organizations are examples of important institutions. A different kind of institution, clearly defined and enforced property rights, is essential to a market economy. (Standard 10)

- There is an economic role for government in a market economy whenever the benefits of a government policy outweigh its costs. Governments often provide for national defense, address environmental concerns, define and protect property rights, and attempt to make markets more competitive. Most government policies also redistribute income. (Standard 16)

Civics and Government (NSCG Standards, Grades 9-12)

- Personal rights. Students should be able to evaluate, take, and defend positions regarding personal rights. (Standard V.B.1)

- Political rights. Students should be able to evaluate, take, and defend positions regarding political rights. (Standard V.B.2)

- Economic rights. Students should be able to evaluate, take, and defend positions regarding economic rights. (Standard V.B.3)

TIME REQUIRED

60 minutes

MATERIALS

- A transparency of Visuals 20.1, 20.2, and 20.3

- A copy of Activity 20.1 for each student

PROCEDURE

1. Tell the students that in this lesson they will examine the economic rights and freedoms that we enjoy in the United States. Ask: Do you recognize the following passage: "We hold these truths to be self-evident, that all men are created equal, that they are endowed by their Creator with certain unalienable Rights, that among these are Life, Liberty and the pursuit of Happiness." *(This passage is from the Declaration of Independence.)*

2. Explain that the Constitution, its Bill of Rights, and subsequent constitutional amendments specify in more detail the freedoms and rights guaranteed to U.S. citizens. Ask the students to identify examples of these rights. *(The students might suggest trial by jury; the right not to be deprived of life, liberty, or property, without due process of law; freedom of speech; freedom of the press; freedom of assembly; freedom to exercise religion; the right to petition the government; the right to bear arms; etc.)*

3. Tell the students that most of these rights can be described as political or personal rights and freedoms. Call on the students to give examples of personal rights *(freedom of expression, freedom of thought, etc.)* and political rights *(freedom of political speech, freedom of petition, etc.)*.

4. Ask: What kind of economic system does the United States have? *(The economic system in the United States is a capitalist system—also known as a market economy. Some students may note that the United States has a mixed economy, since the government is involved—e.g., through taxation and regulations—in economic activity.)*

   Tell the students that two main characteristics of a capitalist system are (1) private ownership of the factors of production and (2) the use of a market system to allocate goods and services.

5. Explain that people living in a capitalist economy expect certain economic rights or freedoms. What might these be? Ask:

What are some examples of economic rights or freedoms that you expect in your everyday lives? *(The right to own private property, to own and operate a business, to choose a career, etc.)*

6. Raise a question about the source or foundation of these economic rights. Where do they come from? *(Discuss responses briefly.)* Display Visual 20.1. Note that many economic rights or freedoms are identified in the U.S. Constitution. *(Property rights are protected by the Fifth Amendment. The First Amendment protects the right of free association, which allows for the formation of unions and other organizations. Article 1, section 8 of the Constitution provides for protection of the intellectual property of authors and inventors. Article 1, section 10 prohibits the government from invalidating contracts.)*

7. Refer again to activities such as owning and operating your own business or pursuing your own career. Point out that these activities are not specifically named in the Constitution. Ask: are they protected rights, nonetheless? *(The students may respond [if they do not, bring the point up yourself] that these rights are implied by the rights specifically listed in the Constitution. For example: protection of the right to own property, guaranteed by the Fifth Amendment, implies a right to own and operate a business, an automobile, etc.)*

8. Introduce a challenge: if the Constitution guarantees my right to own and operate a business, does that mean I can own any kind of business I might want to own, and operate it any way I want to? Could I establish an auto body repair shop or a foundry or a pig farm in a quiet residential neighborhood? *(The students most likely will know that constitutional guarantees of economic freedom do not mean that anything goes. Some businesses are illegal, and some regulations—zoning ordinances, for example—are permissible even as applied to the right to own property.)*

9. Summarize two main points introduced thus far: Yes, the Constitution protects certain economic rights, such as the right to own property; no, this does not mean that people exercising those rights can do whatever they want to do. Where does this leave us? How can government officials, and the citizens to whom they are accountable, decide where to draw the line when the exercise of an economic right may be problematic? *(The students may suggest that a person exercising his or her rights may not impede the rights or freedoms of others.)*

10. Continue the discussion. Ask: Why are the following economic activities prohibited?

    • **Forming a monopoly for the sale of a good.** *(Monopolies restrict production. The restriction of production, which increases the potential profits of monopolists, is inefficient and deprives consumers of the freedom to buy goods at a competitive price. For this reason, trusts are prohibited by federal laws, based on the federal government's constitutional authority to regulate interstate commerce.)*

    • **Paying someone to vote for a certain candidate in a presidential election.** *(This is prohibited under the Voting Rights Act of 1965, which is grounded in the Fifteenth amendment. In this example, allowing one person to use his or her money to buy votes would interfere with the political rights of others. Instead of the idea of one person, one vote, a candidate for office would be elected, in effect, by economic interests.)*

11. By reference to the examples above, explain that some people believe that the U.S Constitution and its Bill of Rights are not sufficient as a source of economic rights for U.S. citizens. According to this view, it is not enough that the Constitution limits the power of government to interfere with people's right to own property, enter into contracts, establish labor unions, and so on. Over and above such protection from government interference, this argument holds, the American people should be guaranteed a certain level of results or outcomes—in housing, jobs, and health care, for example. One well-known proponent of this view was Franklin Delano Roosevelt (FDR), the 32nd president of the United States. Tell the students that they are going to participate in an activity in which they examine an Economic Bill of Rights proposed by former President Roosevelt in 1944.

12. Organize the students into groups of three or four. Distribute a copy of Activity 20.1, FDR's Economic Bill of Rights, to each student. Explain that material quoted on the Activity has been excerpted from FDR's State of the Union Address in 1944. (As appropriate, provide a brief review of the Great Depression and World War II to put FDR's message in context.)

13. Ask the students to read Activity 20.1 and, working in their groups, to answer the Questions for Discussion. When the students have finished their work, discuss their answers in class.

    (Possible answers: 1. FDR argues that people who have no economic security are not truly free, despite the existence of political freedoms. 2. To some degree, many of FDR's proposed rights are enjoyed by U. S. citizens. Antitrust laws protect people from unfair competition; low-income citizens can obtain assistance for food and medical care; farmers benefit from various agricultural programs; the Social Security System pays for assistance to many elderly and disabled citizens; and elementary and secondary schooling is publicly funded. On the other hand, some citizens are homeless, some are without a job, and some are without health insurance. 3. According to FDR, the capitalist economic system alone does not guarantee that people will be able to reach the outcomes listed in his economic bill of rights. In his view, government should play a role in helping people to achieve these outcomes.)

14. In discussion of the students' answers, emphasize the distinction between rights that guarantee an economic **opportunity** and rights that guarantee specific economic **outcomes**. In a capitalist system, people have a right to own property—a home, a grocery store, a farm, a hair salon, and so on. Owning property creates an **opportunity** for people to earn money—by selling the house at a profit, for example, or by doing well in the grocery business, in farming, in hair styling, and so on. But owning and using property does not guarantee any particular **outcome**. A house may gain or lose value over time, and a business may flourish or go bad.

15. Display Visual 20.2. Explain that the transparency lists several economic rights (or proposed rights), including some mentioned in FDR's Bill of Economic Rights. Go through the list; for each item, ask the students to identify those rights that emphasize economic opportunity and those that emphasize an economic outcome.

(Right to acquire, own, and use private property – economic opportunity. Right to pursue one's own career – economic opportunity. Right to join a labor union – economic opportunity. Right to own and operate a business – economic opportunity. Right to own and enjoy protection for intellectual property – economic opportunity. Right to have contracts enforced – economic opportunity. Right to hold a useful job – economic outcome. Right to earn enough money (minimum wage) to provide food, clothing, and recreation – economic outcome. Right to be free from unfair competition and monopoly – economic opportunity. Right to live in a decent home – economic outcome. Right to receive adequate medical care – economic outcome. Right to protection in one's old age or in a condition of disability – economic outcome. Right to a good education –Uncertain: One might emphasize either the opportunity or the outcome inherent in a good education.)

16. Take stock of the analysis up to this point. Ask:

- Are most of FDR's proposed economic rights aimed at providing economic outcomes or economic opportunities? *(Most are aimed at providing economic outcomes.)*

- Why do you think FDR said that "Necessitous men are not free men."? *(This statement expresses FDR's view that people without adequate food, clothing, housing, and so on, are unable to enjoy the benefits of freedom.)*

17. On an overhead projector, display the top portion of Visual 20.3. Ask: which of these hungry persons is experiencing economic freedom? *(The first person has chosen hunger and is therefore experiencing freedom. The second person is unable to make an economic choice to overcome hunger and is therefore not experiencing economic freedom.)*

18. Display the remaining portion of Visual 20.3. Note that both of the people described here did not vote. Ask: which of these people is experiencing political freedom? *(The second person has chosen not to vote and is therefore experiencing political freedom. The first person could have voted, but if she had voted she would have lost some pay. Students may suggest that this person has limited political freedom; even though she had the right to vote, this right was compromised in such a way that she decided she could not vote.)*

19. Explain that the examples in Visual 20.3 are based on ideas presented by 1998 Economics Nobel Prize winner Amartya Sen. Sen has contended that without economic security, people do not have the "capability" to exercise their other rights, even if they have the liberty to do so. To be free, Sen states, one must have the capability to pursue happiness—an idea that FDR also states. Sen suggests that economic deprivation is one of the ways in

which a person's freedom may be reduced; political and social conditions may also reduce freedom. (Sen states and explains these ideas in *Development as Freedom* [*New York:* Anchor Books, 1999].)

20. Sen also argues that different rights reinforce one another. To explore this idea, ask the following questions:

- Could legislators in the United States adopt economic policies that would create famine and leave many U.S. citizens without food? What might prevent legislators from doing that? *(Among other things, the legislators would most likely get thrown out of office; people would exercise their right to vote them out and elect somebody else. Sen has argued that famines rarely occur in countries where people can exercise political rights.)*

- Why do people in the United States who are economically secure tend to be more politically active than others who are less secure? *(Students may respond variously. Among the possibilities: with economic security, people can more easily take time to become politically active.)*

21. Conclude by underscoring the important relationship illustrated by these examples: political rights reinforce economic rights, and economic rights reinforce political rights.

22. Remind the students that the lesson began with a quotation from the Declaration of Independence: people have the right to "Life, Liberty and the Pursuit of Happiness." Ask the students, in light of this lesson, how they would answer the following question:

What rights must people be afforded in order to have the freedom to pursue their own happiness? *(Answers will vary, but the lesson suggests that economic and political rights are essential to the pursuit of happiness, and that people must have adequate economic security in order to exercise these rights.)*

CLOSURE

Summarize the lesson by asking the following questions:

- Are political rights alone sufficient to guarantee freedom? *(Answers will vary, but the lesson suggests that economic rights are also essential.)*

- Are economic rights alone sufficient to guarantee freedom? *(Answers will vary, but the lesson suggests that political rights are also essential.)*

- Which of FDR's proposed economic rights, if any, do you believe are necessary to guarantee freedom? *(Answers will vary depending on how much weight students give to the importance of economic outcomes as opposed to economic opportunities.)*

- Are people free if they have rights but have no capability to exercise them? *(Answers will vary. Amartya Sen suggests that people must have the capability to exercise rights in order to enjoy the benefits of economic and political freedom.)*

ASSESSMENT

Multiple-Choice Questions

1. Which of the following is an economic right mentioned in FDR's Economic Bill of Rights?

   A. The right to vote

   B. The right to have contracts enforced

   C. **The right to a decent home**

   D. The right to free speech

2. Which one of the following economic rights is intended to guarantee an economic outcome?

   A. The right to have contracts enforced

   B. The right to choose your own career

   C. **The right to adequate medical care**

   D. The right to own property

Constructed-Response Questions

1. Which rights are necessary for a person to be free? *(There is no correct answer here. A good answer should discuss personal, political, and economic rights. The distinction between the right to an economic opportunity and the right to an economic outcome should be incorporated into the answer in some fashion.)*

2. According to FDR, what is necessary in today's society for the pursuit of happiness? *(FDR argued that political rights were sufficient to guarantee life and liberty; but in order to pursue one's happiness, economic security is also necessary.)*

VISUAL 20.1
EXAMPLES OF ECONOMIC FREEDOMS AND RIGHTS

The freedom or right to . . .

- Acquire, own, and use private property
- Choose and pursue your own career
- Join labor unions or other professional organizations
- Own and operate a business
- Own intellectual property, knowing that it will be protected
- Enter into contracts, knowing that they will be enforced

VISUAL 20.2

GUARANTEE OF ECONOMIC OPPORTUNITIES OR GUARANTEE OF ECONOMIC OUTCOMES?

The right to . . .	Guarantee of an Economic Opportunity?	Guarantee of an Economic Outcome?
Acquire, own, and use private property		
Pursue one's own career		
Join a labor union		
Own and operate a business		
Own intellectual property		
Enter into contracts, knowing that they will be enforced		
Hold a useful job*		

VISUAL 20.2, CONTINUED

GUARANTEE OF ECONOMIC OPPORTUNITIES OR GUARANTEE OF ECONOMIC OUTCOMES?

The right to . . .	Guarantee of an Economic Opportunity?	Guarantee of an Economic Outcome?
Earn enough money to provide adequate food and clothing*		
Be free from unfair competition and monopoly*		
Live in a decent home*		
Receive adequate medical care*		
Be assured of protection in old age and in case of disability*		
Be assured of a good education*		

* Mentioned in FDR's Economic Bill of Rights

VISUAL 20.3

ECONOMIC FREEDOM? POLITICAL FREEDOM?

ECONOMIC FREEDOM

In your view, is either one of the following people experiencing economic freedom?

- A person who is earning $55,000 a year in the United States goes on an inadvisable diet, does not eat for three days, and is very hungry.
- A person in sub-Saharan Africa has not been able to find or buy food for three days, and is very hungry.

POLITICAL FREEDOM

In your view, is either one of the following people experiencing political freedom?

- A citizen in the United States is working at a minimum-wage job. Since this worker is paid hourly, she could not take time off to vote in a presidential election without a decrease in her much needed pay.
- A citizen in the United States is earning a salary of $45,000 a year. He does not bother to vote in a presidential election, even though he could easily have voted during his lunch hour. He simply is not interested in politics, he says.

ACTIVITY 20.1
FDR's ECONOMIC BILL OF RIGHTS

The following is an excerpt from the State of the Union speech President Franklin Delano Roosevelt delivered on January 11, 1944.[1]

It is our duty now to begin to lay the plans and determine the strategy for the winning of a lasting peace and the establishment of an American standard of living higher than ever before known. We cannot be content, no matter how high that general standard of living may be, if some fraction of our people—whether it be one third or one fifth or one tenth—is ill-fed, ill-clothed, ill-housed, and insecure.

This Republic had its beginning, and grew to its present strength, under the protection of certain inalienable political rights—among them the right of free speech, free press, free worship, trial by jury, freedom from unreasonable searches and seizures. They were our rights to life and liberty.

As our Nation has grown in size and stature, however—as our industrial economy expanded— these political rights proved inadequate to assure us equality in the pursuit of happiness.

We have come to a clear realization of the fact that true individual freedom cannot exist without economic security and independence. 'Necessitous men are not free men.' People who are hungry and out of a job are the stuff of which dictatorships are made.

In our day these economic truths have become accepted as self-evident. We have accepted, so to speak, a second Bill of Rights under which a new basis of security and prosperity can be established for all regardless of station, race, or creed.

Among these [proposed new rights] are:

> The right to a useful and remunerative job in the industries or shops or farms or mines of the Nation;
>
> The right to earn enough to provide adequate food and clothing and recreation;
>
> The right of every farmer to raise and sell his products at a return which will give him and his family a decent living;
>
> The right of every businessman, large and small, to trade in an atmosphere of freedom from unfair competition and domination by monopolies at home or abroad;
>
> The right of every family to a decent home;
>
> The right to adequate medical care and the opportunity to achieve and enjoy good health;
>
> The right to adequate protection from the economic fears of old age, sickness, accident, and unemployment;
>
> The right to a good education.

All of these rights spell security. And after this war is won we must be prepared to move forward, in the implementation of these rights, to new goals of human happiness and well-being.

America's own rightful place in the world depends in large part upon how fully these and similar rights have been carried into practice for our citizens. For unless there is security here at home there cannot be lasting peace in the world.

---

[1] The speech is widely available. See, for example, the Franklin and Eleanor Roosevelt Institute website: http://www.feri.org/archives/speeches/jan1144.cfm.

ACTIVITY 20.1, CONTINUED

FDR's ECONOMIC BILL OF RIGHTS

QUESTIONS FOR DISCUSSION

1. According to FDR, are political rights sufficient to secure freedom?

2. Which of FDR's proposed economic rights, if any, have been given to U.S. citizens?

3. Does a capitalist economic system alone guarantee FDR's proposed economic rights?

FOCUS: UNDERSTANDING ECONOMICS IN CIVICS AND GOVERNMENT © COUNCIL FOR ECONOMIC EDUCATION, NEW YORK, NY